THIS EDITION WRITTEN AND RESEARCHED BY

Abigail Blasi

welcome to Malta & Gozo

Prehistoric & Futuristic

Malta and Gozo are home to some of the world's most impressive prehistoric sites, including gigantic temples set atop sea cliffs, and the Hal Saflieni Hypogeum – the 5000-year-old underground necropolis carved perfectly from the living rock. A visit to any of them will stay with you long after you've left the island.

It's also remarkable to visit somewhere where the history of savage warfare – all due to Malta's geographical significance – is so enduringly evident. The islands have an embattled feel, even in today's peaceful times, with their walled cities, great fortresses, fortifications running over remote hills and myriad underground tunnels that became homes away from home during WWII bombardment.

Though building upon an already overcrowded landscape is a favoured activity of the Maltese, many parts of the island still manage to retain a sense of timelessness. This back-in-time atmosphere is even more pronounced on Gozo, where horses and carts are sometimes seen on country lanes, and quiet villages combine Italianate architecture with incongruous English red post boxes and blue police lamps. Lately, however, Malta's beautiful 17th-century capital, Valletta, has received some substantial 21st-century sparkle. The city has a new Renzo Piano–designed gateway, parliament building and open-air auditorium built on the elegiac ruins of the city's opera house.

The Maltese Islands are like nowhere else. Here you'll find great prehistoric temples, fossil-studded cliffs, glittering hidden coves, thrilling diving opportunities and a history of remarkable intensity.

(left) Mgarr harbour (p114), Gozo
(below) Tranquil street, Mdina (p85)

The Deep Blue Sea

You're never far from the Mediterranean here; in Gozo you can see the sea from almost everywhere. The islands' beaches are small and perfectly formed; there are also some breathtakingly beautiful coves to swim in. This is also one of the world's finest places to go diving, with sites ranging from sunken WWII bombers to dramatic undersea caves. To cap it all, much of what you'll eat will come from the sea's bounty.

A Mediterranean Cocktail

People here are warm and welcoming, but also have a certain gentle reserve. It's the kind of place where if you ask for direc-tions you'll get a cheerful reply and maybe even be guided part of your way for good measure.

The country is staunchly Roman Catholic, with mighty churches towering over diminutive villages. But there's also the beguiling mix of cultures that's stewed over generations. The Malti language sounds Arabic, but is speckled with Italian, French and English words, and local food packs in Sicilian and Middle Eastern flavours, while making use of local ingredients like rabbit and honey. Even the local fishing boats resonate with history, their prows painted with eyes as their Phoenician predecessors' were several millennia ago.

Malta & Gozo

Dwejra
Stunning coastline carved by wind, sea and time (p119)

Victoria
Cultural and gastronomic delights abound (p110)

San Blas Bay
Secluded cove for swimming and snorkelling (p125)

Blue Lagoon
Oft-crowded yet undeniably lovely swimming spot (p126)

Northern Beaches
Malta's most alluring seaside holiday destination (p72)

Dingli Cliffs
Windswept walks and clifftop views (p94)

GOZO

San Dimitri Point
Žebbuġ
Marsalforn
Gharb
Ramla Bay
San Blas Bay
Dwejra Point
Dwejra Bay
Xagħra
Dahlet Qorrot
Wardija Point
Xlendi Bay
VICTORIA (RABAT)
Xewkija
Nadur
Qala
Munxar
Għajnsielem
Mġarr
Sannat
Ta' Cenċ
Ta'Ċenċ Cliffs
Fort Chambray
North Comino Channel
COMINO
Mġarr ix-Xini
Cominotto
South Comino Channel
Aħrax Point

Ċirkewwa
Paradise Bay
Marfa Peninsula
Mellieħa Bay
MELLIEĦA
Anchor Bay
Mellieħa Ridge
Bajda Ridge
Ras il-Waħx
Golden Bay
Wardija
Ras il-Pellegrin
Għajn Tuffieħa
Mġarr
Fomm ir-Rih Bay
Żebbie
Ras ir-Raħeb
Victoria

MEDITERRANEAN SEA

ELEVATION

250m
200m
150m
100m
50m
0

0 —— 4 km
0 —— 2 miles

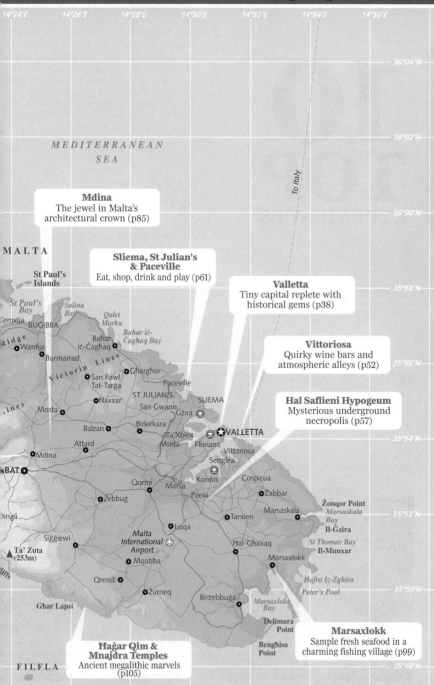

14°24'E 14°26'E 14°28'E 14°30'E 14°32'E 14°34'E 14°36'E

*MEDITERRANEAN
SEA*

To Italy

36°04'N
36°02'N
36°00'N
35°58'N
35°56'N
35°54'N
35°52'N
35°50'N
35°48'N

Mdina
The jewel in Malta's
architectural crown (p85)

**Sliema, St Julian's
& Paceville**
Eat, shop, drink and play (p61)

Valletta
Tiny capital replete with
historical gems (p38)

Vittoriosa
Quirky wine bars and
atmospheric alleys (p52)

Hal Saflieni Hypogeum
Mysterious underground
necropolis (p57)

Marsaxlokk
Sample fresh seafood in a
charming fishing village (p99)

**Haġar Qim &
Mnajdra Temples**
Ancient megalithic marvels
(p105)

MALTA

St Paul's
Islands

*St Paul's
Bay*
Xemxija BUĠIBBA
Ridge ○Wardija
○Burmarrad
*Salina
Bay* *Qalet
Marku*
Baħar
iċ-Ċagħaq *Baħar iċ-
Ċagħaq Bay*
Victoria Lines
○San Pawl
Tat-Tarġa ○Għargħur
Paceville
Dingli
Lines ST JULIAN'S
○Naxxar San Ġwann SLIEMA
○Mosta Birkirkara Gżira
○Balzan Ta'Xbiex
Attard Msida Floriana ★○VALLETTA
○Mdina Vittoriosa
Senglea
BAT○ Qormi Kordin Cospicua
○Żebbuġ Marsa Paola ○Żabbar
Dingli Tarxien Marsaskala *Marsaskala
Bay*
Siġġiewi ○Luqa Hal-Għaxaq *Żonqor Point*
▲Ta' Żuta
(253m) *Malta
International
Airport* Marsaxlokk Il-Gżira
St Thomas Bay
Il-Munxar
○Mqabba
Ġħar Lapsi Qrendi○ Żurrieq○ Birżebbuġa *Marsaxlokk
Bay* *Hofra Iz-Zghira*
Peter's Pool
*Delimara
Point*
*Benghisa
Point*
FILFLA

10 TOP EXPERIENCES

Dwejra

1 The thrilling coastline of Dwejra (p119), in Gozo, features some astoundingly beautiful rock formations that have been sculpted by the wind and sea. From here you can take a boat trip through the Azure Window, an arch of rock that forms a doorway to the open sea. There's also the Inland Sea, which is a wonderful place to swim and snorkel when the sea is calm. Close to the coast, the great chunk of Fungus Rock rears from the piercing blue Mediterranean. Azure Window, Dwejra

Valletta

2 Malta's capital (p36) is a remarkable city. It's the size of a small town – easy to explore on foot, and laid out in a harmonious grid formation. The tall, gracious houses are distinctive for their wood-and-glass balconies, which give them a top-heavy look. The hills mean some of the roads are so steep they have to be stepped, and the roller-coaster streetscape allows mesmerising views along the straight, narrow lanes and out to sea. Street looking down to the sea, Valletta

ALLARD SCHAGER/GETTY IMAGES ©

FOTOSOL FOTOSOL/GETTY IMAGES ©

Victoria

3 The Il-Kastell of Victoria (p110) is an evocative place to wander – this tiny *medina* (walled city) almost seems to grow out of its rocky outcrop. It was built after a particularly devastating raid on the island, when almost every Gozitan was carried off to slavery; there was a time when the entire population of around 3000 used to sleep here at night. Sweeping views can be had from its battlements. Cathedral of the Assumption, Victoria, Gozo

Sunday Lunch in Marsaxlokk

4 It gets packed every Sunday at the small coastal town of Marsaxlokk (p99). Locals and tourists throng to visit the buzzing fish market, where you can buy all manner of sea bounty, from colourful rock fish to baby sharks. The harbour bobs with colourful fishing boats painted with the eye of Osiris – a tradition that's thought to hark back to the Phoenician era. The seafront, lined by excellent fish restaurants, is a great place for a long lazy lunch – a favourite activity of locals as well as visitors. Harbour scene, Marsaxlokk

Mdina & Rabat

5 Malta's tiny sometime capital (p85) is a walled city perched on a hilltop, filled with beautiful honey-coloured buildings. A treasure trove of museums, artefacts and churches (including Malta's other cathedral), it's also appealingly mysterious at night, when everything's closed and the city is dimly lit and empty. Wander around after most people have left and you'll understand why it's known as the 'Silent City'. Mdina adjoins Rabat (p90), itself a lovely town with some fascinating sights, many of them underground. Medieval street, Mdina

Ħaġar Qim & Mnajdra Temples

6 These great prehistoric structures (p105) are among Malta's finest and most atmospheric, partly due to their breathtaking location – they are set high up on the edge of coastal cliffs that are carpeted by wild flowers in spring. There are magnificent views out to sea and over to the distant islet of Filfla, and marked nature trails around the surrounding countryside. Ħaġar Qim temple

Comino

7 This small, rocky island (p126) has a beautiful coastline and an eclectic history, having served as a hermit's hideaway, a cholera isolation zone and a prison camp. It was written of by Ptolemy, and today it attracts huge numbers of visitors to its Blue Lagoon. This serene sea pool is so blue that it looks like an over-saturated image – if you manage to see it without the crowds, it's breathtaking. Comino is an equally beautiful place to walk, with easy paths around the island leading up to the 17th-century watchtower and around the coast to the island's sole hotel. Blue Lagoon, Comino

Vittoriosa's Backstreets

8 Vittoriosa (p52) – known locally as Birgu, its name before the Great Siege of 1565 – is the most fascinating of the Three Cities. This small town, perched on its small lip of land, has stunning views all around it and perfectly preserved ancient streets within. It was the original home of the Knights of St John, but it's no museum – this is a living, breathing city with a strong sense of community. You're in luck if you've timed your visit to see Birgu by Candlelight in October, when the streets are lit by candles. Street in Il Collachio district, Vittoriosa

7

VICTOR PAUL BORG/ALAMY ©

ARCAID IMAGES/ALAMY ©

NICK SERVIAN/GETTY IMAGES ©

Hal Saflieni Hypogeum

9 Visiting these ancient underground burial chambers (p57) is a unique, mysterious and awe-inspiring experience. Amazingly preserved, the sacred spaces hollowed out from the rock are around 5000 years old, yet painted ochre patterns are still visible decorating the ceilings of some sections. It's a window into a mysterious ancient world, which leaves a beguiling and perplexing resonance. You'll need to book several weeks ahead.

St John's Co-Cathedral

10 The austere exterior of Valletta's cathedral (p38) is no preparation for the frenzy of baroque gold and lavish decoration in its interior. The floor alone is a carpet of many-coloured marble tombs, in which symbolic pictures are delicately rendered in stone. The chapels, each pertaining to an auberge, vie to outdo each other in opulence. The outstanding highlight is Caravaggio's *Beheading of John the Baptist* in the Oratory – the largest work ever produced by the artist. Interior, St John's Co-Cathedral

need to know

When to Go

Victoria (Rabat)
GO Apr–Jun & Sept–Oct

St Julian's
GO Apr–Jun & Sept–Oct

Valletta
GO Apr–Jun & Sept–Oct

Mdina
GO Apr–Jun & Sept–Oct

Marsaxlokk
GO Apr–Jun & Sept–Oct

Warm to hot summers, mild winters

High Season
(Jun–Aug)

» Many resort hotels are booked solid and beaches are very busy.

» Daytime temperatures in July and August can reach more than 35°C.

» This is also the main season for festas (feast days).

Shoulder
(Apr–Jun, Sep–Oct)

» Warm and sunny, with the occasional rainfall or hot and humid wind.

» The sea is considerably warmer in autumn than in spring.

» Holy Week is a wonderful time to be in Malta.

Low Season
(Nov–Feb)

» Temperatures in November and December average from 12°C to 18°C.

» January and February are the coldest months.

» Christmas to New Year is a mini-high season.

Your Daily Budget

Budget less than
€60

» Hostel or guesthouse accommodation €20

» Simple restaurant meals, bakeries and self-catering

» Buy one-day or weekly bus tickets, and enjoy free activities

Midrange
€60–100

» Hotel with air-con and a swimming pool €60 to €140 for two people.

» Allow extra for car rental (average of €25 per day).

» Buy a MaltaCard to save money on sights.

Top End more than
€100

» Luxury hotel €140 to €350 for two people.

» Eat at the best restaurants (meal for two from €100)

» Do a diving course or hire a jeep.

Money

» ATMs are widespread. Credit cards are used in larger hotels and upmarket restaurants, but otherwise most smaller hotels and eateries only accept cash.

Visas

» Visas are not required for citizens of EU and EEA countries. Other nationalities check www.foreign.gov.mt.

Mobile Phones

» Malta uses the GSM900 mobile network (not compatible with the USA and Canada's GSM1900).

Transport

» An efficient Arriva bus system has revolutionised travel around the islands. Regular ferries and water taxis ply the waters and connect Malta with Gozo.

Websites

» **Lonely Planet** (www.lonelyplanet. com) Destination information, hotel bookings, traveller forum and more.

» **Malta Tourism Authority** (www. visitmalta.com) Huge official site that makes a good first port of call.

» **Gozo** (www.gozo. com) All about Gozo.

» **Restaurants Malta** (www. restaurantsmalta.com) Travel your tastebuds and expand your waistline.

» **Maltese Islands** (www.malteseislands. com) Nicely designed site with plenty of general information.

Exchange Rates

Australia	A$1	€0.79
Canada	C$1	€0.78
Japan	¥100	€0.98
New Zealand	NZ$1	€0.63
UK	£1	€1.24
United States	US$	€0.77

For current exchange rates, see www.xe.com.

Important Numbers

Drop the 0 when dialling an area code from abroad.

International access code	☏00
Country code	☏356
Directory enquiries	☏1182
Directory Enquiries (Go Mobile)	☏1187
Directory Enquiries (Vodafone)	☏1189
Emergency	☏112

Arriving in Malta

» **Malta International Airport**
Buses – Six express services and other buses serve all Malta's main towns from around 5am to midnight.
Night buses – The N71 runs to St Julian's.
Airport shuttle – MaltaTransfer (☏2133 2016; www.malta transfer.com) operates services to major hotels.
Taxis – €15 to Valletta (25 mins).

Sightseeing Tip

If you're planning to visit more than a few of Malta and Gozo's cultural treasures, it's a good idea to purchase a multisite pass from Heritage Malta. Admission fees can easily mount up, considering that a single adult ticket to the Armoury and State Rooms in Valletta costs €10, the Ħaġar Qim & Mnajdra Temples cost €9, and most other sites cost €5 to €6 – a pass will allow you to save satisfying amounts of euros.

The pass offers 30 days of free admission to most Heritage Malta sights (see www. heritagemalta.org for a full list). An adult pass costs €30, while a family ticket (two adults and two children) is an even better bargain at €65.

if you like...

Eventful History

Malta are Gozo are small islands, but their rich past has left them with an unparalleled historical legacy. Of the many influxes of peoples to these islands, perhaps most significant was the arrival of the swashbuckling Knights of Malta, who so famously withstood their besiegement by 30,000 Turks. Another fascinating and resonant era of Malta's history is the island's stoic performance during WWII.

Valletta Malta's capital is crammed with emblems of the island's history, from St John's Co-Cathedral to the Malta War Museum (p36)

Mdina & Rabat Mdina's evocative walled city sits alongside an excavated Roman Villa and Rabat's catacombs and necropoli (p85)

Vittoriosa This historic walled town was the original home of the Knights, and contains the Inquisitor's Palace and the Malta at War Museum (p52)

The coastal towers The islands' coastlines are lined by a chain of watchtowers built largely in the 17th century (p61)

Amazing Sea

The islands of Malta, Gozo and Comino offer some of the best diving opportunities in the world. The lack of tides and the islands' size and position mean that water is remarkably clear. There's also a wide range of fascinating sights below the water: natural rock formations, WWII bombers and boats sunk to create artificial reefs. Plus watery fun is by no means limited to beneath the surface. You can hire all sorts of boats here, from canoes to yachts; explore the cave-pocked coast and offshore islets by boat; and go para-sailing, water-skiing and banana boating.

Dive sites Spectacular dive sites for beginners, experts and everyone in between (p22)

Watersports Malta isn't just for divers: swimming, snorkelling and sailing opportunities abound in these waters (p20)

Boat trips You'll discover an enormous range of cruises and boating activities accessible from various towns (p177)

Prehistoric Relics

It's not only Malta's recent history that's fascinating, but also the remarkable evidence of its more distant past. There is an incredible wealth of prehistoric temples and necropoli here: mysterious structures on a breathtaking scale, some around 5000 years old. These huge, freestanding structures were constructed here a millennium before the Egyptian pyramids.

Underground Don't miss the fantastic Hypogeum, a 5000-year-old subterranean necropolis masterfully carved out of the living rock; book ahead (p57)

Ħaġar Qim & Mnajdra Extraordinary clifftop temples (p105)

National Museum of Archaeology Valletta's museum houses Malta's most dazzling and refined prehistoric relics (p43)

Ġgantija Temples on Gozo seemingly built by giants (p122)

» Produce from Gozo (p113)

Sublime Swimming Spots

Rather than being ringed by beaches, the rocky islands of Malta and Gozo proffer splendid swimming from rocky, picturesque coves into the warm waters of the dark azure Mediterranean sea. There are some lovely scenic sandy stretches as well: these tend to be small, if picturesque.

Golden Bay & Għajn Tuffieħa Bay Malta's best two beaches have ochre sand and picturesque backdrops (p72)

The Inland Sea Swim amid extraordinary rock formations on Gozo (p119)

Ramla Bay & San Blas Bay Gozo has two lovely beaches on its northwest coast: Ramla Bay and the less-visited (it's further to walk) San Blas Bay (p125)

Mġarr ix-Xini & Wied il-Għasri Explore the gorgeous little coves of Gozo, lapped by azure water (p115, p120)

The Blue Lagoon Malta's most sublime swimming spot, in the brilliant turquoise waters off Comino – though be warned that it gets packed in summer (p126)

Family Days Out

Malta and Gozo make an ideal family destination. Children are welcomed warmly at all most restaurants, and there's plenty for all ages to do. Besides bucket-and-spade beach fun and guaranteed sunshine, there are plenty of activities to do around the coast, including boat trips and water parks.

Comino Have a perfect day combining boat trips, swimming and exploring the barely inhabited, tower-topped island (p126)

Popeye Village This former film set is a pretty huddling of buildings above a dramatic bay; younger kids will love it (p72)

Valletta Malta's diminutive capital has choreographed fountains, relaxed restaurants, the National War Museum, gardens and forts (p43)

Mediterraneo Marine Park A chance to see sea lions, parrots and reptiles (p83)

Buġibba There are loads of family activities on offer in this tourist hub, including glass-bottomed boat trips and the much anticipated Malta National Aquarium (p78)

Food

Malta and Gozo's cuisine is an enticing mix of influences, and the cooking here includes Italian, French, British and Arabic flavours. The most obvious inspiration is neighbouring Italy – pasta and pizza are ubiquitous menu items, albeit often with a Maltese twist. To sample the local cuisine, try the various excellent Maltese restaurants focusing on local ingredients. You can also take your pick from seafood, fusion and international restaurants.

Valletta Head to the capital to try some of Malta's finest Slow Food restaurants (p46)

Sliema & St Julian's Eat out where locals head for its great mix of eateries and happening buzz (p63)

Mġarr ix-Xini At a beachside eatery, sample delicious fish fresh out of the Gozitan waters (p115)

Home-made jams Buy locally made liqueurs, jams and honey on Gozo (p113)

Fresh fish Queue up with Gozitan locals to buy fresh-from-the-sea fish (p115)

month by month

February

As the winter draws to a close on Malta and Gozo, the islands celebrate Carnival with notable verve.

Carnival
A week of vibrant celebrations preceding Lent, with traditional processions of floats, fancy dress and grotesque masks. Carnival is celebrated throughout the islands but the main procession is in Valletta (www.visitmalta.com/carnival).

March

Holy Week sees Malta's most spectacular and important celebrations.

Good Friday
Life-size statues depicting scenes from the Passion of the Christ are carried shoulder high in processions along the main streets of towns and villages, accompanied by men and women dressed as biblical characters.

Easter Sunday
In contrast to the solemnity of Good Friday, this is a day of joy. Early in the morning processions bear the statue of the Risen Christ – in the three harbour towns of Vittoriosa, Senglea and Cospicua, the statue bearers actually *run* with the statue.

April

Temperatures begin to warm and wild flowers carpet the countryside. It's too cold to swim for all but the hardiest, but early spring is a glorious time to be in Malta.

Fireworks Festival
A noisy and colourful festival of fireworks, folk music and entertainment (www.visitmalta.com/malta-fireworks-festival), set against the awesome views of Grand Harbour's bastions.

Medieval Mdina
Mdina forms the perfect backdrop for a weekend of medieval events, including human chess, birds of prey, archery and cookery at the Medieval Mdina Festival (www.medievalmdina.eu).

May

Malta's weather reaches a lovely pitch in May, with warm sunshine making the occasional dip inviting, yet it's not too hot to sightsee and sights remain uncrowded.

Lejlet Lapsi Notte Gozitana
The run-up to the feast of the Ascension of Our Lord is celebrated with a weekend of music, arts, tours and craft events in Gozo.

June

Malta begins to hot up, and early summer is a great time to visit for piercing-blue skies and less-busy beaches, plus there are several great music events.

L-Imnarja
Harvest festival with an agricultural show and traditional horse races; festivities are centred on and around Rabat.

Malta Music Week
A week of gigs on Gozo at the end of June, all leading

up to the Isle of MTV festival event in Floriana, starring mainstream international acts (www.isleofmtv.com; www.maltamusicweek.com).

 Għanafest
Traditional Maltese folksongs are celebrated with three days of live music in Floriana's Argotti Gardens (www.maltafolk musicfestival.org).

July

High summer might be the hottest and busiest period, but it's also a joyous time of year, packed with interesting festivals.

 Malta Jazz Festival
This increasingly popular event , with outdoor performances for jazz cats, is held beneath the bastions of Valletta in the third weekend in July (www.maltajazz festival.org).

 Farsons Great Beer Festival
Ten days of free live gigs on two stages at Ta'Qali central Malta, with Maltese artists performing, food stalls, a 'Kids Fantasyland' and a focus on local and international beer (www.farsons. com/beer festival/).

 **Malta Arts Festival**
For three weeks from early July, this arts festival (www. maltaartsfestival.org) incorporates music, dance, theatre and literature performances and art exhibitions at various venues in and around Valletta and Argotti Gardens in Floriana.

September

In Autumn the crowds ebb away, the dust settles, occasional storms quench the land, and temperatures cool; the sea has been warmed over the summer, so it's better for swimming than the spring.

 Notte Bianca
On 1st October, Valletta's museums, historical buildings and cultural institutions are open free of charge till late, and there are free live gigs all over the city.

 Malta International Air Show
An exhibition of visiting aircraft and aerial displays takes place over a weekend in late September at the Luqa airfield (www.maltair show.com).

October

Malta's autumnal months are an ideal time to visit, with greenery returning to the parched landscape, and sunny weather.

 BirguFest
Three days of cultural activities including music, dance and pageantry in Vittoriosa, culminating in the exquisitely beautiful 'Birgu by Candlelight' when the electric lights are switched off and the historic streets are lit by thousands of candles (www.birgu.gov.mt).

 Mdina Grand Prix
Mdina's classic car event and race event takes place in the stunning location of Mdina and Rabat (www. vallettagrandprix.com).

 Malta Military Tattoo
A weekend performance of precision marching, gymnastic displays and military music at the convention centre in Ta'Qali (www. maltamilitarytattoo.org).

 Rolex Middle Sea Race
This offshore sailing classic starts and finishes at the Royal Malta Yacht Club (www.rolexmiddlesea race.com).

 Mediterranea
Gozo's Arts Festival features concerts and opera, mostly in Victoria (www. mediterranea.com.mt).

November

There tends to be more rain in late Autumn, but it's still a great time of year for some guaranteed sunshine, few crowds, low prices and to sightsee.

 Mediterranea
This 10-day festival of culture on Gozo celebrates the history, art, crafts, opera and music of the island (www.mediter ranea.com.mt).

December

Although it's cold and damp at this time of year, the Christmas period is an enchanting time to visit.

 Christmas
Christmas is celebrated with fervour all over this Catholic country; miniature and even life-size nativity scenes are set up in churches or on the streets.

itineraries

Whether you've got six days or 60, these itineraries provide a starting point for the trip of a lifetime. Want more inspiration? Head online to lonelyplanet. com/thorntree to chat with other travellers.

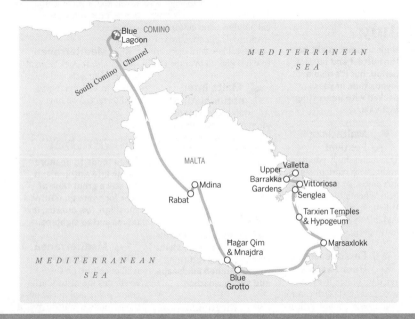

One week
Malta's Magic

> Malta's diminutive dimensions mean that you can cover a lot of ground while taking it easy. Having your own car is an asset; otherwise, base yourself in Valletta, Sliema, Mdina or St Julian's for the easiest bus connections.
>
> Begin by taking in **Valletta** – explore the narrow streets and walk around the fortifications. Feast your eyes on the views from the **Upper Barrakka Gardens**. On the second day explore the charms of **Vittoriosa** and **Senglea**, ideally taking a water taxi to make the dramatic harbour crossing from Valletta. On day three visit the **Tarxien Temples** and **Hypogeum**, close to Valletta in the suburb of Paola, en route south for a seafood lunch at **Marsaxlokk**. On day four spend the morning at the **Blue Grotto** and the temples of **Ħaġar Qim** and **Mnajdra**, and the afternoon in exquisite **Mdina** and **Rabat**. Day five would be best spent relaxing on a beach in the northwest, recharging your batteries for some physical activity on day six – a clifftop walk or maybe a scuba-diving taster. End on a high with a day trip to Comino's spectacular **Blue Lagoon**.

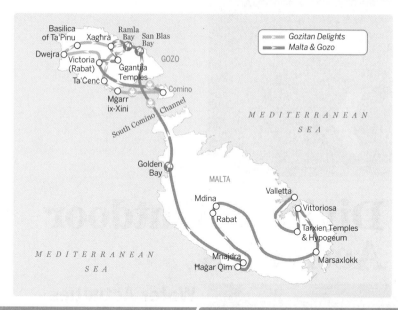

Five days to one week
Gozitan Delights

The island of Gozo (14km by 7km) is much smaller than Malta, but you still need time to do it justice. Because of its modest size, you could base yourself anywhere to follow this itinerary, particularly if you have your own set of wheels (recommended). To get the most out of your stay, rent a rambling, idyllic Gozitan farmhouse.

Ideally your trip should start with a day exploring **Victoria**, wandering around majestic **Il-Kastell** and the laneways of **Il-Borgo**. Spend day two walking, swimming and snorkelling at **Dwejra** after paying your respects at the grand **Basilica of Ta'Pinu**. Begin day three with a visit to the temples and other attractions of **Xagħra**, then spend the afternoon reclining on **Ramla Bay**, where red sands meet blue water. Day four could be set aside for walking around **Ta'Ċenċ**, and for seeking out a lesser-known spot for swimming and snorkelling (nearby **Mġarr ix-Xini** is lovely, and a great place for a leisurely lunch). Spend day five visiting **Comino**, discovering the tiny island on foot and swimming in crystal-clear water. There's five days covered – but why not allocate a week and spend a few days relaxing poolside?

Two to three weeks
Malta & Gozo

If you have more time to play with, you can explore the best of Malta and Gozo.

Start your odyssey by taking in **Valletta**. On day two, visit the **Tarxien Temples** and the **Hypogeum**, going on to wander around the narrow, unspoilt streets of **Vittoriosa**. Try to visit the colourful harbour town of **Marsaxlokk** on a Sunday, when the fish market is in full swing. On day four you can explore the many sights of **Mdina** and **Rabat**. Your next must-sees on Malta are the amazing temples of **Ħaġar Qim** and **Mnajdra**, before you chill out on a charming beach like **Golden Bay**.

Next slooow your pace and take the ferry over to Gozo for some relaxation. Spend your first day on gorgeous **San Blas Bay**, or on **Ramla Bay**'s russet sands. The following day explore the attractive small town of **Xagħra**, visiting the **Ġgantija Temples**. The next you could explore the hilltop citadel at **Victoria**. On your ninth day, take a trip to **Comino**, to swim, snorkel and ramble around the beautifully rocky island. The rest of your time take it easy, walking around the coast, visiting churches, relaxing by a pool, and exploring Gozo's many delightful coves.

Diving & Outdoor Activities

Best Time to Go

» **Diving** Possible year-round

» **Sailing** April and November

» **Walking** October to early June

Best Dive Sites

» Ċirkewwa Arch

» Blue Hole

» Fungus Rock

» Blue Lagoon

Best Swimming Spots

» Golden Bay

» Blue Lagoon

» Mellieħa Bay

Marine Life Spotting

» Seahorses around the coast

» Dolphin sightings from cruise boats

» Multiple shark species

Water Activities

Diving

The Maltese Islands – and Gozo in particular – offer some of the best scuba-diving in Europe and have many advantages for divers (especially beginners), including a pleasant climate; a calm sea, which makes for excellent visibility; warm water; a wide range of interesting dive sites (caves, reefs, wartime wrecks), many of them accessible from the shore; and a large number of dive schools with qualified, professional, multilingual instructors. There are also sites perfect for experienced open-water and cave divers. Even in winter, the water temperature rarely drops below 13°C, making the islands a good destination all year round.

Most schools in Malta offer courses that lead to qualifications issued by one or more of the internationally recognised diving bodies, the most common being Professional Association of Diving Instructors (PADI) courses. The following organisations' websites offer general information about diving and dive qualifications, plus details of accredited diving schools in Malta:

» **British Sub-Aqua Club** (BSAC; www.bsac.com)

» **Confédération Mondiale des Activités Subaquatiques** (CMAS; www.cmas.org)

» **Professional Association of Diving Instructors** (PADI; www.padi.com)

Requirements

If you want to learn to dive in Malta, there are a few things required of you, not the least of which is the ability to swim. Restrictions on minimum age are at the instructor or operator's discretion, but operators usually teach junior open water diving from 10 years of age; note that those under 18 must have written parental consent. Some dive schools operate PADI 'Bubblemaker' programs designed to introduce kids aged eight and nine to breathing underwater.

Medical bureaucracy has relaxed a little in recent times. All persons registering at a dive centre are now required to fill out a self-assessment medical questionnaire to show that they are medically fit to dive. If this questionnaire highlights any medical condition that may restrict your diving practices, you will be requested to have a medical examination, and a physician will determine your fitness. The medical can be organised by the dive school, usually at a cost of €20 to €25. Alternatively, you can come prepared with recent certification from a diving doctor. You should also heed medical warnings and not fly within 24 hours of your last dive. Your last day in Malta should be spent reacclimatising to sea-level pressures.

Qualified divers wishing to lead their own groups must do so through a licensed dive centre, and must be at least an advanced open-water diver, with certification. The instructor will first have to register with a dive centre, presenting an instructor qualification and a current copy of an annual medical examination by a doctor specialising in diving medicine. You can rent cylinders and other equipment from dive centres.

Courses & Qualifications

Most schools offer a 'taster course' or 'beginner's dive', which begins with one or two hours of shore-based instruction on the workings of scuba equipment and safety procedures. You will then be introduced to breathing underwater in a pool or shallow bay and will end up doing a 30-minute dive in the sea. This kind of taster course should cost around €35.

A two or three resort-based scuba course gives you shore-based instruction plus open-water dives accompanied by an instructor and costs around €190. Such a course would qualify you up to 12m, and with two days more instruction you can upgrade it to an open-water diving qualification.

A course that will give you an entry-level diving qualification (CMAS One-Star Diver, PADI Open Water Diver, BSAC Ocean Diver) should take three to five days and cost around €315 to €350.

For certified divers, guided dives usually cost around €35 for one dive (including all equipment), but multidive packages are a better option, costing around €140 to €200 for six dives (price dependent on the amount of gear included). Transport to dive sites may be included in these packages, but if you're staying in Malta, boat trips to Gozo or Comino will often be an additional cost (this varies depending on your location).

Unaccompanied diving is possible for those in possession of a minimum qualification of a CMAS two-star or PADI advanced certificate; a six-day dive package that includes use of cylinder, weight belt and unlimited air fills costs around €75.

Dive Schools

There are more than 40 dive school operators in Malta. The majority are members of the **Professional Diving Schools Association** (PDSA; www.pdsa.org.mt), an organisation dedicated to promoting high standards of safety and professionalism.

The following dive schools all offer a similarly comprehensive menu of PADI-, BSAC- or CMAS-approved training and education courses, guided diving and the rental of scuba equipment to experienced divers. Some are based at large resorts; many can organise packages covering diving, accommodation and possibly airport transfers and car rental, should you require them.

Note that Nautic Team diving centre in Gozo specialises in diving for people with disabilities.

Sliema & St Julian's Area

» **Dive Systems** (Map p62; ☑2131 9123; www.divesystemsmalta.com; Exiles, Triq it-Torri, Sliema)

» **Diveshack** (Map p62; ☑2133 8558; www.divemalta.com; Ix-Xatt Ta'Qui-si-Sana, Sliema)

» **Divewise** (Map p66; ☑2135 6441; www.divewise.com.mt; Westin Dragonara Resort, St Julians)

Northwest Malta

» **Buddies Dive Cove** (Map p80; ☑2157 6266; www.buddiesmalta.com; 24/2 Triq il-Korp Tal-Pijunieri, Buġibba)

» **Dive Deep Blue** (Map p80; ☑2158 3946; www.divedeepblue.com; 100 Triq Ananija, Buġibba)

» **Subway Dive Centre** (Map p80; ☑2157 0354; www.subwayscuba.com; Triq il-Korp Tal-Pijunieri, Buġibba)

» **Meldives Dive School** (☑2152 2595; www.meldivesmalta.com; Tunny Net Complex, Mellieħa Bay)

» **Paradise Diving** (☑2157 4116; www.paradise diving.com; Paradise Bay Resort Hotel, Cirkewwa)

Gozo

» **Atlantis** (Map p121; ☑2155 4685; www. atlantisgozo.com; Atlantis Hotel, Triq il-Qolla, Marsalforn)

» **Calypso Diving Centre** (Map p121; ☑2156 1757; www.calypsodivers.com; Triq il-Port, Marsalforn)

» **Nautic Team** (Map p121; ☑2155 8507; www.nauticteam.com; Triq il-Vulcan, Marsalforn)

» **Frankie's Gozo Diving Centre** (☑7900 9575; www.gozodiving.com; Triq Mġarr, Xewkija)

» **Moby Dives** (☑2156 4429; www.moby divesgozo.com; Triq il-Gostra, Xlendi)

» **St Andrews Divers Cove** (☑2155 1301; www.gozodive.com; Triq San Ximun, Xlendi)

Comino

» **Comino Dive Centre** (☑2152 9824; Comino Hotels, operated by Subway Dive Centre)

Safety

Speedboat and ferry traffic can be quite heavy, especially in peak summer months and in the Gozo Channel area. For their own protection, divers are required to fly the code-A flag and use a surface-marker buoy. Boats are required to keep a distance of over 100m from divers' buoys, but it's wise to remain vigilant.

Divers should ensure that their travel insurance policy covers them for diving. Some policies specifically exclude 'dangerous activities', which can include scuba-diving.

Malta's public general hospital is Mater Dei Hospital (p67), southwest of Sliema; there is a decompression chamber here. Staff at the hospital can be contacted for any diving incidents requiring medical attention on ☑2545 5269 or by calling the emergency number ☑112. There is another decompression chamber at Gozo's General Hospital (p113).

Top Diving & Snorkelling Spots

Northwest Malta

» **Aħrax Point** (average depth 7m, maximum depth 18m) Caverns and a tunnel opening up to a small inland grotto with good coral growth. Suitable for all levels of diving experience. Shore dive, but it can also be viewed by snorkelling.

» **Anchor Bay** (average depth 6m, maximum depth 12m) Not much to see in the bay itself, but around the corner are good caves. Suitable for all levels of diving experience. Shore dive.

» **Ċirkewwa Arch** (average depth 10m, maximum depth 36m) Underwater walls and a magnificent arch, where divers can encounter a variety of fish and sometimes seahorses. Suitable for all levels of diving experience.

» **Marfa Point** (average depth 12m, maximum depth 18m) Large dive site with caves, reefs, promontories and tunnels. Can be accessed from the shore. Decent snorkelling opportunities.

» **P29** (average depth 30m, maximum depth 37m) Former minesweeper deliberately sunk in Paradise Bay in 2007, close to *Tugboat Rozi*.

» **St Paul's Islands** (multiple sites, average depths 6m to 12m, maximum depth 25m) Popular dive sites with a wreck between the shore and inner island, a reef on the eastern side of the northernmost island, and a valley between the two islands. Suitable for all levels of diving experience. The wreck can be accessed from the shore.

» **Tugboat Rozi** (average depth 30m, maximum depth 36m) A boat deliberately sunk in 1991 as an underwater diving attraction and now colonised by thousands of fish.

Valletta Area

» **Carolita Barge** (average depth 12m, maximum depth 22m) Possibly mistaken for a submarine, this barge was hit by a torpedo in 1942 and sank immediately. Well preserved and home to grouper and octopus. Popular training site for divers and therefore busy. Suitable for all levels of diving experience. Shore dive.

» **HMS Maori** (average depth 13m, maximum depth 18m) Below Fort St Elmo is the wreck of the *HMS Maori*, sunk in 1942. Silted up, but home to fish and octopus. Suitable for all levels of diving experience. Shore dive.

Southeast Malta

» **Blenheim Bomber** (average depth 42m, maximum depth 42m) Exciting dive to explore the well-preserved wreck of a WWII bomber, with engine and wings intact. For experienced divers only.

» **Delimara Point** (average depth 12m, maximum depth 25m) Usually excellent visibility for divers, with vertical cliffs and many caverns. Varied and colourful flora and fauna. Suitable for all levels of experience. Shore dive.

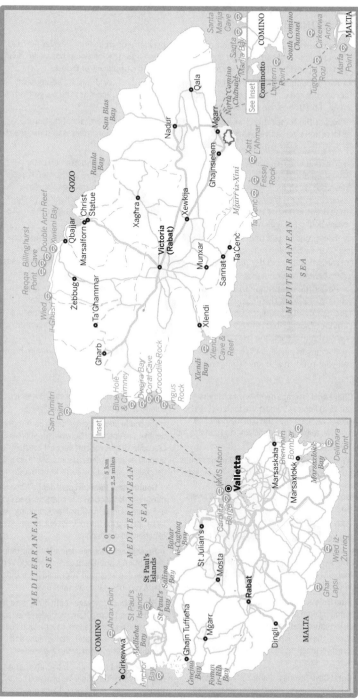

Diving & Snorkelling Malta & Gozo

MEDITERRANEAN SEA

COMINO

Ahrax Point

St Paul's Islands

Mellieħa Bay

Anchor Bay

Ċirkewwa

St Paul's Bay

Salina Bay

Għajn Tuffieħa

Mġarr

Gnejna Bay

Fomm ir-Riħ Bay

Baħar ic-Cagħaq Bay

St Julian's

Mosta

Wied iz-Żurrieq

Għar Lapsi

Dingli

Rabat

MALTA

Dellimara Point

Marsaxlokk Bay

Marsaxlokk

Marsaskala

Blenheim Bomber

HMS Maori

Carolita

Barge

Valletta

Inset

MEDITERRANEAN SEA

San Dimitri Point

Reqqa Point

Billinghurst Cave

Double Arch Reef

Xwien Bay

Qbajjar

Marsalforn

Christ Statue

Żebbuġ

Ta'Għammar

Xagħra

Għarb

Wied il-Għasri

GOZO

Victoria (Rabat)

Xagħra

Xewkija

Munxar

Sannat

Ta'Ċenċ

Xlendi

Xlendi Bay

Xlendi Cave & Reef

Blue Hole & Chimney

Dwejra Bay

Coral Cave

Crocodile Rock

Fungus Rock

San Blas Bay

Ramla Bay

Qala

Nadur

Għajnsielem

Mġarr

Xatt l-Aħmar

Mġarr ix-Xini

Ta'Ċenċ

Fessej Rock

Santa Marija Cave

Santa Marija Bay

North Comino Channel

COMINO

Cominotto

Lantern Point

South Comino Channel

Marfa Point

Tuġboat Rozi

Ċirkewwa Arch

MALTA

Marfa Bay

See Inset

MEDITERRANEAN SEA

RESPONSIBLE DIVING

The popularity of diving is placing immense pressure on many sites – over 40,000 divers a year visit the Maltese Islands. Please consider the following tips when diving and help preserve the ecology and beauty of Malta's underwater world:

» Avoid touching living marine organisms with your body or dragging equipment across the rocks. Be conscious of your fins – even without contact the surge from heavy fin strokes can damage delicate organisms.

» Resist the temptation to feed fish. You may disturb their normal eating habits, encourage aggressive behaviour or feed them something detrimental to their health.

» Minimise your disturbance of marine animals.

» Practise and maintain proper buoyancy control. Make sure you are correctly weighted and that your weight belt is positioned so that you stay horizontal. If you have not dived for a while, have a practice dive in a pool before taking to the sea. Be aware that buoyancy can change over the period of an extended trip: initially you may breathe harder and need more weight; a few days later you may breathe more easily and need less weight.

» Take great care in underwater caves. Spend as little time within them as possible as your air bubbles may be caught within the roof, leaving previously submerged organisms high and dry. Taking turns to inspect the interior of a small cave will lessen the chances of damaging contact.

» Resist the temptation to collect or buy shells or other remains of marine organisms. Aside from the ecological damage, taking home marine souvenirs depletes the beauty of a site and spoils the enjoyment of others. The same goes for marine archaeological sites (mainly shipwrecks). Respect their integrity; some sites are protected from looting by law.

» Plastics in particular are a serious threat to marine life. Ensure that you take home all your rubbish and any litter you may find as well.

» **Għar Lapsi** (average depth 6m, maximum depth 15m) Popular training site for divers. Safe, shallow cave that winds through the headland. Shore dive, reasonable snorkelling and suitable for all levels of experience.

» **Wied iż-Żurrieq** (average depth 9m, maximum depth 30m) Close to the Blue Grotto. Underwater valley and labyrinth of caves. Shore dive, reasonable snorkelling and suitable for all levels of experience.

Gozo

» **Billinghurst Cave** (average depth 20m, maximum depth 35m) Long tunnel leading to a cave deep inside the rock, with a multitude of coloured sea sponges. There's very little natural light (torch required). For experienced divers only.

» **Blue Hole & Chimney** (average depth 20m, maximum depth 45m) The Blue Hole is a natural rock formation and includes a large cave plus a fissure in the near-vertical wall. Popular, busy site. Shore dive, excellent snorkelling and suitable for all levels of experience.

» **Coral Cave** (average depth 25m, maximum depth 30m) Huge semicircular opening with a sandy bottom, where divers can view varied and colourful flora and fauna. Shore dive.

» **Crocodile Rock** (average depth 35m, maximum depth 45m) Rocky reef between the shore and crocodile-shaped rock off the west coast. Natural amphitheatre and deep fissures. Shore dive, decent snorkelling and suitable for all levels of experience.

» **Double Arch Reef** (average depth 30m, maximum depth 45m) Site characterised by a strange formation, with an arch dividing two large openings in the rock. Prolific marine life. For experienced divers only.

» **Fessej Rock** (average depth 30m, maximum depth 50m) A prominent column of rock. Vertical wall dive descending to 50m amid large shoals of fish. A very popular deep-water dive.

» **Fungus Rock** (average depth 30m, maximum depth beyond 60m) Dramatic underwater scenery with vertical walls, fissures, caverns and gullies. Good site for underwater photography and suitable for all levels of diving experience.

» **Reqqa Point** (average depth 25m, maximum depth beyond 70m) Near-vertical wall cut by fissures, caves and crevices. Large numbers of

» (above) Divers emerging from the sea by the Azure Window, Gozo (p119)
» (left) Rock climbing (p28), Malta

small fish, plus groups of amberfish and grouper if conditions are favourable. Shore dive and good snorkelling.

» **San Dimitri Point** (average depth 25m, maximum depth beyond 60m) Lots of marine life and exceptional visibility (sometimes exceeding 50m). Good snorkelling and suitable for all levels of experience.

» **Ta'Ċenċ** (average depth 25m, maximum depth 35m) Sheltered bay – access is by 103 steps from car park of nearby hotel. Canyon with large boulders, plus cave. Good marine life, but visibility can occasionally be poor. Good spot for night dives. Shore dive and suitable for all levels of experience.

» **Wied il-Għasri** (average depth in cave 12m, maximum depth 30m) A deep, winding cut in the headland makes for a long, gentle dive. Possible to view seahorses in the shallows. Cave with a huge domed vault and walls covered in corals. Can be done as a shore dive. Very good snorkelling and suitable for all levels of experience.

» **Xatt l'Aħmar** (average depth 9m, maximum depth 30m) Small bay, excellent for observing a large variety of fish including mullet, grouper, sea bream, octopus and cuttlefish. Shore dive, OK snorkelling and suitable for all levels of experience. Two vessels were scuttled here in August 2006 to create an artificial dive site.

» **Xlendi Cave & Reef** (average depth 6m, maximum depth 25m) Easy cave dive in shallow water and popular with beginners. Brightly coloured cave walls. Rocky headland dips steeply to the sea. An abundance of flora and fauna. Shore dive, OK snorkelling.

Comino

» **Blue Lagoon** (average depth 6m, maximum depth 12m) Easy site to the north of the sheltered lagoon, very popular with divers and snorkellers. Plenty of boat traffic. Shore dive. Suitable for all levels of experience.

» **Lantern Point** (average depth 30m, maximum depth 45m) Very popular dive site. Dramatic dive down a vertical wall. Rich fauna and an abundance of colour. OK snorkelling.

» **Santa Marija Cave** (average depth 7m, maximum depth 10m) Large cave and cavern system, and one of the most popular sites for cave dives. An abundance of fish in the area. Very good snorkelling and suitable for all levels of experience.

Snorkelling

If you don't fancy scuba-diving, you can still sample the delights of the underwater world by donning mask, snorkel and fins and exploring the rocks and bays around Malta's coastline. The only qualification necessary is the ability to swim. You can usually rent or buy the necessary equipment from hotels, lidos (recreational facilities with a swimming pool) and watersports centres in all the tourist areas.

Top snorkelling spots are off Comino and Gozo and include the Blue Lagoon (where you can rent snorkelling equipment from the kiosk) and the crags and caves east of **Santa Marija Bay** on Comino; the cave-riddled coastline at **Dwejra**; the long, narrow inlet at **Wied il-Għasri** off Gozo; and along the salt pan rocks west of **Xwieni Bay** near Marsalforn on Gozo.

Malta's Marine Life

Malta's location in the narrows between Sicily and North Africa, far away from the pollution of major cities and silt-bearing rivers, means that its marine life is richer than in many other parts of the Mediterranean.

Invertebrates including brightly coloured bryozoans, cup corals, sea anemones, sponges, starfish and sea urchins encrust the underwater cliffs and caves around the shores of Malta and Gozo. The countless nooks and crannies in the limestone provide shelter for crabs, lobsters, common octopuses and white-spotted octopuses. By night, cuttlefish graze the algal beds below the cliffs.

Most divers who visit Malta hope to catch sight of a seahorse. The maned seahorse is

---

DIVE GOZO

Over the past decade, EU funding has been channelled towards promoting diving as a niche tourism market for Gozo, which is regarded as one of Europe's top diving spots. To add to the catalogue of dive sites off Gozo's shores, two vessels were scuttled in the waters around Gozo and Comino to serve as an artificial reef for the visiting divers, followed by two more vessels in 2007 and 2009, landing in perfect positions on the seabed 30m to 35m underwater to create artificial dive sites. The locations were chosen in part because they are sheltered from the strong prevailing winds that can make popular sites like Dwejra and Marsalforn inaccessible.

fairly common around the Maltese coast, preferring shallow, brackish water; they grow up to 15cm in length and feed on plankton and tiny shrimps. Seahorses mate for life and display an unusual inversion of common male and female reproductive roles. Using her tube-like ovipositor, the female deposits her eggs in a brood pouch in the male's abdomen, where they are fertilised. Here the eggs develop and finally hatch before the male 'gives birth' by releasing the live brood into open water.

Migratory shoals of sardine, sprat, bluefin tuna, bonito, mackerel and dolphin fish – a Maltese delicacy known locally as *lampuka* – pass through the offshore waters in late summer and autumn. Swordfish are fairly common all year round. Sea bream, sea bass, grouper, red mullet, wrasse, dogfish and stingray frequent the shallower waters closer to shore, where moray and conger eels hide among the rocks and venture out at night to feed on octopus and fish.

The seas around Malta are known among shark-watchers as one of the 'sharkiest' spots in the Med. In April 1987 a great white shark caught by local fisherman Alfredo Cutajar off Filfla was claimed to be a world record at 7.13m in overall length. However, later investigations brought the accuracy of the original measurements into doubt (still, be it 7m or 7.13m, it's still *big*!).

Other shark species known to haunt Maltese waters include the blue, thresher and mako. However, bathers and divers should not be unduly alarmed, as shark sightings in inshore waters are extremely rare. Indeed, the great white is considered to be an endangered species, and the decrease in its numbers is thought to have resulted from dwindling stocks of tuna, its main food source.

The loggerhead turtle is another endangered species that is occasionally sighted in Maltese waters, but the lack of secluded, sandy beaches means that they do not nest on the Maltese Islands. The common dolphin – known as *denfil* in Malti – and the bottlenose dolphin are fairly common in Maltese waters and are occasionally seen from cruise boats and dive boats.

Swimming

Don't go to Malta expecting miles of sandy beaches – there are only a handful of sandy stretches, and these get very busy. However, there are numerous rocky bays and coves that offer swimming in crystal-clear waters

SUPERLATIVE SWIMMING SPOTS

The country built its holiday reputation on sunny weather and beaches, but Malta's coastline tends to be rocky rather than lined by silky sands. Its beaches tend to be small and perfectly formed, but tend to get packed out in summer. Often a better option is to do as the locals do and swim off the rocks. Here are some of the islands' loveliest places to swim.

» **Golden Bay** (p72), Northwest Malta

» **Blue Lagoon** (p126), Comino

» **Mellieħa Bay** (p75), Northwest Malta

» **Għajn Tuffieħa Bay** (p72), Northwest Malta

» **Ġnejna Bay**, Northwest Malta

» **Paradise Bay**, Northwest Malta

» **Għar Lapsi**, Southeast Malta

» **St Peter's Pool** (p99), Southeast Malta

» **Ramla Bay** (p125), Gozo

» **Wied il-Għasri** (p120), Gozo

» **Mġarr ix-Xini**, Gozo

(take a snorkel along), and these are the preferred summer haunts of the Maltese. There are also several natural pools around the islands, which are also favoured by locals as great swimming spots.

Sailing

Malta is a major yachting centre, with a large marina at Msida, a smaller one at Gozo's Mġarr harbour, and two slick modern marinas – one at the Portomaso development in St Julian's, the other, called Grand Harbour Marina, at Vittoriosa. Many yacht owners cruise the Med in summer and winter their vessels in Malta.

A full program of races and regattas is held between April and November each year (great for participants and spectators). The popular Rolex Middle Sea Race (www.rolexmiddlesearace.com) is a highly rated offshore classic staged annually in October. The race route is 606 nautical miles long, starting from Malta's Grand Harbour and sailing anticlockwise around Sicily before finishing back in Malta. For details of events and opportunities for crewing, contact the **Royal Malta Yacht Club** (2133 3109; www.rmyc.org; Ta'Xbiex Seafront) or check the website.

If a yacht seems a little too much to handle, sailing dinghies can be rented by the hour at most tourist resorts for around €13 an hour. However, qualified sailors are able to hire a yacht by the day or the week from one of several charter companies. If you don't have a RYA Coastal Skipper qualification you'll need to pay extra for a skipper (around €80 to €100 per day). Try the following:

» **Captain Morgan Yacht Charter** (2346 3333; www.yachtcharter.com.mt; per week low/mid/high season from €1100/2700/3000 for an eight-berth Oceanis Clipper 411 sailing yacht)

» **S & D Yachts** (2133 1515; www.sdyachts.com; per week low/mid/high season from €1375/1625 for a six-berth Bavaria 31 sailing yacht)

Windsurfing

Windsurfing is enjoyed year-round in Malta. Equipment hire and instruction are available at the main tourist resorts. Mellieha Bay, Ghallis Rock (close to St Julian's) and St Thomas Bay are popular venues. A good place for information is the website at www.holidays-malta.com/windsurf.

Other Activities

Birdwatching

Where to Watch Birds & Other Wildlife in the Maltese Islands, written by Alex Casha and published by BirdLife Malta, is a comprehensive guide.

BirdLife Malta (2134 7646; www.birdlife malta.org) is the best contact for birders visiting Malta. The organisation manages the Ghadira Nature Reserve (p75) at Mellieha Bay and the Is-Simar Nature Reserve (p78) at Xemxija, and monitors activity that threatens wild birds. Its website details recent sightings, and documents the campaign against illegal hunting.

Rock Climbing

There are more than 1300 established rock-climbing routes in the Maltese Islands (all on limestone), with some of the most popular sites for climbers below the Dingli Cliffs in the west, at Ghar Lapsi and near the Victoria Lines below Naxxar. **The Malta Rock Climbing Club** (www.climbmalta.com) can provide information for visiting climbers.

Malta Activities (9942 5439; www.maltaout doors.com) facilitates sessions for experienced climbers and taster half-days for beginners. Trips include opportunities to traverse sea cliffs, and all equipment is provided.

Walking

There is some good walking to be enjoyed on the winding back roads and cliff-top paths of Malta and Gozo, although fences, dogs and bird-shooters can occasionally prove to be a nuisance. Distances are small and you can easily cover much of the islands on foot. A circuit of Gozo is a good objective for a multiday hike. You can also download walking routes from www.visitmalta.com/country_walks_gozo.

A great source of information is the **Ramblers' Association of Malta** (www.ramblers malta.org), which organises informal guided country walks for like-minded folk from October to early June (the best time for walking). This organisation is dedicated to safeguarding public access to the Maltese countryside in the face of threats like hunting and commercial development; read about their campaigns on the comprehensive website.

Horse Riding

Horses have long played an important part in Maltese life, and you can often see owners out exercising their favourite trotting horses. The quieter back roads offer enjoyable riding. Instruction and horse hire can be organised through most major hotels. Recommended stables include Golden Bay Horse Riding (p72) in Golden Bay and Lino's Stables (p125) on Gozo.

Travel with Children

Best Regions for Kids

Valletta
A perfectly child-sized capital, with a pedestrianised centre. War museum, forts and armoury will tickle some children's fancy.

Gozo
Malta's neighbour is fun to get to (by ferry) and once there you can slow your pace, swim, explore, snorkel, boat and dive.

Comino
A fantastic day out to an almost-deserted island with plenty of trails, a fortified tower and the glorious Blue Lagoon for swimming.

Northwest Malta
This region harbours Malta's best beaches, with lots of water-sports facilities, boat-trip opportunities and several theme parks.

Buġibba
This cheap and fairly cheerful resort might feel less Maltese and more generic than elsewhere, but kids will love the tacky shops and boating opportunities, and from 2013 it's home to the Malta National Aquarium.

Mdina & Rabat
The Natural History museum may be fusty, but enjoyable nevertheless. The Mdina Experience will appeal to older kids, as will Rabat's catacombs.

Sun and sea; boat trips and snorkelling; countryside and caves; pedestrianised walled towns and a child-friendly capital; forts, castles and fossil-packed museums; swords and suits of armour: Malta and Gozo have plenty to offer kids of all ages. There's also something about Malta's small size that makes it a particularly family-friendly destination – even if you want to visit myriad places, you'll never end up spending hours in the car or on the bus. A great thing about the islands is that grown ups can enjoy themselves while keeping the kids happy, as there's so much of interest to do. Add to the list of attractions those pitched specifically for children, like water and theme parks, and you'll find plenty of ingredients for a great family holiday.

Malta for Kids
The Maltese have a great affection for children, and as in Italy or Spain, families will receive a warm welcome. There's a good healthcare system here and many people speak not only Malti, but English, Italian, and sometimes French, which is a help if you run into any difficulties. The **Malta Baby & Kids Directory** (www.maltababyandkids.com) lists lots of useful information, including days out, activities and general advice. You can buy the directory online (€8) or register to obtain its listings.

Open Spaces

Although Malta's main roads are busy, village and town squares and promenades are sometimes pedestrianised, which means there's plenty of space to run about. This is especially the case on Gozo, which is a lot more rural than Malta. Most towns have a children's playground; there are large ones at Sliema and Mdina. Valletta also has a couple of parks and a pedestrianised centre.

Dining Out

Children are welcome at all but the grandest restaurants. Even places that don't look like typical family places, Gozo's Restaurant Ta'Frenċ (p120) and Tatita's (p118), for example, are very easy going and family friendly. High chairs are usually available and there's normally a children's menu. Still, children's menus tend to offer a similar roll call of chicken nuggets, pizza, and so on; if you want to provide more variety, ask for an adult half portion instead.

Children's Highlights
Theme Parks and Aquariums

» **Splash & Fun Park** Waterslides and playground, at Baħar iċ Ċagħaq.

» **Mediterraneo Marine Park** Watery park that includes displays by sea-lions and dolphins. Be mindful, however, that the presence of dolphins here is controversial.

» **Sweethaven** This theme park is in an ageing film set from the 1980 film *Popeye,* and is popular with younger children, even if they've never heard of Popeye himself.

» **Malta National Aquarium** This new complex in Buġibba (under construction at the time of research) promises to be a state-of-the-art glimpse into the world of the sea.

BABYSITTING

If you're in need of a breather, large hotels will usually offer a babysitting service, or you can enquire at your guesthouse or apartment complex whether they provide babysitting. Otherwise, try **Stepping Stones Early Learning Centre** (www.steppingstonesmalta.com) on Malta.

Museums, Forts & Underworlds

» **Fort Rinella, near Valletta** This costumed fort features guided tours by volunteers, and cannon- and rifle-firing demonstrations.

» **Inquisitor's Palace, Vittoriosa** Children will be intrigued by the prison cells at this palace, and the cesspits are likely to be of particular fascination.

» **Red Tower, Marfa Peninsula** The mini-fortress Red Tower is a nicely child-sized castle.

» **Hal Saflieni Hypogeum, Paola** This mysterious underworld will appeal to older children.

» **Catacombs, Rabat** Older children will enjoy these mysterious caverns.

» **National War Museum, Valletta** Children intrigued by war and history will enjoy this museum's military hardware.

» **Armoury, Grandmaster's Palace, Valletta** The armour and weaponery here will appeal to children with a military fascination.

» **Pomskizillious Museum of Toys (Xagħra) and Toy Museum (Valletta)** Both museums house historic toys in glass cases.

» **Maritime Museum, Vittoriosa** It's a bit old-fashioned here, but younger children might enjoy the model boats or role-playing in the mock sailors' bar.

» **Caves, Xagħra** Gozo's Xerri's Grotto is an appealing place to visit, with stalagmites and stalactites in myriad shapes.

» **Old Prison, Victoria** Prison cells in Gozo's castlelike capital – more suitable for older children.

Beaches & Coves

» **Golden Bay, Malta** A lovely, safe, gentle, sandy beach with lots of facilities.

» **Għajn Tuffieħa Bay, Malta** A bit hard to reach (steps down to it) but gentle and sandy.

» **Mellieħa Bay, Malta** Sandy, with safe paddling and swimming, and lots of facilities.

» **St Peter's Pool, Malta** Limpid sea pool.

» **Għar Lapsi, Malta** Natural sea swimming pool, popular with locals.

» **Ramla Bay, Gozo** A lovely red-sand beach with cafes. There can be currents here, though – look out for the flag signals.

» **San Blas Bay, Gozo** Another great beach, less crowded than Ramla – once again, look out for currents.

» **Mġarr-ix-Xini, Gozo** A gorgeous little cove with good swimming.

» **Wied il-Għasri, Gozo** Great cove with azure sea and adventurous steep approach.

» **Blue Lagoon, Comino** The ultimate sea-swimming pool, but crowded in summer.

Outdoor Activities

» **Boat trips** Round-island, in a glass bottomed boat, to see coves, or to Comino and Gozo: the choices are endless.

» **Diving** Malta and Gozo are great places to learn to dive, and there are centres dotted all over the islands. Most diving centres will teach children from age 10.

» **Horse Riding** Golden Bay is a particularly good place for horse riding; there's a popular centre nearby.

» **Jeep Safaris** Many tour companies offer these safaris – and they're a fun way to explore the islands.

» **Watersports** All the major resorts offer sailing, dinghies for hire as well as pedalos and other items.

Exhibitions

» **Audiovisual exhibitions** Cinematic presentations like the Malta Experience (Valletta) and the Mdina Experience will entertain older kids.

Planning
When to Go

The best times to be in Malta and Gozo with kids are spring, early summer and autumn (May, June and September), when you'll definitely be able to swim, the weather won't be at its hottest, prices are lower and places are less crowded. Of course, families with school-age kids will be tied to the holidays. If travelling in the European summer, easy access to the sea or a pool will be a boon. Children will enjoy the colourful parades at Carnival (February) and Easter (March/April), but swimming will be chilly in these months; in March/April pack wetsuits and your children may still enjoy a dip.

Accommodation

As Malta and Gozo are such family-centred destinations, there are lots of suitable, reasonably priced accommodation options. The farmhouses for rent on Gozo are ideal; they offer plenty of space and often a pool (for more information see the Accommodation chapter). Note that some places only have shower facilities, which is something to investigate if your child only takes baths.

What to Pack

You'll find everything you need available for sale in Malta, so don't panic about forgetting something: formula milk, nappies, wipes, clothes, toys and English-language children's books are all easy to find.

regions at a glance

Valletta, Malta's beautiful little capital, is rich in history and culture and is also a great place to eat out. Nearby lie Sliema, St Julian's and Paceville, seafront settlements that together form Malta's gastronomic and nightlife capital. To the northwest are Malta's best beaches and the island's major resorts. Central Malta is the most traditional-feeling area of the island, encompassing the historically fascinating and evocative towns of Mdina and Rabat, and a breathtaking coastline. The southeast of the island has more fine coast, a vibrant fish market and some of Malta's finest prehistoric temples. The smaller islands of Gozo and Comino are good for anyone who enjoys nature, walking, eating out, diving, or just relaxing and enjoying the slower pace.

Valletta

History
Food
Prehistory

History
Valletta was built after the triumph of the Knights of St John at the Siege of Malta in 1565. The city's narrow grid of streets and fortifications remains intact, while the Knights' original heartland lies just across the glittering harbour.

Food
You can dine spectacularly in Malta's capital, which includes some of the island's loveliest restaurants. Regional specialities are fresh local produce and Maltese dishes with a twist.

Prehistory
The Hal Saflieni Hypogeum and Tarxien Temples are two of Malta's most amazing prehistoric sites. The former is a beautifully carved 5000-year-old necropolis, the latter a temple complex with extraordinary carvings.

p36

Sliema, St Julian's & Paceville

Food
Nightlife
Boat Trips

Food
Buzzing Sliema and St Julian's are packed full of restaurants – Maltese, Italian and fusion cuisine – and bars; there's an after-dark sparkle here that's unmatched elsewhere on the island.

Nightlife
If you're under 25 and looking for a party, Paceville could be heaven, with a fiesta-style atmosphere on summer nights, as swarms of international students, tourists and young locals back for the holidays descend.

Boat Trips
Sliema's promenade has one of the best views in Malta. From here you can explore the harbours by boat – or go further afield, encircling the entire island or taking a trip to Gozo and Comino.

p59

Northwest Malta

Beaches
Views
Food

Central Malta

History
Architecture
Scenery

Southeast Malta

Food
Prehistoric Sites
Coastline

Gozo & Comino

Swimming
Scenery
Activities

Beaches
Malta is ringed by rocks, rather than by beaches, but its finest sandy fringes lie on the northwestern coast. The beaches here may not be huge, but they are beautiful curves of golden sand, particularly off-season.

Views
Take a trip around the Marfa Peninsula and you'll be rewarded by some jaw-dropping views. You may think it's hard to get away from it all on Malta, but a short drive or walk along the headland to Ras il-Qammieħ will leave you feeling like you've reached the end of the world.

Food
The resort town of Mellieħa has escaped the development seen on other parts of the coast, and you can dine on Maltese haute cuisine at some excellent restaurants.

p69

History
Central Malta is the best place on the island to feel as if you have travelled in time. Here is the silent city of Mdina; the Roman villa excavated at Rabat; and Rabat's intriguing catacombs, full of mystery and atmosphere.

Architecture
Whether it's the jumble of medieval and baroque architecture in Mdina and Rabat, or the great Rotonda at Mosta, Central Malta yields some illustrious architectural splendours.

Scenery
The Dingli Cliffs feature some of the island's most sumptuous scenery. The 60m cliffs drop down into royal-blue sea, and their heights offer soul-searing views over the Mediterranean.

p84

Food
Southeast Malta is the place to go for fresh seafood. The seafront at ancient fishing village Marsaxlokk is lined by restaurants overlooking bobbing boats while Marsaskala, off the tourist path, is a favourite of foodie locals.

Prehistoric Sites
Ħaġar Qim and Mnajdra temples have the most thrilling location of any of Malta's prehistoric sites. The great ruins, with their slabs of limestone pitched precisely to catch the sun's rays, are perched on sea cliffs overlooking the Islet of Filfla.

Coastline
There are some lovely spots along the southeast coast, from where you can take trips to the Blue Grotto, swim in the natural pool of Għar Lapsi and seek out St Peter's Pool.

p98

Swimming
As well as its distinctive red-sand beaches on the northeast coast, Gozo has some glorious rocky bays to swim in, including the coves of Mġarr-ix-Xini and Wied il-Għasri.

Scenery
Nineteenth-century nonsense artist and poet Edward Lear invented new words to describe the beautifully strange landscapes of Gozo, calling it 'pomskizillious and gromphiberous'.

Activities
Gozo is a particularly beguiling destination for underwater exploration, and also yields fantastic horse riding, boat trips and other watersport opportunities.

p107

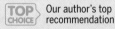
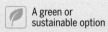

See the Index for a full list of destinations covered in this book.

On the Road

Valletta

Includes »

Best Places to Eat

» Ambrosia (p46)
» Trattoria da Pippo (p46)
» Rubino (p46)
» Salvino's (p46)

Best Places to Stay

» Valletta Suites (p130)
» Palazzo Vittoriosa (p131)
» Palazzo San Pawl (p130)

Why Go?

Valletta is Malta's Lilliputian capital, measuring 600m by 1000m. When it was built by the Knights of St John in the 16th and 17th centuries, its founder decreed that it should be 'a city built by gentlemen for gentlemen', and it retains much of this elegance. Despite its small size, there's a mass of things to see here: when Unesco named Valletta a World Heritage Site, it described it as 'one of the most concentrated historic areas in the world'.

Now is the time to visit: Valletta's lately undergone more changes than it has for centuries, with the brand-new Renzo Piano–designed main gate and parliament building, as well as the renovation of the bombed-out Opera House. There are plenty of bars and restaurants here too; just don't expect Valletta to be buzzing all night – its tranquility is a large part of its charm.

When to Go

April, May, June, September and October are the balmiest months, with lower prices, sunshine and fewer crowds. In April there's the Malta Firework Festival, and in June Ghanafest celebrates traditional music. However, summer is hot and lively with the Malta Arts and Jazz festivals in July. Look out also for the Notte Bianca in September, when Valletta stays up unusually late.

Valletta Highlights

1 Exploring the nooks and crannies of **Valletta** (p38)

2 Checking out the view that puts the grand in Grand Harbour, from the **Upper Barrakka Gardens & the Saluting Battery** (p44)

3 Discovering the glories of **St John's Co-Cathedral** (p38)

4 Admiring the delicate modelling of the 'fat ladies' at the **National Museum of Archaeology** (p43)

5 Asking the unanswerable questions (who? why? how?) at the remarkable **Hal Saflieni Hypogeum** (p57) – book ahead!

6 Exploring Vittoriosa's charming **Il Collachio** (p56) district, followed by a cruise of the **Grand Harbour** (p53)

VALLETTA SIGHTS

History

Before the Great Siege of 1565, the Sceberras Peninsula was uninhabited and unfortified, except for Fort St Elmo at its furthest point. Fearing another attack by the Turks, Grand Master Jean Parisot de la Valette (of the Knights of St John) began the task of building a new city on what was then just a barren limestone ridge. Valletta was the first planned city in Europe, with buildings tall enough to shade the streets from the hot sun, and straight streets to allow cooling sea breezes to circulate. A great ditch – 18m deep, 20m wide and nearly 1km long – was cut across the peninsula to protect the landward approach, and massive curtain walls were raised around the perimeter of the city. Spurred on by the fear of a Turkish assault, the Knights completed the fortifications in a mere five years.

◉ Sights

St John's Co-Cathedral   CHURCH

(⌨2122 0536; www.stjohnscocathedral.com; Triq ir-Repubblika; adult/child €6/free, incl museum admission; ⏱9.30am-4.30pm Mon-Fri, 9.30am-12.30pm Sat, last admission 30 min before closing, closed Sun, public holidays & during services) St John's Co-Cathedral, Malta's most impressive church, was designed by the architect Gerolamo Cassar. It was built between 1573 and 1578, taking over from the Church of St Lawrence in Vittoriosa as the place where the Knights would gather for communal worship. It was raised to a status equal to that of St Paul's Cathedral in Mdina – the official seat of the Archbishop of Malta – by a papal decree of 1816, hence the term 'co-cathedral'.

Visitors should dress appropriately for a house of worship. Stiletto heels are not permitted, in order to protect the marble floor.

The plain facade renders the interior even more of a surprise: it's a colourful treasure house of Maltese baroque. The nave is long and low and every wall, pillar and rib is encrusted with rich ornamentation, giving the effect of a dusty gold brocade. The floor is a vast patchwork quilt of marble tomb slabs, and the vault is covered in paintings by Mattia Preti illustrating events from the life of St John the Baptist. The altar is dominated by a huge marble sculpture depicting the Baptism of Christ, with a painting, *St John in Heaven,* by Preti above it.

There are six bays on either side of the nave, eight of which contain chapels allocated to the various langues (or divisions, based on nationality) of the Order of St John and dedicated to the patron saint of the particular langue. The first bay you'll encounter upon entering and walking to your right is the Chapel of Germany.

Opposite is the Chapel of Castille & Portugal, with monuments to Grand Masters Antonio Manoel de Vilhena and Manuel Pinto de Fonseca. Next is the Chapel of Aragon, the most splendid of all. The tombs of the brothers (and consecutive Grand Masters) Rafael and Nicolas Cotoner compete for the title of most extravagant sculpture.

VALLETTA IN...

Two Days

Start the day with alfresco coffee and *pastizzi* (filled pastry) at Caffe Cordina (p48), before wandering Valletta's history-loaded streets – be sure to pop in to major attractions St John's Co-Cathedral (p38), the Grand Master's Palace (p39) and the National Museum of Archaeology (p43), then rest your legs at the view-enriched Upper Barrakka Gardens (p44). On the second day, take a tour of the Hal Saflieni Hypogeum (p57) – having prebooked a few weeks' ahead – then spend the afternoon exploring the intriguing Three Cities area. Take in an evening show in Valletta at Manoel Theatre (p49) or St James' Cavalier Centre for Creativity (p49).

Four Days

Shake and add water to the two-day itinerary, then stir in the following: visit the National War Museum (p43) to learn of Malta's WWII heroism and hardships, and in the evening see a show at the former Royal Opera House (Triq ir-Repubblika), now converted into an outdoor amphitheatre. The next day, venture further afield – take a bus to Mdina, Marsaxlokk or the northern beaches for some swimming, or take a ferry across to Sliema.

St John's Co-Cathedral

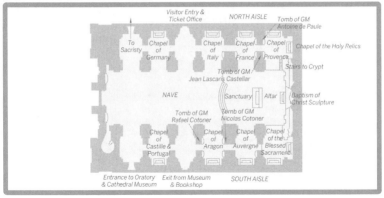

Visitor Entry & Ticket Office
NORTH AISLE
Tomb of GM Antoine de Paule
To Sacristy
Chapel of Germany
Chapel of Italy
Chapel of France
Chapel of Provence
Chapel of the Holy Relics
Stairs to Crypt
Tomb of GM Jean Lascaris Castellar
NAVE
Sanctuary
Altar
Baptism of Christ Sculpture
Tomb of GM Rafael Cotoner
Tomb of GM Nicolas Cotoner
Chapel of Castile & Portugal
Chapel of Aragon
Chapel of Auvergne
Chapel of the Blessed Sacrament
Entrance to Oratory & Cathedral Museum
Exit from Museum & Bookshop
SOUTH AISLE

The last bay in this aisle, past the Chapel of Auvergne, contains the Chapel of the Blessed Sacrament (also known as the Chapel dedicated to the Madonna of Philermos), closed off by a pair of solid silver gates. It contains a 15th-century crucifix from Rhodes and keys of captured Turkish fortresses.

Opposite is the dark, moody Chapel of Provence, containing the tombs of Grand Masters Antoine de Paule and Jean Lascaris Castellar. The cathedral crypt (usually closed to the public) can be reached by the stairs at the back. Here the first 12 Grand Masters of Malta – from 1523 to 1623 – are interred. The reclining effigies include Jean Parisot de la Valette, hero of the Great Siege and the founder of Valletta, and his English secretary Sir Oliver Starkey, the only man below the rank of Grand Master to be honoured with a tomb in the crypt. Darker still is the Chapel of the Holy Relics (also known as the Chapel of the Anglo-Bavarian Langue), which contains a wooden figure of St John that is said to have come from the galley in which the Knights departed from Rhodes in 1523.

The austere Chapel of France, with a Preti altarpiece of St Paul, was stripped of its baroque decoration in the 1840s. Preti's painting, The Mystic Marriage of St Catherine, hangs in the Chapel of Italy, looking down on a bust of Grand Master Gregorio Carafa.

The first bay in the south aisle of St John's gives access to the Cathedral Museum (☎2122 0536; Triq ir-Repubblika, entrance through St John's Co-Cathedral; admission included in cathedral ticket price; ⊘same opening hr), the first room of which is the Oratory, built in 1603. It is dominated by its altarpiece, the menacing Beheading of St John the Baptist (c 1608) by Caravaggio, which is the artist's largest painting. The executioner and Salome with her platter are depicted with chilling realism (note that the artist signed his name in the blood seeping from St John's severed neck). On the east wall hangs Caravaggio's St Jerome, another work of great power and pathos.

The rest of the Cathedral Museum houses some beautiful 16th-century illuminated manuscripts and a fine collection of Flemish tapestries based on drawings by Rubens.

Grand Master's Palace   HISTORIC BUILDING

(Pjazza San Ġorġ, visitor entrance on Triq il-Merkanti; €10/5, includes State Apartments & Armoury, plus free Armoury audio guide; ⊘Armoury 9am-5pm, State Apartments 10am-4pm Fri-Wed) Like St John's Co-Cathedral, the stern exterior of the 16th-century Grand Master's Palace conceals a sumptuous interior. This was once the residence of the Grand Masters of the Knights of St John. Since Malta's independence in 1964 the building served as the seat of Malta's parliament, but this is set to change as they move into their new Renzo Piano-designed building close to the City Gate. The Grand Masters' Palace remains the official residence of the Maltese president.

The right-hand arch is the public entrance; a ticket office between the two courtyards sells tickets to visit the Armoury and the State Apartments (☎2124 9349; adult/child €10/5 joint admission; ⊘9am-5pm);

Valletta

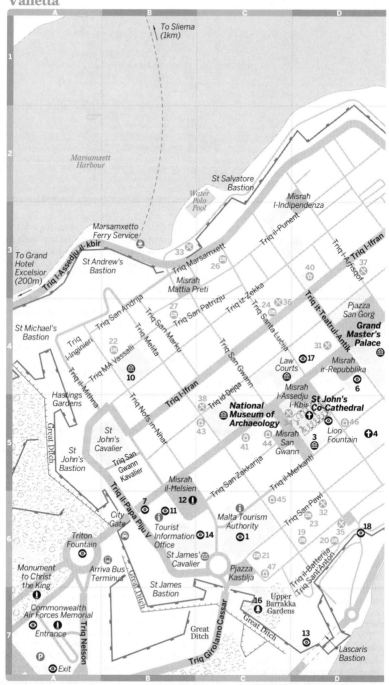

To Sliema
(1km)

Marsamxett
Harbour

St Salvatore
Bastion

Misrah
I-Indipendenza

Water
Polo
Pool

Triq il-Punent

Triq I-Arrisqof

Triq I-Ifran

Marsamxetto
Ferry Service

33

Triq l-Assedju il-kbir

St Andrew's
Bastion

Triq Marsamxett

26

Misrah
Mattia Preti

Triq tz-Zekka

40

Pjazza
San Gorġ

To Grand
Hotel
Excelsior
(200m)

Triq l-Assedju il-Kbir

27

Triq San Andrija

Triq San Patrizju

24   36

Triq it-Teatrul-Antik

Grand
Master's
Palace

St Michael's
Bastion

Triq
I-Inginieri

22

Triq Melita

Triq San Marku

Triq Santa Lucija

31

Triq MA Vassalli

10

Triq San Gwann

Law
Courts

17

Misrah
ir-Repubblika

6

Hastings
Gardens

Triq il-Mithna

Triq I-Ifran

Triq id-Dejqa

38

National
Museum of
Archaeology

Misrah
I-Assedju
I-Kbir

St John's
Co-Cathedral

St John's
Cavalier

Triq Nofs in-Nhar

43

41

44

Misrah
San
Gwann

3

34

Lion
Fountain

46

4

St John's
Bastion

St
John's
Cavalier

Triq San
Gwann Kavalier

Misrah
il-Helsien

12

Triq San Zakkarija

Triq il-Merkanti

45

Triq San Pawl

32

23

Great Ditch

Triq Il-Papa Piju V

7

11

City
Gate

Tourist
Information
Office

14

Malta Tourism
Authority

1

19

20

35

18

Triq il-Batterija

Triq Sant'Anton

Triton
Fountain

St James'
Cavalier

21

47

Monument
to Christ
the King

Arriva Bus
Terminus

Pjazza
Kastilja

Commonwealth
Air Forces Memorial

Entrance

Triq Nelson

St James
Bastion

16

Upper
Barrakka
Gardens

Triq Girolamo Cassar

P

Exit

Great
Ditch

Great Ditch

13

Lascaris
Bastion

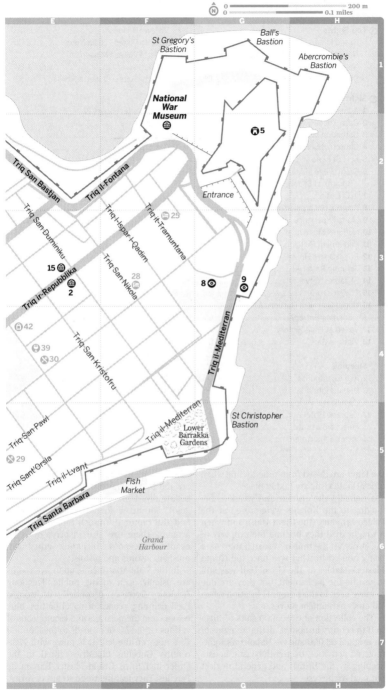

St Gregory's Bastion

Ball's Bastion

Abercrombie's Bastion

National War Museum

5

Entrance

Triq San Bastjan

Triq il-Fontana

Triq San Duminku

Triq l-Ispar l-Qadim

Triq it-Tramuntana

25

15

Triq ir-Repubblika

Triq San Nikola

28

2

8

9

42

39

Triq San Kristofru

Triq il-Mediterran

30

Triq San Pawl

Triq il-Mediterran

St Christopher Bastion

Lower Barrakka Gardens

29

Triq Sant'Orsla

Triq il-Lvant

Fish Market

Triq Santa Barbara

Grand Harbour

Valletta

the latter are closed from time to time when official state visits are taking place.

Originally, the armour and weapons belonging to the Knights were stored at the Palace Armoury (the Great Hall), and when a Knight died they became the property of the Order. At the time of research they were being housed in what was once the Grand Master's stables as the Great Hall was still in use by the parliament, but they are due to move back to their original location when Valletta's parliament moves.

The collection of over 5000 suits of 16th- to 18th-century armour is all that remains of an original 25,000 suits – Napoleon's light-fingered activities, over-enthusiastic house-keeping by the British and general neglect put paid to the rest.

Some of the most interesting pieces are the breastplate worn by la Valette, the beautifully damascened (steel inlaid with gold) suit made for Alof de Wignacourt and the captured Turkish Sipahi (cavalry) armour. There are also displays of some beautiful weapons, including crossbows, muskets, swords and pistols.

In the State Apartments, up to five rooms are usually open to the public. The long **Armoury Corridor**, decorated with trompe l'oeil painting, scenes of naval battles, blue colours and the portraits and escutcheons of various Grand Masters, leads to the **Council Chamber** on the left. It is hung with 17th-century Gobelins tapestries gifted to the Order in 1710 by Grand Master Ramon de Perellos. They feature exotic scenes of Africa,

India, the Caribbean and Brazil, including an elephant beneath a cashew-nut tree; an ostrich, cassowary and flamingo; a rhino and a zebra being attacked by a leopard; and a tableau with palm trees, a tapir, a jaguar and an iguana.

Beyond lie the State Dining Room and the Supreme Council Hall, where the Supreme Council of Order met. It is decorated with a frieze depicting events from the Great Siege of 1565, while the minstrels' gallery bears paintings showing scenes from the Book of Genesis. At the far end of the hall a door gives access to the Hall of the Ambassadors, or Red State Room, where the Grand Master would receive important visitors, and where the Maltese president still receives foreign envoys. It contains portraits of the French kings Louis XIV, Louis XV and Louis XVI, the Russian Empress Catherine the Great and several Grand Masters. The neighbouring Pages' Room, or Yellow State Room (despite the abundance of greenish tones), was used by the Grand Master's 16 attendants.

National Museum of Archaeology   MUSEUM
(☑2122 1623; Triq ir-Repubblika; adult/child €5/2.50; ☺9am-7pm) The National Museum of Archaeology is housed in the formidable Auberge de Provence.

In the downstairs galleries the exhibits include delicate stone tools dating from 5200 BC, and there's an amazing temple model from Ta' Ħaġrat – a prehistoric architectural maquette. More impressive still are the well-preserved voluptuous figurines, or 'fat ladies', found at Ħaġar Qim, with massive rounded thighs and arms, but tiny, doll-like hands and feet, wearing pleated skirts and sitting with legs tucked neatly to one side. The so-called *Venus de Malta*, also from Ħaġar Qim, is about 10cm tall and displays remarkably realistic modelling – it resembles a prehistoric Lucien Freud. Best of all is the *Sleeping Lady,* found at the Hypogeum, which is around 5000 years old. It shows a woman lying on her side with her head propped on one arm, apparently deep in slumber. There are also beautiful stone friezes from the Tarxien temples.

Upstairs the new displays showcase the coarser pottery from the Bronze Age, animal figurines and jewellery, as well as information on the island's mysterious cart ruts.

National War Museum   MUSEUM
(☑2122 2430; Triq il-Fontana; adult/child €6/3; ☺9am-5pm) This impressive collection, based

appropriately at Fort St Elmo, commemorates the country's ordeal during WWII. It includes the Gloster Gladiator biplane called *Faith* (minus wings) the sole survivor of the three planes that so valiantly defended the island when Italy declared war in 1940, the jeep *Husky* used by General Eisenhower, and the wreckage of a Spitfire and a Messerschmitt Me-109 fighter aircraft recovered from the seabed. The pictures of bomb damage in Valletta give some idea of the amount of rebuilding that was needed after the war. Pride of place goes to the replica George Cross medal that was awarded to the entire population of Malta in 1942.

National Museum of Fine Arts   MUSEUM
(☑2122 5769; Triq Nofs in-Nhar; adult/child €5/2.50; ☺9am-5pm) Take the icing-sugar-style sweeping staircase to begin your exploration of the fine art collections, which range from the 15th to 20th centuries. Highlights include room 8, with Guido Reni's *Risen Christ,* and the sinister *Judith & Holophernes* by Valentin de Boulogne, as well as rooms 12 and 13, which display works by Mattia Preti. Look out for the dramatic *Martyrdom of St Catherine* and St John the Baptist dressed in the habit of the Knights of St John.

Downstairs, room 14 contains portraits of several Grand Masters by the 18th-century French artist Antoine de Favray, including one of the imperious Manuel Pinto de Fonseca. Room 18 has scenes of Malta by 19th-century British artists, including lovely paintings of Gozo by poet Edward Lear,

VALLETTA FOR CHILDREN

Valletta is a great city to wander through with kids. Much of the centre is closed to traffic, and there are plenty of child-friendly restaurants. The Upper Barrakka Gardens (p44) are a good place for a run around, and kids will particularly love the choreographed fountains in Misraħ San Ġorġ (St George's Square). Those with an interest in battles will get a kick out of the Armoury (p39) and the National War Museum (p43). Older kids may enjoy the Malta Experience (p45), historical reenacts at Fort St Elmo (p44), and exhibitions like Great Siege of Malta & the Knights of St John (p46) or the Knights Hospitallers (p45). Water taxi and ferry rides will also be a hit.

CARAVAGGIO IN MALTA

The Italian painter Michelangelo Merisi (1571–1610) is better known by the name of his home town, Caravaggio. His realist depiction of religious subjects and dramatic use of light and shade shocked and revolutionised the 16th-century art world.

He made his name in Rome with a series of controversial works, but was also notorious for his volatility and violence. Numerous brawls culminated in Caravaggio murdering a man during an argument over a tennis game. He fled Rome and went into hiding in Naples for several months. Then, towards the end of 1607, he moved to Malta.

In Malta, Caravaggio was welcomed as a famous artist and produced several works for the Knights of St John, including the famous *The Beheading of St John the Baptist* for the Oratory of St John's Co-Cathedral (p38). In July 1608 he was admitted into the Order as a Knight of Justice, but only two months later he was arrested for an unspecified crime, and he was promptly imprisoned in Fort St Angelo.

He escaped to Sicily, but was expelled from the Order and spent the next two years on the run. He created some of his finest paintings – ever darker and more twisted – during this period. He died in Italy; the cause of his death remains unknown.

and a small Turner watercolour depicting a Grand Harbour scene (1830) – the museum's pride and joy. Curiously enough, Turner never visited Malta; the work is based on scenes painted by another artist.

St James' Cavalier   ARTS CENTRE

(This 16th-century fortification has been transformed into a dazzling arts centre. Recent exhibitions have encompassed British artists including Lucian Freud, David Hockney and Stanley Spencer, and the photographs of Steve McCurry (famous for his iconic photograph of an Afghan girl). To gain a sense of the contemporary scene, step inside to see what's on in its various galleries. There's also a cinema and theatre (p49).

Upper Barrakka Gardens
& Saluting Battery   PARK

These colonnaded gardens perched high above Grand Harbour were created in the late 16th century as a relaxing haven for the Knights from the nearby Auberge d'Italie. They provide a shady retreat from the bustle of the city, and the balcony has one of the best views in Malta.

The terrace below is occupied by the Saluting Battery (2180 0992; www.wirtartna. org; adult/child €5/3; 10am-1pm, guided tours at 11am & 12.15pm), where a cannon once fired salutes to visiting naval vessels, and now fires every day at noon. The sight was under renovation at the time of research, but will have reopened by the time you're reading this. Guided tours are usually available, demonstrating how the cannon is loaded and fired, the network of tunnels within the St Peter

and Paul Bastion, and a series of displays on the history of time-keeping and signalling. A new panoramic lift has also been constructed, which connects the gardens with the Lascaris ditch, replacing a British-built lift that started operating in 1905 and was decommissioned in 1973.

Manoel Theatre   THEATRE

(2124 6389; www.teatrumanoel.com.mt; 115 Triq it-Teatru l-Antik; tours €4) Malta's national theatre was built in 1731 and is one of the oldest theatres in Europe. Take an entertaining guided tour (conducted in English, French, Italian and German) to see the restored baroque, gilt-twinkling auditorium with its huge chandelier. Tours begin at 10.15am, 11am, 11.45am, 12.30pm, 1.15pm, 2pm, 3pm, 3.30pm and 4.30pm Monday to Friday, and 12.30pm on Saturday.

Fort St Elmo   FORTRESS

Guarding the entrance to both Marsamxett and Grand Harbours is Fort St Elmo, named after the patron saint of mariners. Although now much altered and extended, this was the fort that bore the brunt of Turkish arms during the Great Siege of 1565. It was built by the Knights in 1552 to guard the entrances to the harbours on either side of the Sceberras Peninsula. The courtyard outside the entrance to the fort is studded with the lids of underground granaries.

It's pitched for renovation, but is currently home to Malta's police academy and is open to the public only for historical reenactments, held at 11am on most Sunday mornings except from mid-July to late September.

In Guardia (☎2123 7747; adult/child €5/3) is a colourful and photogenic military pageant in 16th-century costume, which includes a cannon-firing demonstration. Alarme! (☎2123 7747; adult/child €5/3) is a reenactment of a military encounter between French and Maltese troops. Check upcoming dates at the tourist office.

Church of St Paul's
Shipwreck CHURCH

(Triq San Pawl, enter from Triq Santa Luċija; admission free, donations welcome; ⊗9am-7pm) In AD 60 St Paul was shipwrecked on Malta and brought Christianity to the population. Don't be fooled by this church's 19th-century facade; it dates from the 16th century and houses many treasures, including a dazzling gilded statue of St Paul, carved in Rome in the 1650s and carried shoulder-high through the streets of Valletta on the saint's feast day (10 February). There's also a golden reliquary containing some bones from the saint's wrist, and part of the column on which he is said to have been beheaded in Rome.

Casa Rocca Piccola HISTORIC BUILDING

(☎2122 1499; www.casaroccapiccola.com; 74 Triq ir- Repubblica; adult/child €9/3) The 16th-century palazzo Casa Rocca Piccola is the family home of the Marquis de Piro, who has opened part of the palazzo to the public. Guided tours on the hour (10am to 4pm Monday to Saturday) give a unique insight into the elegant, privileged lifestyle of the aristocracy, and include a visit to the family WWII air-raid shelters underground.

Toy Museum MUSEUM

(☎2125 1652; 222 Triq ir-Repubblika; adult/child €3/free; ⊗10am-3pm Mon-Fri, to 1pm Sat & Sun) This doll-sized museum houses an impressive private collection of model planes and boats from the 1950s, as well as Matchbox cars, farmyard animals, train sets and dolls.

DISCOUNT CARDS

If you're going to visit more than a few historical sites in Valletta, it's well worth investing in a multisite pass from Heritage Malta (☎2295 4000; www.heritage malta.org; multisite pass adult/family (2 adults, 2 children) €30/65). This covers you for admission to sites including the Palace State Rooms, the Armoury, the National War Museum, the National Museum of Fine Arts and the National Museum of Archaeology.

Audiovisual Shows & Exhibitions

Malta Experience AUDIOVISUAL ATTRACTION
(☎2124 3776; www.themaltaexperience.com; Triq il-Mediterran; adult/child €10/5, plus tour €4/free; ⊗hourly 11am-4pm Mon-Fri, 11am-2pm Sat & Sun) This 45-minute audiovisual presentation, available in 13 languages, showcases the country's long history and highlights its scenic attractions. It's screened in the basement of the Mediterranean Conference Centre, which occupies the Sacra Infermeria, the 16th-century hospital of the Order of St John. Here surgeons performed advanced operations as well as the more routine amputations and treatment of war wounds. For a small extra charge you can take a worthwhile tour of the hospital, visiting its Grand Hall that once housed around 300 patients. A Knights Hospitallers Exhibition (☎2124 3840; Triq it- Tramuntana; adult/child €4.50/2; ⊗9.30am-4.30pm) which goes heavy on the waxworks, records the achievements of these medieval medics.

Valletta Living History AUDIOVISUAL ATTRACTION
(☎21222225; www.maltaattraction.com; The Embassy Complex, Triq St Lucia; €9.75/4 adult/child; ⊗10:00am,shows at 10:45am, 11.30am, 12.15pm,

---

VALLETTA WATERFRONT

The Valletta Waterfront (also known as Pinto Wharf; www.vallettawaterfront.com) was once a run-down dockside area, now renovated and lined with waterside restaurants. Most of the services here, including shops, restaurants and bars, cater to the passengers of the cruise ships that dock here. There's a small tourist information booth, plus operators offering bus and boat trips around Valletta. In theory you should be able to catch Malta Water Taxis (p179) from here to Vittoriosa, but call ahead to check.

It's a steep haul up to Valletta from here, but the new panoramic lift from Lascaris to the Upper Barakka Gardens will make the connection much easier. Presently there's a vintage Maltese bus that runs intermittently between the waterfront and the town (€1.50).

1pm, 1.45pm, 2.30pm, & 3.15pm) A glossy, entertaining 35-minute sweep (eight languages available) through Malta's eventful history. This is especially worthwhile if you have the Maltapass (maltapass.com.mt), which grants free entry.

Great Siege of Malta & the Knights of St John   AUDIOVISUAL ATTRACTION

(☑2124 7300; www.greatsiege.com.mt; Misraħ ir-Repubblika; adult/child €7.50/3.75; ⊘10am-4.30pm Mon-Fri, 10am-3pm Sat) The Great Siege of Malta and the Knights of St John, beside the entry to the Bibliotheca, is a 30-minute walk-through diorama-with-audio-guide and light and sound effects, featuring re-creations of battle scenes from the 1565 siege – don't expect any great insights.

Tours

Hop-on, hop-off bus Citysightseeing Malta (p180)'s South Tour makes a circuit of Valletta before heading to the Three Cities, Għar Dalam cave, Marsaxlokk, the Blue Grotto, the Ħaġar Qim and Mnajdra temples, Montekristo winery and the Malta Falconery Centre. The North Tour goes from City Gate to San Anton Gardens, Ta'Qali Crafts Village, Mosta, Mdina, Golden Bay, Mediterraneo Marine Park, Buġibba, St Julian's and Sliema.

QUICK EATS

Cheap, tasty fare can be found at the kiosks beside the Valletta bus terminus. Millennium (Map p52; pastizzi €0.30), just to your right after you exit the city sells hot *pastizzi* (pastry parcels filled with either ricotta cheese or mushy peas); next door, the Dates Kiosk (Map p52; mqaret €0.20) sells traditional *mqaret* (pastries stuffed with spiced dates and deep-fried).

Follow your nose to a couple of friendly, hole-in-the-wall places on Triq San Pawl where you can pick up a fresh hot *pastizza* from around 7.30am Monday to Saturday. Agius Confectionery & Pastizzerija (273 Triq San Pawl; pastizza €0.30) opposite the Church of St Paul's Shipwreck, and Carmelo Azzopardi Pastizzerija (310 Triq San Pawl; pastizza €0.30) are both recommended.

Myguide Valletta   AUDIO TOUR

(www.myguide.com.mt; €8) You can hire a Valletta audio guide from the National Museum of Archaeology (p43) or the Grand Master's Palace (p39), and see the city's main sights at your own pace.

Eating

TOP CHOICE Ambrosia   MEDITERRANEAN €€

(☑2122 5923; 137 Triq l-Arċisqof; mains €14-23; ⊘lunch Mon-Sat, dinner Tue-Sat) This is one of Valletta's loveliest restaurants, with paintings covering the walls and a relaxed, intimate feel. Locals love this place and the welcome is warm (the chef might just pop by to see how you enjoyed your meal). It uses mainly local produce, farmed and cooked according to the Slow Food philosophy, and creates Maltese dishes that play with traditions.

TOP CHOICE Trattoria da Pippo   MEDITERRANEAN €€

(☑2124 8029; Triq Melita ; mains around €20; ⊘lunch Mon-Sat) This hidden-away, informal Valletta hub, all green woodwork and gingham tablecloths, is a local favourite, with something an old boys' club feel. The food is a delightful mix of Maltese, Sicilian and Italian. Book ahead.

Rubino   MEDITERRANEAN €€

(☑2122 4656; 53 Triq l-Ifran; mains €10-22; ⊘lunch Tue-Fri & Sun, dinner Tue-Sat) Rubino earns rave reviews for reinventing Maltese cuisine while staying true to its roots. There's no menu, just a selection of the day's dishes depending on seasonal produce, with taste sensations like *sfinec ta l-incova*, a deep-fried savoury doughnut with anchovies. Leave room for dessert – the house speciality, *cassata siciliana* (sponge cake soaked in liqueur, layered with ricotta cheese), is particularly recommended. Tuesday night is usually *fenkata* (a communal meal of rabbit) night; bookings are advised.

Salvino's   MEDITERRANEAN €€

(☑2124 6437; www.salvinos.eu; 32 Triq L-Arcisqof; mains €12-22; ⊘lunch Mon-Fri, dinner Wed-Sat) Salvino's has a sophisticated seasonal menu and proffers excellent meat and fish dishes. Its arched cellar-like interior, hung with paintings, is also a welcoming place to eat.

Cockneys   MEDITERRANEAN €€

(☑2123 6065; Marsamxett Wharf; mains €8-24; ⊘lunch & dinner daily, winter dinner Sat & Sun

START CITY GATE
FINISH UPPER BAR-
RAKKA GARDENS &
SALUTING BATTERY
DISTANCE APPROX
2.25KM
DURATION ONE HOUR

Walking Tour
Valletta

> This walk explores some of Valletta's back-
streets, and affords some great views.

Begin at ① **City Gate**. Misrah il-Ħelsien
(Freedom Square), just inside the gate, is the
site of the new, Renzo Piano–designed
② **Parliament House**; beyond it is the
ruined ③ **Royal Opera House**. Built in the
1860s, it was destroyed during a German
air raid in 1942. After passing the Opera
House, turn right into Triq Nofs In-Nar, and
then turn left at Tri il-Merkanti. You'll see the
④ **Palazzo Parisio** on your right, where
Napoleon stayed during his six days on Malta,
and the ⑤ **Auberge d'Italie**, built in 1574,
on your left. Continue walking and you'll see
⑥ **Palazzo Castellania**, once Valletta's law
courts. The figures either side of the first-
floor balcony represent Justice and Truth.
Look for the pillory stone at the building's
corner. Turn right into Triq San Gwann, then
left into Triq San Pawl, passing the 16th-
century ⑦ **Church of St Paul's Shipwreck**.
Follow Triq San Pawl until you reach Triq San
Duminku then turn right; turn left into Triq

Il-Mediterran, turning left to see the Knights'
16th-century ⑧ **Sacra Infermeria**.

As you double back along Triq il-Mediterran,
on your left you'll see a small park and a
pillared cupola. This is the ⑨ **Siege Bell
Memorial**, commemorating those who lost
their lives in the convoys of 1940 to 1943.
Then follow Triq il-Mediterran past the
⑩ **Lower Barrakka Gardens**, which contain
a little Doric temple commemorating Sir
Alexander Ball, the naval captain who took
Malta from the French in 1800.

Continue along Triq Santa Barbara, a
charming tree-lined street with great harbour
views. Cross the bridge above Victoria Gate
and head through a sun-trap of a square,
usually home to a handful of cafe tables.
Turn left and climb up steep Triq il-Batterija
to reach the ⑪ **Upper Barrakka Gardens
& Saluting Battery** and view a magnificent
panorama of Grand Harbour.

NEW LOOK VALLETTA

Little has changed architecturally in Valletta since it was constructed in the 17th century, so it's unsurprising that Renzo Piano's dramatic new additions, completed in 2012, have created something of a rumpus. The Italian architect's designs encompass a new gateway, parliament building, and amphitheatre.

The new City Gate echoes the dimensions of the original 1633 entrance, rather than the 1960s gate that it replaces. Piano's designs intended to return it to a sense of how it was, with access from here down to the ditch that was excavated by the knights.

Beyond the gate is the new parliament building, which is set to house a state-of-the-art interactive Museum of Maltese History and Political Development. The design is formed of two massive volumes of stone, supported by stilts that create an impression that the building is suspened in the air.

Finally, the ruins of the Opera House (it was bombed in 1942) are so much a feature of the Valletta landscape that they have been retained to act as a framework for an open-air performance space. Critics have protested that an alfresco theatre makes no sense in Valletta, as the summer nights are filled with noisy fireworks displays, but supporters hope that this new space will attract international stars and galvanise cultural life. When the theatre is unused, the place is intended to be an open piazza with a seating deck.

only) Cockneys, in a great location just next to the water taxi and ferry stop, is a Valletta institution. There's a boat-like wooden cabin with a cosy interior, and a sunny terrace with yellow awnings. Food is tasty and traditional, including dishes like spaghetti with rabbit.

La Sicilia ITALIAN €€
(☑2124 0659; 1a Triq San Ġwann; mains €7-20; ☻9am-5pm, lunch noon-3pm Tue-Sat) You're sure to find something to fill a gap at this unpretentious eatery overlooking a tranquil little square. There are lots of hearty Italian pasta dishes (under €8), grilled meats and fish.

Kantina CAFE €
(☑2723 0096; Triq San Ġwann; mains €4-10; ☻8am-10pm Mon-Sat 8am-3pm Jan-Apr) This friendly cafe has a great location – its outdoor tables are scattered under the trees in the pedestrianised area outside St John's Co-Cathedral. The menu stretches from bagels, *ftira* (Maltese bread), sandwiches and salads to cocktails and local wines.

Caffe Cordina CAFE €
(☑2123 4385; 244 Triq ir-Repubblika; mains €5-12; ☻8am-7pm Mon-Sat, 8am-3pm Sun) There's some prime people-watching on Misraħ ir-Repubblika, where several cafes command the ranks of tables around the statue of Queen Victoria. This is the oldest (and busi-

est) option, established in 1837 and now a local institution. You have the choice of waiter service at the sunshaded tables in the square or inside, or joining the locals at the zinc counter inside for a quick caffeine hit. Be sure to look up; the ceiling is exquisite.

 Drinking

Valletta feels half-asleep after 8pm, but there are a handful of cafe-bars – you just need to know where to look. Closing times vary depending on how busy the venue is.

Trabuxu WINE BAR
(☑2122 3036; 1 Triq id-Dejqa; ☻7.30pm-midnight Tue-Sat, restaurant noon-3pm Tue-Fri, 7pm-midnight Fri & Sat) Trabuxu's name means 'corkscrew'. This 350-year-old cellar is decorated with great B&W shots and musical instruments, and its menu includes perfect platters to accompany much wine quaffing. The owners have now also opened the recommended Trabuxu restaurant nearby.

The Pub PUB
(☑7980 7042; 136 Triq l-Arċisqof; ☻from 11am) Fans of the late British actor Oliver Reed might want to raise a glass to their hero in this succinctly named watering hole. This is the homely little hostelry where the wild man of British film enjoyed his final drinking session before last orders

were called forever in 1999. A pint costs from €2.80.

☆ Entertainment

Manoel Theatre THEATRE
(✆2124 6389; www.teatrumanoel.com.mt; 115 Triq it-Teatru l-Antik) This beautiful place is Malta's national theatre, and the islands' principal venue for drama, concerts, opera, ballet and the much-loved Christmas pantomime. The performance season runs from October to May, and the theatre also hosts regular lunchtime and evening concerts. Programs are available at the booking office (◎10am-1pm & 5-7pm Mon-Fri, 10am-1pm Sat).

**St James' Cavalier Centre
for Creativity** ARTS CENTRE
(✆2122 3200; www.sjcav.org; Triq Nofs in-Nhar; tickets adult/child from €2.50/1; ◎10am-9.30pm) The Centre for Creativity has a cinema that occasionally screens alternative and arthouse films, and also a theatre-in-the-round, which hosts live music and theatre performances.

🛍 Shopping

Triq Santa Luċija, behind Misraħ ir-Repubblika, is home to a number of jewellery stores offering silver filigree – the most popular souvenir here is a silver eight-pointed Maltese Cross on a chain.

[TOP CHOICE] **Blush & Panic** VINTAGE
(http://panic-at-strait-street.tumblr.com; 46a Triq Melita ; ◎10am-6pm Mon-Fri, 10.30am-2pm Sat) This is a gorgeous clothes shop selling exquisite vintage and vintage-inspired clothes, as well as wonderfully unusual pieces of costume jewellery. These are beautiful quality items – there's no musty second-hand feel here. It's mainly womenswear, but they stock some select menswear.

Malta Crafts Centre CRAFTS
(✆2122 4532; Misraħ San Ġwann) This place offers a small but beautiful range of locally produced crafts, including glassware, ceramics, jewellery and lace.

Agenda BOOKSHOP
(✆2123 3621; 26 Triq ir-Repubblika) A cramped shop with an excellent selection of history books, travel guides, reference and fiction.

Mdina Glass CRAFTS
(✆2141 5786; 14 Triq il-Merkanti) Mdina Glass features handblown glass produced by craft workshops near Mdina, in a range of styles and colours from traditional to decidedly modern – vases, bowls, paperweights, collectables and more.

Word for Word BOOKSHOP
(✆2559 4603; 4 Pjazza Kastilja) An upmarket bookshop with armchairs, and shelves stocked with travel, fiction, nonfiction, cooking and gastronomy, biographies and Maltese interest.

Aquilina BOOKSHOP
(✆2123 3774; www.maltabook.com; 58 Triq ir-Repubblika) This long-running bookshop sells an excellent selection of history books, travel guides, reference and fiction; most are available to buy online.

Street Market MARKET
(Triq il-Merkanti; ◎around 7am-1pm Mon-Sat) A crowded street market set up between Triq San Ġwann and Triq it-Teatru l-Antik sells mainly clothes, shoes, watches, jewellery, pirated CDs and computer games.

ℹ Information

Emergency
Police Station (✆2122 5495; 111 Triq L-Arċisqof)

Internet Access
Ziffa (✆2122 4307; 194 Triq id-Dejqa; per 30 min €2.40, per 60 min €3.30; ◎8am-8pm) Plenty of computers, fast internet access, wi-fi and good rates for overseas phone calls.

Medical Services
Royal Pharmacy (✆2123 4321; 271 Triq ir-Repubblika; ◎8.30am-2pm Mon-Sat, 3-7pm Mon-Fri) Central pharmacy.

Money
There are plenty of ATMs, plus places to change money and cash travellers cheques on and near Triq ir-Repubblika in Valletta.

Bank of Valletta (cnr Triq ir-Repubblika & Triq San Ġwann; ◎8.30am-2pm Mon-Thu, 8.30am-3.30pm Fri, 8.30am-12.30pm Sat) Foreign exchange machine and ATMs.

Post
Main Post Office (Pjazza Kastilja; ◎8.15am-3.45pm Mon-Fri, 8.15am-12.30pm Sat) Found under the St James' Cavalier, opposite the Auberge de Castile.

Tourist Information
Heritage Malta (Triq il-Merkanti & Triq San Kristofru) Provides information on national museums and heritage sites.

Tourist Information Branch (☑2369 6073; Malta International Airport, arrivals hall; ⊙10am-9pm)

Tourist Information Office (☑2291 5214; www.visitmalta.com; Auberge d'Italie, Triq il-Merkanti; ⊙9am-5.30pm Mon-Sat, 9am-1pm Sun & public holidays)

Travel Agencies

National Student Travel Service (NSTS; ☑2558 8257; www.nsts.org; 220 Triq San Pawl, Valletta; ⊙8.30am-4.30pm Mon-Fri) Special-ises in student and youth travel; can arrange budget holiday packages, watersports facilities and English-language courses.

SMS Travel & Tourism (☑2123 2211; 311 Triq ir-Repubblika) A good general agency, offering excursions, guided tours, currency exchange and plane and ferry tickets.

❶ Getting There & Away

Air

Harbour Air (p177) operates a floatplane service between Valletta and Mġarr Harbour on Gozo. There are two flights daily (weather and sea conditions permitting), with a flight time of 10 minutes. At the time of research, all flights were grounded while they replaced their fleet; when they're functioning again fares will cost approxi-mately €150 return.

Boat

The Marsamxetto Ferry Service (p179) crosses frequently between Valletta and Sliema. The crossing takes only about five minutes and there are departures every half-hour from 7am to 6pm Monday to Saturday, and from 10am to 4pm from Valletta to Sliema and to 6pm in the other direction on Sundays. The fare one way/return is €1/3. To reach the ferry departure point in Valletta, follow Triq San Marku all the way to the north, then go under the overpass and down to the water.

Valletta also has an on-demand water taxi service – the most scenic way to reach the Three Cities. In principle, Malta Water Taxis (p179) operates from 7am to midnight daily, and charges €2.50 per person (minimum two people) from Valletta to anywhere in Grand Harbour, and €6 per person to Sliema. How-ever, at the time of research, it was much more evident on the Sliema–Valletta route than from Valletta to the Three Cities, so it's wise to call ahead.

Bus

The Valletta **bus terminus** has 17 bus bays with buses to places all over the island. The informa-tion office opens from 7am to 9pm. Bays serve particular destinations, as follows.

DESTINATION	ROUTE NOS	BAY
Airport	X4, X5	16
Birgu	2, 3	14
Buġibba	12, 31	1A, 4
Ċirkewwa	41, X6	17
Marsaxlokk	81	11
Marsaxlokk	81	11
Mellieħa	41, X6	17
Naxxar	31, 21, 23, 35, 43	4, 5, 7
Paceville	12, 13	1A, 1
Rabat	51, 52, 53	9
St Julian's	12, 13	1A, 1
Zurrieq	71, 73	14, 15

❶ Getting Around

To/From the Airport

Arriva express buses run to/from the airport. X1 serves Ċirkewwa (for Gozo ferries; 65 minutes; half-hourly), via Mellieħa; X2 connects with St Julian's (55 minutes; half-hourly) and Sliema; X3 runs to/from Buġibba (1 hour, 20 minutes; half-hourly), via Rabat; and X4 connects with Valletta (25 minutes; every 15 minutes). Regular route 135 goes to Marsaskala (30 minutes, half-hourly); 201 goes to Rabat (70 minutes, hourly); and 71 and 72 connect with Valletta (25 minutes, every 20 minutes). As for everywhere in Malta, buses cost €2.20/2.60 for a single/day ticket.

You can arrange for a direct transfer from the airport to most hotels in Malta using **Malta-Transfer** (☑2133 2016; www.maltatransfer.com), who has a desk in the airport baggage re-claim hall. Fares per person as far as Buġibba and Xemxija are €10/20 one-way/return; to Mellieħa and Ċirkewwa (for Gozo ferries) it's €12/24. Book your transfer in advance using the website.

You'll find a taxi information desk in the airport arrivals hall and you can organise and pay for your taxi there. The set fare for a taxi from the airport to Valletta or Floriana is €15.

To/From the Sea Passenger Terminal

It's long been difficult to travel between Valletta and the **Sea Passenger Terminal** at the Valletta Waterfront. If you're travelling by ferry from Sic-ily, it's probably best to arrange a transfer when booking your passage.

However, with the development of the new panoramic lift linking the harbour area with Valletta's Upper Barrakka Gardens, steep hauls uphill or waiting around for buses should be a thing of the past.

If you decide to walk to Valletta, you face a steep climb. There are two options: follow the waterfront northeast, under the Lascaris Bastion, then veer left and climb the steps up at **Victoria Gat**. Alternatively, walk northeast along the waterfront then take a sharp left up It-Telgħa Tal-Kurċifiss (Crucifix Hill). Halfway up you'll encounter Il Taraġ Tal-Kalkara (Kalkara Steps) – climb these to reach the war memorial; from here it's a few minutes' walk north to Valletta's City Gate. Allow at least 15 minutes for either journey.

As at the airport, there's a **taxi information kiosk** on Valletta Waterfront where you organise and pay the set rate for your taxi journey upfront. The cheapest fare (to an address in Valletta or Floriana) is a ridiculously overpriced €10. The *karrozzin* (traditional horse-drawn carriage) drivers loitering here will charge even more (usual rates are €35 per 35 minutes).

Car & Motorcycle

If you're driving, the best thing to do is use the big underground car park just outside the City Gate in Floriana, near the Hotel Phoenicia. It's difficult to park within the city walls and there are lots of restrictions. Valletta is eminently walkable so you don't need your car here.

Taxi

There is a taxi rank just outside City Gate.

Smart Cabs (7741 4177) is a fleet of eco-friendly electric-powered taxis that ply the streets of Valletta from 8am to 7pm daily. Fares cost from €3 to €5 within the city walls, but trips can be extended outside the walls on request; book a cab by phone (at least 15 minutes' notice needed), or hail one in the street.

Bus

Bus 133 is a circular bus route that zips half-hourly around Valletta city walls, calling at Castille, Marsamxett and Polyclinic at Floriana. As well as being a good way to get around, this route offers some great views.

AROUND VALLETTA

Floriana

POP 2550

The threat of a Turkish attack in 1634 prompted Grand Master Antoine de Paule to begin the construction of a second line of landward defences, the Notre Dame Ditch, about 1km southwest of Valletta's Great Ditch. These were designed by the Italian engineer Pietro Paolo Floriani, who gave his name to the town (Floriana) that grew up within these walls in the 18th century. The northern part is taken up with government buildings and offices, while the south side is mostly residential.

Eating & Drinking

Pegasus Brasserie   MEDITERRANEAN €€€

(2291 1083; Phoenicia Hotel, Il-Mall; mains €9-29; ☺dinner Wed-Mon) This relaxed and informal brasserie in the grand-old-dame Phoenicia Hotel offers upmarket fare using seasonal local ingredients, with dishes including pappardelle with local prawns, fennel, hazelnuts and shellfish bisque. There's also a lounge in the lobby serving all-day sandwiches and snacks (right down to scones for a civilised afternoon tea).

Tom Bar   GAY BAR

(7906 1572; www.tombarmalta.webs.com; 1 It-Telgħa Tal-Kurċifiss; ☺from 8.30pm Tue-Sun year-round) It's not the most likely location for one of Malta's prime gay nightspots, but this two-storey bar is enduringly popular and appeals to a mix of ages. Tom Bar has space upstairs for chilling out and downstairs for dance music.

Information

The Malta Police headquarters (p171) is at Pjazza San Kalċidonju.

Getting There & Away

Floriana is just a five-minute walk from Valletta. All buses to and from Valletta also pass through Floriana.

There are two ferry terminals in Floriana. The **Gozo cargo ferry** (used primarily by trucks, but with some foot passengers) departs from Sa Maison wharf at Pieta Creek in Marsamxett Harbour, while passenger ferries to/from Sicily dock at the **Sea Passenger Terminal** by the Valletta Waterfront, where cruise liners moor when in town.

The Three Cities

This trio of towns Vittoriosa, Senglea and Cospicua are close-knit working communities largely dependent on their dockyards for employment. Despite their picturesque narrow streets and stunning views, they are surprisingly off the tourist radar and – for now, at least – offer a welcome escape from the commercial hustle of Valletta and Sliema.

The controversial Cottonera Waterfront (www.cottonerawaterfront.com) development in Vittoriosa now includes a chichi casino, half a dozen restaurants, and a yacht-filled marina. It's a pleasant place to eat or have a drink on a sunny afternoon.

VALLETTA FLORIANA

Floriana

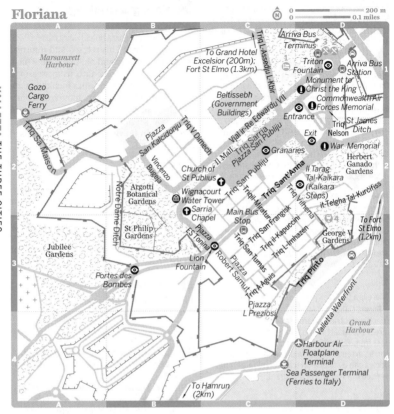

For tourist information, head to the *dgħajsa* (traditional rowing boat or water taxi; pronounced *dye*-sa) information kiosk on the waterfront. There are a couple of excellent accommodation choices in Vittoriosa, and the number of eating and drinking venues is growing.

History

When the Knights of St John first arrived in Malta in 1530, they made their home in the fishing village of Birgu, on a finger of land on the south side of Grand Harbour, overlooking the inlet (now known as Dockyard Creek) that was called the Port of the Arab Galleys. Here they built their auberges and repaired and extended the ancient defences. By the 1550s, Birgu (Fort St Angelo) and the neighbouring point of L-Isla (Fort St Michael) had been fortified, and Fort St Elmo had been built on the tip of the Sceberras Peninsula.

From this base, the Knights withstood the Turkish onslaught during the Great Siege of 1565, but in the years that followed, they moved across the harbour to their new city of Valletta. During WWII, throughout 1941 and 1942, the Three Cities and their surrounding docks were bombed almost daily, and suffered terrible damage and bloodshed.

VITTORIOSA
POP 3035

Vittoriosa is only 800m long and 400m at its widest, so it's hard to get lost – it's a sheer pleasure to wander aimlessly its flower-bedecked alleys, and there's a real sense of community in this small enclosed town. There are several interesting sights, and stunning views across to Valletta. There's good information on Vittoriosa at www.birgu.gov.mt.

Floriana

Sights & Activities

Inquisitor's Palace   HISTORIC BUILDING
(☎2182 7006; Triq il-Mina l-Kbira; adult/child €6/3; ☺9am-5pm) The Inquisitor's Palace was built in the 1530s and served as law courts until the 1570s, when it became the tribunal (and prison) of the Inquisition, whose task it was to find and suppress heresy. Today the palace houses the a small ethnographic museum. However, the most fascinating part of the building is the former prison cells, with elaborate carvings by prisoners on the walls. The building was strengthened in 1698, as before this one prisoner managed to dig his way out eight times in one year. Outside the prison warden's room there is a delicate sundial, carved by an 18th-century warden. Particularly sinister is the torture chamber, with its rope contraptions for extracting confessions.

Malta at War Museum   MUSEUM
(☎2189 6617; www.wirtartna.org; Couvre Port; adult/child €8/6; ☺10am-5pm Tue-Sun) This museum, housed in an 18th-century barracks and the underground tunnels that lie beneath it, pays testament to Malta's pivotal part in WWII, and brings vividly to life the suffering of the islanders. As well as displays in glass cases, there is a stirring film, with lots of original footage, narrated by Sir Lawrence Olivier. Plus you have the opportunity to descend into the former air-raid shelters, bringing to life the underground existence necessary during the islands' fierce bombardment.

Harbour Cruises   BOAT TOUR
(☎2180 6921; www.maltesewatertaxis.com; ☺9am-5pm, or until dark in summer) Cruises are operated by the friendly folk at A&S Water Taxis, who have a kiosk set up on the waterfront, in front of the Freedom Monument. They provide maps of the Three Cities and helpful tourist information, and also organise good-value 35-minute cruises of Grand Harbour in a restored dgħajsa for €10 per person. These boatmen can also act as a water taxi to take you to either Senglea (€2) or Valletta (€5); the drop-off point is not far from the base of the Lascaris Bastion.

Maritime Museum   MUSEUM
(☎2166 0052; adult/child €5/2.50; ☺9am-5pm) The old naval bakery, built in the 1840s, now houses a wealth of material on Malta's maritime past. The collection includes huge Roman anchors, traditional Maltese fishing boats, and models of the Knights' galleys. The small details of naval life are among the most fascinating: bone dye and hashish pipes used for whiling away hours at sea, plus local prostitutes' licenses indicating the lifestyle back on land.

Fort St Angelo   FORTRESS
The tip of the Vittoriosa peninsula has been fortified since at least the 9th century, and before that it was the site of Roman and Phoenician temples. The Knights took over the medieval fort in 1530 and rebuilt and strengthened it – Fort St Angelo served as the residence of the Grand Master of the Order until 1571 and was the headquarters of la Valette during the Great Siege.

Further defences were added in the late 17th century by the talented engineer Don Carlos Grunenberg, whose florid coat of arms still sits above the gate overlooking St Angelo Wharf.

The British took over the fort in the 19th century, and from 1912 until 1979 it served as the headquarters of the Mediterranean Fleet, first as HMS *Egmont* and from 1933 as HMS *St Angelo*. The upper part of the fort, including the Grand Master's Palace and the 15th-century Chapel of St Anne, is now occupied by the modern Order of St John. The remainder of the fort is officially closed to visitors due to its poor state of repair; a long rehabilitation project is in progress.

Eating & Drinking

There are several restaurants lining the sun-splashed Cottonera Waterfront development facing the marina in Vittoriosa, which are great for a light meal and a snack. For something more distinctive, head into the town.

TOP CHOICE **Taverna Sugu**   MALTESE €
(☎2788 1122; www.sugu.com.mt; Triq Papa Alessandru VII; tasting menu €15; ☺dinner Tue-Sat) This

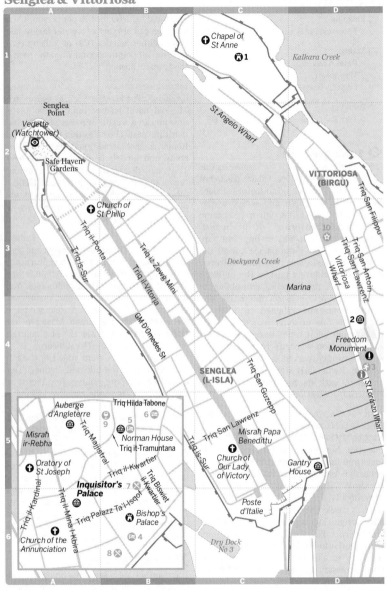

Chapel of
St Anne
1

Kalkara Creek

St Angelo Wharf

Senglea
Point
Vedette
(Watchtower)

Safe Haven
Gardens

**VITTORIOSA
(BIRGU)**

Church of
St Philip

Triq San Filippu

Triq San Antoin

Triq it-Ponta

Triq iż-Żewġ Mini

Triq il-Vitorja

Triq is-Sur

10

Dockyard Creek

Triq San Lawrenz

Vittoriosa Wharf

Marina

GM D'Omedes St

2

Freedom
Monument

**SENGLEA
(L-ISLA)**

Triq San Ġużepp

St Lorenzo Wharf

Triq San Lawrenz

Misraħ Papa
Benedittu

Church of
Our Lady
of Victory

Gantry
House

Triq is-Sur

Poste
d'Italie

*Dry Dock
No 3*

Auberge
d'Angleterre
9

Triq Hilda Tabone

5   6

Misraħ
ir-Rebħa

Triq Majjistral

Norman House
Triq it-Tramuntana

Oratory of
St Joseph

Triq il-Kwartier

Triq Biswet il-Kwartier

**Inquisitor's
Palace**

7

Triq il-Kardinal

Triq il-Mina l-Kbira

Triq Palazz Ta'l-Isqof

Bishop's
Palace

4

Church of the
Annunciation

8

---

lovely restaurant is tucked away down a Birgu backstreet in a 17th-century townhouse, and features authentic Maltese and Gozitan food. The six-course tasting menu allows a splendid array of dishes, like *roti tal-bragjoli* (slices of beef olives stuffed with egg, smoked streaky bacon and garlic), all served with flair by chef David Darmamin.

Tal-Petut   MALTESE €€
(Map p54; ☏7942 1169; www.talpetut.com; 20 Triq Pacifiku Scicluna ; 3/5-course menu €20/28;

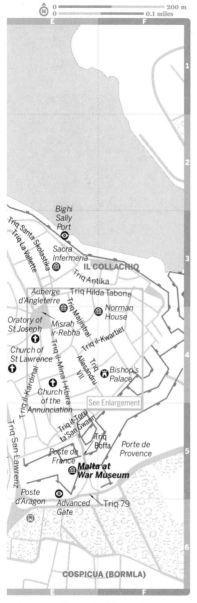

dishes and produce, including rabbit or slow-cooked pork.

Il-Forn WINE BAR

(☑2182 0379; 27 Triq it-Tramuntana; mains €6-15; ☉7.30pm-late Tue-Sun) Il-Forn, an alluring wine bar in Il Collachio (almost opposite the Norman House), also functions as an art gallery, with plenty of fabulously colourful art on display by the bar's Austrian-born owner. It's well worth a look, and you can enjoy traditional snacks, pasta and a choice of over 100 wines in one of the courtyards.

☆ Entertainment

Casino di Venezia CASINO

(☑2180 5580; www.casinovenezia.it; admission €5; ☉tables 3.30pm-2.45am Mon-Fri, to 3.15am Sat, from 4pm mid-Jun–Aug) Vegas meets Venice: travellers looking for a chance to make (or blow) some holiday dough should head to this ritzy casino beside the marina. Visitors must be aged at least 18, be smartly dressed and carry a passport or ID card. Casinos in Malta draw many gamblers from Sicily, which doesn't have any casinos of its own.

❶ Getting There & Away

Bus 2 from Valletta will take you to Vittoriosa/Birgu (30 minutes, half-hourly), via Paola. It's also possible to travel between Valletta and

☉dinner Tue-Sat, Sat & Sun) Intimate, characterful restaurant Tal-Petut occupies a former grocery but feels like a home from home. It is presided over by the host-with-the-most Donald, who's passionate about the restaurant's emphasis on seasonal local

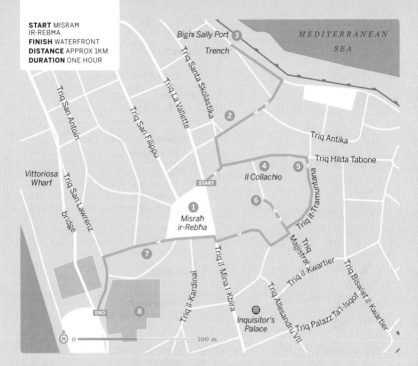

MEDITERRANEAN SEA

Bigħi Sally Port ③

Trench

Triq Santa Skolastika

Triq La Vallette

Triq San Filippu

Triq San Antoin

②

Triq Antika

Triq Hilda Tabone

④ ⑤

Il Collachio

Triq it-Tramuntana

Vittoriosa
Wharf

Triq San Lawrenz

bridge

START

⑥

① Misraħ
ir-Rebħa

Triq Majjistral

Triq il-Kwartier

⑦

Triq il-Mina l-Kbira

Triq il-Kardinal

Triq Alesandru VII

Triq il-Kwartier

Triq Biswiet il-Kwartier

END

⑧

Inquisitor's
Palace

Triq Palazz Ta' l-Isqof

Ⓝ 0 ————————— 100 m

Walking Tour
Vittoriosa

❯ Start at ① **Misraħ ir-Rebħa** (Victory
Sq) with its two monuments: the Victory
Monument, erected in 1705 in memory of
the Great Siege; and a statue of St Lawrence,
patron saint of Vittoriosa, dating from 1880.
You'll notice a magnificent building on the
eastern side of the square; this dates from
1888 and is home to the Band Club of St
Lawrence.

From the square head east on Triq Hilda
Tabone, then take the first left (Triq Santa
Skolastika) towards the massive blank walls
of the ② **Sacra Infermeria**, the first hospital
to be built by the Knights on their arrival in
Malta. It now serves as a convent. Turn right
down an alley (signposted Triq il-Miratur) and
walk along the wall's perimeter. The stepped
ramp descending into a trench in front of the
Infermeria leads to the ③ **Bigħi Sally Port**,
where the wounded were brought by boat
to the infirmary under the cover of darkness
during the Great Siege.

Next, head back onto Triq Hilda Tabone.
To your right lies a small maze of charming

alleys, collectively known as ④ **Il Collachio**,
with some of the city's oldest surviving
buildings. Wander up Triq it-Tramuntana to
the so-called ⑤ **Norman House** at No 11
(on the left) and look up at the 1st floor. The
twin-arched window, with its slender central
pillar and zigzag decoration, dates from the
13th century and is in a style described as
Siculo-Norman. Also in this area are the first
auberges built by the Knights in the 16th
century – the ⑥ **Auberge d'Angleterre** on
Triq il-Majjistral, the auberge of the English
Knights, now serves as the local library. From
here, turn back to Misraħ ir-Rebħa, from
where you can walk down to the waterfront.
Turn left into the nearby chapel where the
little ⑦ **Oratory of St Joseph** contains relics of Grand Master la Valette, and continue
down past the ⑧ **Church of St Lawrence**.
Built on the site of an 11th-century Norman church, St Lawrence's served as the
conventual church of the Knights of St John
from 1530 until the move to St John's Co-
Cathedral in Valletta.

Birgu via Malta Water Taxis (p179) or A&S Water Taxis (p53), both whom charge €5 to take two people across the harbour by boat.

SENGLEA
POP 3500

Senglea is even more difficult to get lost in than Vittoriosa, as the streets form a grid pattern. The town was pretty much razed to the ground during WWII, so little of historic interest remains, but there are great views of Valletta and Vittoriosa, and the little vedette (watchtower) at the tip of the peninsula is one of the classic sights of Malta.

❶ Getting There & Away

Bus 1 runs between Valletta and Senglea (25 minutes, half-hourly Mon-Sat). It's a 15-minute walk from the main gate at Vittoriosa around to the main gate at Senglea.

Hal Saflieni Hypogeum & Tarxien Temples

The suburb of Paola, about 2km southwest of Cospicua, conceals two of Malta's most important prehistoric sites. The Hal Saflieni Hypogeum (☑2180 5019; Triq iċ-Ċimiterju; adult/child €20/12) is a subterranean necropolis, discovered during building work in 1902. Visiting is like stepping into a mysterious and silent world. Its halls, chambers and passages, immaculately hewn out of the rock, cover some 500 sq metres; it is thought to date from around 3600 to 3000 BC, and an estimated 7000 bodies may have been interred here. The ancient workers mimicked built masonry in carving out these underground chambers, and exploited the rock's natural weaknesses and strengths to carve out the spaces by hand and create a safe underground structure.

Excellent 50-minute tours (over 6s only) of the complex are available daily at 9am, 10am, 11am, 1pm, 2pm, 3pm and 4pm. The visit starts with a brief exhibition and multilingual film, which provides an introduction before you descend into the dimly lit, chilly underworld that lies beneath.

Carbon dioxide exhaled by visiting tourists did serious damage to the delicate limestone walls of the burial chambers of the Hypogeum, and it was closed to the public for 10 years, reopening in mid-2000. It has been restored with Unesco funding, and its microclimate is now strictly controlled. For this reason, the maximum number of visitors to the site is limited (10 per tour).

Tickets are understandably in demand, and prebooking is *essential* (usually at least two weeks before you wish to visit, or up to a month in advance for busy periods like summer's peak, Easter and Christmas). Tickets are available in person from the Hypogeum and the National Museum of Archaeology (p43), or online through www.heritagemalta.org. If you're desperate, you might decide to try your luck for cancellations – you'll need to turn up before the first scheduled tour.

The remarkable Tarxien Temples (☑2169 5578; Triq it-Templi Neolitiċi; adult/child €6/3; ☺9am-5pm), pronounced tar-*sheen,* are Malta's most complex network of temples, incongruously hidden up a back street several blocks east of the Hypogeum. These megalithic structures were excavated in 1914 and are thought to date from between 3600 and 2500 BC. There are four linked structures, built with massive stone blocks up to 3m by 1m by 1m in size, decorated with spiral patterns and pitting, and reliefs of animals including bulls, goats and pigs. Aerial photographs show clearly the interlinked and coherent structure. The large statue of a broad-hipped female figure was found in the right-hand niche of the first temple, and a copy remains in situ (the original is in the National Museum of Archaeology, p43).

❶ Getting There & Away

Myriad buses pass through Paola, including buses 1,2 and 3 from Valletta (15-20 minutes). They stop at various points around the main square, Pjazza Paola.

From the main square, the Hypogeum is a five-minute walk; the Tarxien Temples are 10 minutes away.

Fort Rinella

Built by the British in the late 19th century, Fort Rinella (☑2180 9713; Triq Santu Rokku; adult/child/family €8/7/18; ☺10am-5pm Tue-Sun), 1.5km northeast of Vittoriosa, was one of two coastal batteries designed to counter the threat of Italy's new ironclad battleships. The batteries (the second one was on Tigné Point in Sliema) were equipped with the latest Armstrong 100-tonne guns – the biggest muzzle-loading guns ever made. Their 100-tonne shells had a range of 6.4km and could penetrate 38cm of armour plating. The guns acted as a powerful enough deterrent never to be fired in anger, and were retired

MOVIE-MAKING IN MALTA

From the road to Fort Rinella visitors have a good view of the huge water tanks of the Mediterranean Film Studios (not open to the public). There's not a lot to see, but these are the biggest film-production water facilities in Europe – the two main water tanks have a clear horizon behind them, allowing directors to create the illusion that on-screen characters are miles out to sea. Water scenes from such films as *The Spy Who Loved Me* (1977), *Raise the Titanic* (1980), *White Squall* (1996), *U-571* (2000) and *The League of Extraordinary Gentlemen* (2003) were shot here.

But it's not just the water tanks that have drawn film crews to Malta. The country's fortresses have long been popular with location scouts – the basement and casemates of Fort St Elmo were used for the Turkish prison scenes in the 1978 film *Midnight Express*, and Fort St Elmo has doubled as locations in Marseille and Beirut. Also out near Fort Rinella is Ricasoli Fort (also closed to the public), where a large portion of the 2004 Trojan War epic *Troy* was filmed on specially crafted sets. Scenes from another sandals-and-swords blockbuster, *Gladiator* (2000), were also filmed here.

Comino's St Mary's Tower appears in *The Count of Monte Cristo* (2002), as do Mdina and Vittoriosa, while the Blue Lagoon provides a great backdrop to the less-great film *Swept Away* (2002), starring Madonna and produced by her then-husband, Guy Ritchie.

Valletta's harbour appeared in *Alexander* (2004); the island stood in for most of the Mediterranean and Middle Eastern locales in Steven Spielberg's 2005 movie *Munich* (look out for Malta's distinctive yellow buses in a number of scenes) and appeared in a handful of flashback scenes involving the murderous albino monk in the 2006 film *The Da Vinci Code*. More recently, Malta has featured in *Asterix and Obelix: God Save Britannia*, starring Catherine Deneuve and Gérard Depardieu (2011) and Brad Pitt's zombie movie *World War Z* (2014).

There are some good websites to check out if you're interested in learning more: see Mediterranean Film Studios (www.mfsstudios.com), the Malta Film Commission (www.mfc.com.mt) and the website of the Malta Tourism Authority (www.visitmalta.com).

in 1906. Fort Rinella has been restored by a group of amateur enthusiasts from the Malta Heritage Trust (www.wirtartna.org) and is now one of Malta's most interesting military museums. Guided tours every hour are given by volunteers dressed as late-19th-century soldiers. After the 2pm tour there's a rifle display lasting around 20 to 30 minutes, after which visitors have the opportunity to fire the rifles themselves for an extra €5/10 rifle/cannon (the cannon is not available every day).

❶ Getting There & Away

To get to Fort Rinella, take bus no 3 from Valletta (35 minutes, half-hourly Mon-Sat, hourly Sun), Birgu or Paola. It stops outside the fort.

Sliema, St Julian's & Paceville

Best Places to Eat

» Assaggi (p64)

» Mint (p63)

» Zest (p64)

» Kitchen (p64)

Best Places to Stay

» Hotel Juliani (p133)

» Hotel Valentina (p133)

» Palace Hotel (p132)

» Waterfront Hotel (p132)

Why Go?

Malta's cool crowd flocks to this area to promenade, eat, drink, shop and party. This is also where many tourists base themselves: despite the lack of interesting things to see or any beach to speak of, these three districts form a buzzing base and are well connected by public transport.

St Julian's was once a pretty fishing village, but its original charms have been all but obscured by the five-star hotels and apartment complexes rising along the rocky shoreline. It adjoins the small youth-oriented nightlife enclave of Paceville, which only comes to life after dark; you won't spot many punters aged over 25 here. This is also where many of Malta's English-language schools are located.

Sliema has a more exclusive feel than St Julian's, and has long been associated with the Maltese upper classes. The elegant backstreets remain largely residential and the busy waterfront, while built-up, is dotted by some sophisticated eateries.

When to Go

Come in May, June, September and October if you're looking for lower prices, guaranteed sunshine and few crowds. However, if you're after a party atmosphere and lots of action, then head here during the peak summer months of July and August, when the weather will be at its sultriest and the nightlife at its most frenetic.

Sliema, St Julian's & Paceville Highlights

1 Enjoying the early-evening people parade along Sliema's **waterfront promenade** (p61)

2 Alfresco wining and dining on **Spinola Bay** (p65), Malta's gastronomic epicentre

3 Bar-hopping on a big night out in **Paceville** (p62)

4 Living in luxury in one of the area's fab **five-star hotels** (p132)

5 Taking to the waters on a **boat trip** (p63) out of Sliema

◉ Sights

SLIEMA

The main things to do in Sliema are stroll and eat; there are good views of Valletta from Triq ix-Xatt (the Strand), and boat trips, including harbour tours and ferries to Valletta, are on offer all the way along the promenade. Triq ix-Xatt and Triq it-Torri make for a pleasant waterfront stroll. In the evenings these streets fill up with families out for their daily *passeggiata* (evening stroll) and joggers and dog-walkers doing their thing.

Sliema's beaches are mostly shelves of bare rock, so clambering in and out of the sea can be awkward at times. In places along Triq it-Torri and at Qui-si-Sana, square pools have been cut into the soft limestone. These were made for the convenience of leisure-loving upper-class Maltese ladies, but have since fallen into disrepair. For sun- and water-seekers, there are better facilities at the private lidos scattered along the coast, including swimming pools, sun lounges, bars and watersports; admission costs around €5 to €10 per day.

Tigné Point (the Point) AREA

(www.thepointmalta.com; Tigné Point; ⊙9.30am-7.30pm daily) Tigné Point, a promontory east of Sliema, was one of the sites where the Turkish commander Dragut Reis ranged his cannons to pound Fort St Elmo into submission during the Great Siege in 1565. The tip of the peninsula is still known as Dragut Point. This whole area has undergone massive redevelopment, with construction of residential apartments set around large pedestrianised areas. It's now home to Malta's largest shopping mall, the Point, which houses international chains including Debenhams, M&S, Adidas and many more, plus cafes and restaurants. The previously neglected Tigné Fort, built in 1792 by the Knights of St John, was under restoration at the time of writing. It is slated to be a cultural, heritage and commercial venue.

St Julian's Tower
& Il-Fortizza HISTORIC BUILDINGS

There are two towers on Triq it-Torri. St Julian's Tower is one of the network of coastal watchtowers built by Grand Master de Redin in the 17th century. Il-Fortizza was built by the British in Gothic style in the 19th century. Both now house uninspiring restaurants.

AROUND SLIEMA

Sliema merges southward into the suburb of Gżira.

Manoel Island HISTORIC SITE

Manoel Island, which can be accessed via a short bridge from Gżira, is largely taken up by boat-building yards and the partly restored Fort Manoel. The island was used as a quarantine zone by the Knights of St John; the shell of their 17th-century plague hospital, the Lazzaretto di San Rocco, can still be seen on the south side. More recently, the hospital served as an isolation hospital during WWI and was last used during an epidemic in 1936. Fort Manoel was built in the early 18th century under Grand Master Manoel de Vilhena, and suffered extensive bomb damage during WWII, when nearby Lazzaretto Creek was used as a submarine base. The island is scheduled to be rebuilt as a 'Mediterranean Village' as part of the

SLIEMA, ST JULIAN'S & PACEVILLE SIGHTS

MALTA'S WATCHTOWERS

The Knights of St John concentrated their defences on the Three Cities and Valletta. Up to the 19th century, only the two old capitals – Mdina on Malta and Victoria on Gozo – were fortified, and even their defences were not particularly robust. Farmers on the outskirts of the capitals could shelter within the cities, but villages elsewhere were left to fend for themselves.

Malta had long had watchtowers, but Grand Master Juan de Lascaris-Castellar of the Knights of Malta commissioned five towers from 1637 to 1640; another knight, Grand Master Martin de Redin, subsequently built a string of 13 towers in a similar style around the perimeters of the islands from 1658 to 1659. These were strong enough to withstand a small attack, but not a long siege. They were positioned so Gozo and Malta could signal to each other – with fire, gunfire and flags – if Turkish invaders were sighted off the coast. The towers still stand today, and range from simple, small watchtowers to larger mini-fortresses. One of the most impressive is the Red Tower on the Marfa Peninsula – its walls are nearly 4.5m thick.

Sliema

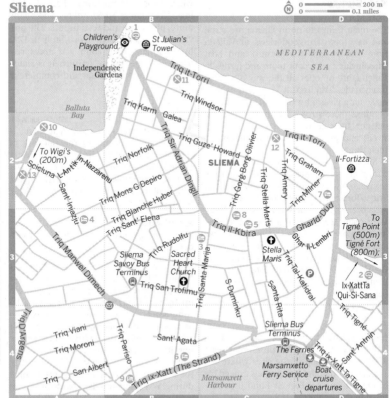

Tigné Point development, but the project has proved controversial and at the time of research seemed unlikely to go ahead.

Ta'Xbiex
AREA

Ta'Xbiex is an upmarket seaside neighbourhood featuring gracious villas, mansions and embassies, and surrounded by yacht marinas.

ST JULIAN'S & PACEVILLE

Paceville
AREA

Paceville is the in-your-face party zone of pubs, clubs and restaurants that forms the focal point for the wilder side of Malta's nightlife. While it comprises only a few narrow streets adjoining St Julian's, this is party-all-night and sleep-all-day territory. The over-25s may feel over-the-hill here. It appeals to a young crowd: a mixture of Maltese back for the holidays from school or college overseas, tourists, and international students studying English at one of the local schools.

Portomaso Apartment & Marina Complex
MARINA

(Map p66) The glitzy development of Portomaso is overlooked by the towering Hilton Hotel, and is ringed by restaurants and bars. It's a popular place to hang out, sip cocktails and dine while watching the sun bounce off the yachts and the water.

Palazzo Spinola
HISTORIC BUILDING

(Map p66) Amid the heaving bars and packed restaurants of central St Julian's lies the elegant Palazzo Spinola, built for the Italian knight Rafael Spinola in the late 17th century. It is surrounded by a walled garden (the entrance is on Triq il-Knisja) and is now home to the Parliamentary Assembly of the Mediterranean.

Villa Dragonara
HISTORIC BUILDING

(Map p66) Villa Dragonara, an aristocratic residence that's found a new lease on life as the Dragonara Casino, is set on the southern headland of St George's Bay. It was built in the late 19th century for the Marquis Scicluna, a wealthy banker.

St Georges Bay
BEACH

Most of the beaches around St Julian's are of the bare rock or private lido variety (the five-star hotels offer beach clubs and watersports), but at the head of St George's Bay there's a genuine, if crowded and nondescript, sandy beach.

🏃 Activities

Water Sports

Traditional touristy stuff like banana rides, paragliding and paddle boats are available at most of the private lidos along the shore. Many also offer waterborne activities, including windsurfing, water-skiing, motorboating, snorkelling and scuba-diving.

Yellow Fun Watersports
WATERSPORTS

(Map p66; ☑2135 0025; www.yellowfunwatersports.com) Yellow Fun Watersports operates from the Portomaso marina in St Julian's, under the Hilton Hotel, and offers a huge menu of activities including jet-ski rental; yacht charter; self-driven boats; water taxis to Sliema, Valletta or Vittoriosa; and trips to Gozo and Comino.

DIVE RIGHT IN

Several local operators can help you explore Malta's excellent dive sites. We recommend the following options:
» Dive Systems (p21)
» Diveshack (p21)
» Divewise (p21)

Boat Trips & Jeep Tours

The average price for a 1½ to two-hour cruise taking in Marsamxett and Grand Harbours costs €16/13 per adult/child, but you may find smaller operators with cheaper rates. Cruise touts line the waterfront at the Ferries in Sliema, from where most cruises depart, and the strip across the road abounds with tour agencies offering island-wide excursions. All these agents can book you on the tours offered by the major operators listed here; prices for half- and full-day cruises usually include hotel transfers.

Captain Morgan Cruises
BOAT TOUR

(☑2346 3333; www.captainmorgan.com.mt) As well as its extensive program of boat trips, from harbour cruises (adult/child under 12 €16/13) to full-day catamaran rides, Captain Morgan Cruises runs popular 4WD jeep safaris exploring the more remote parts of Malta and Gozo (all day combined catamaran and jeep safari adult/child under 12 €69/55).

Hera Cruises
BOAT TOUR

(☑2133 0583; www.heracruises.com) Hera organises various boat tours around Malta, including all-day cruises (adult/child €58/30), and trips to Comino and the Blue Lagoon in a Turkish Gulet (old-style sailing boat; €50/27). It also offers yacht charters (a catamaran costs €800 per day, inclusive of crew) and 4WD jeep tours.

🍴 Eating

SLIEMA

Mint
CAFE $

(☑2133 7177; www.mintmalta.com; Triq Stella Maris; snacks €3-7; ☺8am-7pm Tue-Fri, 9am-7pm Sat & Sun) To see where Sliema's yummiest mummies hang out, head to this chic New Zealand–owned cafe that provides laid-back Kiwi style and home cooking. Its food is smashing, with some really sumptuous snacks – moussaka, savoury muffins, and delicious homemade cakes and cookies. There are some toys and books for kids.

THAI MASSAGE?

Chao Praya Thai Massage & Spa
(Map p66; ☎2137 8666; 52 Triq il-Wilga;
⊙9am-10pm Mon-Sat, 9am-7pm Sun) is
a small, surprising piece of Thailand in
downtown St Julian's – from the smell
of Tiger Balm as you enter the shop-
front to the Thai chatter of the staff.
A half-hour massage costs €25, a full
hour costs €35. You can also submit to
foot massages, reflexology, manicures
and pedicures. It's a real contrast to
the swish day spas of the area's mega-
hotels.

Kitchen   MEDITERRANEAN €€
(☎2131 1112; 210 Triq it-Torri; mains €16-25; ⊙din-
ner Mon-Sat, closed Jan & Aug; ✺) This discreet-
looking place, featuring a narrow, smart
room with a cloth-swathed ceiling, is situated on a none-too-interesting stretch of the
promenade. It's popular with local Sliema
slickers in the know: Kitchen's owner-chef
whips up a small, well-formed menu of ex-
emplary Med-fusion dishes. Mouthwatering
mains include the venison fillet served with
bread and ricotta salata pudding.

Scruples   MALTESE €
(☎2134 1020; Triq il-Kulegg l'Antik; mains €7-14;
⊙10-30am-3pm & 5.30pm-11.30pm Wed-Mon)
This is a wonderful setting for traditional
Maltese cooking. Scruples' interior is tiny,
but outdoor tables on the small piazza are
overlooked by a notable block of original art
nouveau apartments. The kitchen serves national culinary stalwarts like *fenek* (rabbit)
and *qanita* (octopus), as well as excellent
steaks.

Wigi's   ITALIAN €€
(Triq Ġorġ Borg Olivier; mains €15-21; ⊙12.30-
2.45pm daily, 7.30-10.45pm Tue-Sat) Wigi's is the
Malti pronunciation of 'Luigi's'. This much
appreciated, family-run Italian restaurant
offers views over the bay through its large
plate-glass windows. It proffers delicious
steaks, calamari and pork, among other delights; desserts include banofee (banana and
toffee) pie and sticky date pudding.

Barracuda   MEDITERRANEAN €€
(☎2133 1817; 195 Triq il-Kbira; mains €9-22; ⊙din-
ner) This is a traditional, elegant restaurant
set in the drawing room of an early 18th-
century seaside villa on the western fringes

of Sliema and the edge of the water. It's a
picture-perfect place for romance, with brilliant blue sea views framed in the windows,
a sunshaded terrace, professional service
and a menu of carefully prepared Italian
and Mediterranean dishes, with the fish and
seafood reliably first-rate.

La Cucina del Sole   ITALIAN €€
(☎2060 3434; www.lacucinadelsole.com; Tigné
Point; €7-20; ⊙dinner nightly, lunch Sat & Sun) If
you've found yourself sucked into Malta's
biggest mall, the Point (p61), this is a bright
and breezy place to head to eat tasty pizzas,
fresh fish and meat dishes. There are great
views across to Valletta and Manoel Island
and a sunny terrace sheltered by yellow sun-
shades.

ST JULIAN'S & PACEVILLE
The St Julian's and Paceville area is Malta's
gastronomic heartland. While plenty of places
crank out so-so meals, you won't need to
look hard to find some gems.

TOP CHOICE Assaggi   ITALIAN €€€
(☎2133 6625; www.assaggi.net; Triq il-Qaliet;
mains €19-30; ⊙dinner nightly, lunch Sun) Assaggi, tucked away on a backstreet, is a
cut above most local restaurants and is
favoured by sophisticated locals, who rave
about its 35-day dry-aged beef and fresh
fish. The short menu changes daily, according to what's seasonal; the wait staff
are helpful and attentive; and the setting is
cosy yet contemporary, with painting- and
bottle-lined walls.

Zest   FUSION €€€
(☎2138 7600; Hotel Juliani; mains €20-25) To see
and be seen, head to Zest, in the stand-out
boutique Hotel Juliani (p133). This fusion
restaurant is adored by locals. Its menu is
a mix of Japanese, Thai, Indonesian and
European, from which you can order sushi,
teppanyaki or dim sum dishes – and many
other exotic flavours. Book ahead and spec-
ify an outside table if you want a bay view.

Lulu   MEDITERRANEAN €€
(☎2137 7211; 31 Triq il-Knisja; 3-course set menu
€25.50; ⊙dinner Mon-Sat) Lulu's, set on a quiet
side street close to the Portomaso complex,
is informal yet sophisticated. It is prettily
decorated in ochre, white and green, with
a small terrace. Expect friendly service and
modern Med menu, with dishes such as
lamb shank served on steamed couscous
with a rosemary jus, and seared salmon fillet

with red pepper jam and lime and ginger syrup.

Sciacca
ITALIAN €€

(Triq Santu Wistin; mains €9-28; ⊙lunch & dinner daily) On the outskirts of Paceville lies this serene restaurant offering sophisticated Sicilian cooking, with ingredients imported from Malta's near neighbour. Dishes include fettucine with sea urchins, and orecchiette with calamari. The look is chic and contemporary, with leather-look chairs and wooden tables.

Avenue
MEDITERRANEAN €€

(☑2131 1753; Triq Gort; mains €8-20; ⊙lunch & dinner) Enduringly popular Avenue now takes up a sizeable stretch of the street. Despite its size, it's always bustling – the crowds keep coming for its lively atmosphere and good-value, crowd-pleasing menu. It's perfect for families, groups and students, who tuck with relish into simple meals of meat and fish, and huge portions of pizza and pasta. The interior is painted in dazzlingly bright colours and decorated in stained glass; there are also tables outside along the stepped narrow street.

La Spinola
BURGERS €€

(Badass Burgers; ☑2138 4066; www.badassburgers. eu; Triq San Ġorġ; burgers €9-16; ⊙6-11pm Mon-Thu & noon-midnight Fri-Sun) La Spinola, a branch of Badass Burgers, offers Malta's finest burgers. Besides 100% gourmet beef, the menu includes 'Off the Hook' burgers with prawn and haddock, and the 'Maltese' with rabbit and sausage. 'The Daddy' is a ginormous version for ravenous types. All are tasty and top-quality, and the setting is cool, too, an upstairs tented area with a garden feel – it's a very relaxed place to hang out. The kids' menu includes 'three mini-burgers & chips' for €6.50.

Parapett
MEDITERRANEAN €

(☑2135 3394; 125 Triq San Ġorġ; mains €7-13; ⊙6-11pm Tue-Fri, 6-11.30pm Sat noon-3pm & 6.30-11pm Sun) This bright, white-painted, cheerful eatery, dotted by pot plants and hung with watercolours, has a wide ranging menu of freshly prepared pasta, pizza, risotto, salad, seafood and grilled meats. Its relaxed atmosphere makes it a good family choice.

Paparazzi
MEDITERRANEAN €€

(☑2137 4966; 159 Triq San Ġorġ; mains €8-23; ⊙lunch & dinner; ✈) The sunny terrace here is a prime people-watching spot, almost jutting over the water, with a fine view of Spinola Bay. Fight your way through the huge portions on the big, crowd-pleasing menu. It's child- and veggie-friendly, too. Snacks like *ftira* (Maltese bread) are cheaper than the mains but substantial enough for a meal: a good deal.

Drinking

This area has a bar for everyone, from the teenage clubber to the senior citizen. Paceville is the place for full-on partying, with wall-to-wall bars and clubs in the area around the northern end of Triq San Ġorġ (where it turns into the steps of Triq Santa Rita), while the St Julian's and Sliema waterfronts have everything from slick wine bars to traditional British pubs.

Sliema

Muddy Waters
PUB

(☑2137 4155; 56 Triq il-Kbira) Muddy's, on Balluta Bay, has a great jukebox, and regularly hosts DJs and rock and blues bands. It's a great, intimate place to see live music, and a favourite of the student crowd. Things can get pretty rowdy at times – the tables can turn into dance floors.

City of London
PUB

(☑2133 1706; 193 Triq il-Kbira) This tiny pub has been open since 1914. It's packed at weekends and there's a great party atmosphere. It's popular on the gay scene, but everyone is welcome; there's a nicely mixed crowd of expats, locals and students.

St Julian's & Paceville

Level 22
BAR

(☑2310 2222; www.22.com.mt; Level 22, Portomaso Tower; ⊙9.30am-4am Jun-Aug, Wed-Sun Sep-May) Sleek and glitzily chic, lounge-bar Level 22 is well worth a visit if you're in the mood for cocktails with a touch of swank. Situated on the 22nd floor of Portomaso Tower, the bar has an amazing view over the lights of Portomaso and St Julian's and out to sea. It turns into a club on Friday and Saturday nights. Cocktails cost between €6.50 and €13.

Hugo's Lounge
LOUNGE

(☑2138 2264; Triq San Ġorġ; mains €10-15; ⊙daily) Hugo's, in the midst of one of Paceville's main drags, is a lively alfresco designer-style bar. It's great for cocktails and lounging on sofas, and you can soak up the booze with a menu of well-executed Asian food –

St Julian's & Paceville

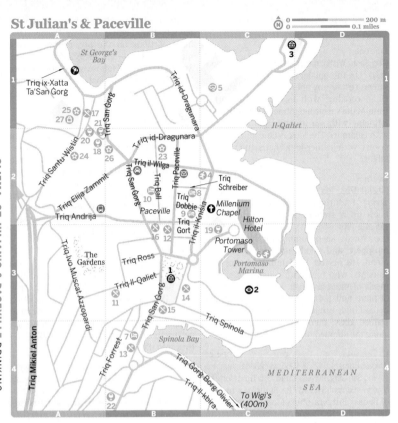

St Julian's & Paceville

sushi, curries, noodles and stir-fries and Thai soups.

Ryan's Irish Pub IRISH PUB
(☑2135 0680; www.ryans.com.mt) Lively pub action can be found at Ryan's Irish Pub, high up overlooking the action on Spinola Bay. It's a popular stop off, crowded, lively, friendly and well-stocked with cold Guinness. The pub also screens live football games.

Native Bar THEME BAR
(Triq San Ġorġ) This Latino-flavoured bar on Paceville's party street is always buzzing. Its indoor and outdoor areas are generally packed out with cocktail- and beer-slurping hedonists. In case the flirtatious action inside and out gets tiresome, there are also live sports on TV.

Nordic BAR
(☑2138 2264; St Rita's Steps) This popular Scandinavian-style bar has more of a club feel than others on Paceville's party strip; like most of the others, it has screens showing live sports.

☆ Entertainment
Nightclubs
There are loads of clubs concentrated at the northern end of Triq San Ġorġ in Paceville (where it turns into Triq Santa Rita), but their names come and go with the seasons. Speaking of seasons, this area is pumping and jam-packed most nights of the week in the high season (June to September), but you won't experience the same level of action in the low season (although weekends year-round are definitely classified as partytime).

The best advice is to wander this area, check out the offerings and see what takes your fancy (the right crowd, the right music, free entry or no need to queue, drinks promotions etc).

You should pick your times to party. Paceville nightlife is the reverse of the expected order of things (ie the younger crowd has the stamina to stay out late and the oldies head home early). Here, the under-21s are out and partying before midnight, then head home early to mum; that's when it's the older crowd's turn (after 1am they have the clubs to themselves).

BJ's Live Music Club LIVE MUSIC
(Map p66; ☑9949 3534; Triq Ball) This local favourite has a great atmosphere, proffers nightly live music (primarily jazz, but also soul, blues and rock). It's a one-off in Paceville – the only place in the area worth hanging out if you're over 25.

Fuego CLUB
(Map p66; ☑2138 6746; www.fuego.com.mt; Triq Santu Wistin) Get hot and sweaty dancing up a storm at this very popular indoor/outdoor salsa bar. The open terraces (covered and heated in winter) are full of people checking each other out – there's something of a meatmarket atmosphere, but it's friendly, fun and not too sleazy. On Wednesdays there are 'foam parties'.

Havana CLUB
(Map p66; ☑2137 4500; 82 Triq San Ġorġ) Free entry, six bars and a mixed menu of R&B, soul and commercial favourites keep the crowds happy here. There are lots of students and tourists chatting each other up, but plenty of locals, too.

Cinemas
Eden Century Cinemas CINEMA
(Map p66; ☑2371 0400; www.edencinemas.com.mt; Triq Santu Wistin) This large complex has 17 screens (on both sides of the road) showing first-run films. Adult tickets cost from €5.50, and all films are in English, or in their original language with English subtitles. See their website or the local newspapers for session details and screening times.

🔒 Shopping
Sliema's Triq ix-Xatt and Triq it-Torri together comprise Malta's prime shopping area. Among the tourist tat are some decent shoe shops and clothing labels, although there's little that's original – you won't need to look too hard to find the big British and European highstreet labels. Tigné Point shopping mall (p61), on the tip of the peninsular, dwarfs all the other competition, with lots of big name chains represented, but other decent hunting grounds for shoppers include the Bay Street Complex (Map p66; Triq Santu Wistin).

ℹ Information
Emergency
Police Station (☑2133 2282; cnr Triq Manwel Dimech & Triq Rudolfu)
Police Station (☑2133 2196; Triq San Ġorġ)

Medical Services
Mater Dei Hospital (☑2545 0000, emergency ☑112; www.ehealth.gov.mt; Tal-Qroqq) Malta's main general hospital is 2km southwest of Sliema, and 3km west of Valletta near the

University of Malta. Staff at the hospital can be contacted for any diving incidents requiring medical attention on ☏2545 5269 or via emergency number ☏112. The hospital can be accessed by numerous buses, including 22, 31, 32, 34 and 35 from Valletta.

Money

There are plenty of banks and ATMs throughout the area. Paceville in particular has plenty of money-exchange offices catering to tourists and international students.

Travelex (☏2132 2747; Il-Piazzetta; ◷8am-5pm Mon-Fri)

Post

Post Office

» **Sliema** (118 Triq Manwel Dimech; ◷7.30am-12.45pm Mon-Sat)

» **Paceville** (Lombard Bank, Triq; ◷8am-1pm Mon-Fri mid-Jun–Sep, 8.30am-2.30pm Oct–mid-Jun)

❶ Getting There & Away

Bus

Bus **21** (15 minutes, every 20 minutes), runs regularly between Valletta and Sliema. Buses **202** and **203** (10-15 minutes, every 30 minutes) run from Sliema to St Julian's and Paceville.

Direct bus services to and from the area – avoiding Valletta – include the following (all routes stop at the Ferries in Sliema, St Julian's and Paceville unless otherwise stated):

202/203 – to Ta'Qali Crafts Village, Rabat & Mdina

12 – along the coast to the Buġibba terminus

222 – Ċirkewwa (for Gozo Ferries)

205 – connects with Naxxar, Mosta, Attard, and Rabat (doesn't call at Sliema)

X2 – between the airport and St Julian's

Night buses, running between midnight and 3am or 4am daily, include:

N11 – running to/from Buġibba, Melieha and Ċirkewwa (for Gozo Ferries)

N13 – between Valletta and St Julian's and Sliema between midnight and 3am daily

N32 – St Julian's to/from Rabat

N81 – St Julian's to/from the Airport (Friday and Saturday only)

Ferry

The **Marsamxetto ferry service** (☏2346 3862; www.vallettaferryservices.com) crosses frequently between Valletta and Sliema. The crossing takes only about five minutes and there are departures every half-hour from 7am to 6pm Monday to Saturday, and from 10am to 4pm from Valletta to Sliema and to 6pm from Sliema to Valletta on Sundays. The fare one way/return is €1/3. Malta Water Taxis (☏7999 0001; www.maltawatertaxis.com.mt) are also available on demand, though it's wise to call ahead. They commute between Sliema and Valletta or Vittoriosa (€6 per person, minimum two people), or from St Julian's (Portomaso Marina or Spinola Bay) to Valletta (€7.50 per person, minimum two people).

❶ Getting Around

Wembley's (p178) provides a reliable 24-hour radio taxi service. Rates are generally cheaper than official taxi rates (to Valletta it's €13, to the airport €18, to the Gozo ferry €28).

There's a busy taxi rank close to the intersection of Triq San Ġġ and Triq il-Wilga in Paceville, which caters to the late-night crowd.

Northwest Malta

Includes »

Best Places to Eat

» Tarragon (p79)

» Giuseppe's Restaurant & Wine Bar (p75)

» Rebekah's (p75)

» il-Barri (p73)

Best Places to Stay

» San Antonio Hotel & Spa (p134)

» Radisson Blu Resort & Spa (p134)

» Splendid Guesthouse (p135)

» Pergola Club Hotel (p135)

Why Go?

It's curious that Malta has such a reputation for bucket-and-spade holidays, when its beaches are few and far between. Certainly the island is surrounded by a tremendous azure sea, but most beaches, such as they are, are concentrated on the Northwest coast. Beach bums should make a beeline for Mellieħa Bay for its facilities and water sports, or either Għajn Tuffieħa Bay or Ġnejna Bay for something more low-key and a chance to hang out with the locals. Scenic Golden Bay offers a choice midway between those two extremes, and is largely unspoilt, with only one five-star hotel. Just be aware that there's little chance of finding solitude on any rock or patch of sand during the high season.

And yet the northwest's list of drawcards extends far beyond holiday resorts. Here you can enjoy myriad water-sports and boat trips, birdwatching, horse riding, lovely walks along the coast and Malta's best family-fun attractions.

When to Go

Malta's major beach zone gets busy over July and August. Schools are out, prices are higher and the weather is at its hottest. If you're after a party scene, it's at its height during this time. If you're looking for sunshine and off-season bargains, travel in April, May, September and October (bear in mind that it'll only be hot enough to swim in May and September).

Northwest Malta Highlights

1 Squeezing yourself into a wetsuit to explore the local marine life while scuba-diving off the **Marfa Peninsula** (p76)

2 Feasting your eyes on the magnificent coastal views from the wild headland of **Ras il-Qammieħ** (p77)

3 Making the long climb down to the near-empty **Għajn Tuffieħa Bay** (p72) on a quiet spring day

4 Letting the locals know that you prefer your bird life alive, not hunted down, by supporting the beautiful birds of **Għadira Nature Reserve** (p75)

MEDITERRANEAN
SEA

St Paul's
Islands

Qawra
Tower

St Paul's Bay

Malta National Aquarium

QAWRA

*Salina
Bay*

Ghallis
Tower

Buġibba

**ST PAUL'S
BAY VILLAGE**

*Qalet
Marku*

Qalet
Marku
Tower

*Baħar
iċ-Ċagħaq
Bay*

Baħarċ-Ċagħaq

Mediterraneo
Marine Park

Splash &
Fun Park

Wardija

Burmarrad

*Church of
San Pawl Milqi*

Madliena Fort

VICTORIA   LINES

Madliena

*To
St Julian's
(250m)*

*Mosta
Fort*

San Pawl

Gharghur

Tat-
Tarġa

*Mosta
Dome*

Naxxar

Mosta

Lija

Balzan

Birkirkara

Mdina

Golden Bay & Għajn Tuffieħa

The fertile Pwales Valley stretches 4km from the head of St Paul's Bay to Għajn Tuffieħa. Here, two of Malta's best sandy beaches draw crowds of sun-worshippers.

◉ Sights & Activities

Golden Bay   BEACH
The lovely – if small – arc of Golden Bay is bustling and well developed, with cafes, watersports and boat trips, and a huge five-star hotel rising above the shoreline.

Għajn Tuffieħa Bay   BEACH
Għajn Tuffieħa Bay (ayn too-*fee*-ha, meaning 'Spring of the Apples') is even lovelier than neighbouring Golden Bay, and less busy, as it's reached via a long flight of 186 steps from the nearby car park. It's a 250m-strip of red-brown sand, backed by slopes covered in acacia and tamarisk trees, and guarded by a 17th-century watchtower. Sun loungers can be hired here.

TOP CHOICE Charlie's Discovery
Speedboat Trips   BOAT TOUR
(☏9948 6949) Charlie is a knowledgeable guide who was twice awarded 'Boatman of the Year'. He'll take you south from his base at Golden Bay to view rugged cliffs, bays and grottoes, including Għajn Tuffieħa, Ġnejna and Fomm ir-Riħ (tricky to reach by land). The one-hour trips leave at noon and 2.30pm daily and cost €11/9 per adult/child. Charlie also operates a daily trip to Comino's Blue Lagoon at 4pm from April to October – a great chance to visit this beautiful spot after the crowds have left. This trip costs €16/12 per adult/child and includes an hour-and-a-half swim. Look out for Charlie and his boat on the northern part of the beach, or ask at Munchies Bar-Pizzeria.

Park Tal-Majjistral   NATURE RESERVE
(www.majjistral.org) The area between Golden Bay and Anchor Bay was once earmarked for a new golf course but opposition from environmental groups led to the creation instead of Malta's only national park, Park tal-Majjistral. The park – essentially a nature reserve – protects a region of wild sea cliffs and limestone boulder scree, home to plants such as euphorbia, Maltese rock centaury and golden samphire, and wildlife that includes Mediterranean chameleons. Information boards show waymarked walking trails; the park arranges regular guided walks (adult/child €5/3). Also available in summer are 2.5-hour snorkelling trips to explore the park (adult/child €12/10; over 9 years only). Check their website and Facebook page for upcoming events, and book by emailing walks@majjistral.org.

Borg Watersports   WATERSPORTS
(☏2157 3272) Borg Watersports is located on the shoreline of Golden Bay (in front of the Radisson) from March to November. It has snorkelling gear, sailboards, jet skis, speedboats, pedalos and canoes available for hire, as well as powerboating (€200), sailing (€30), parakiting (€50) or water-skiing (€40).

Golden Bay Horse Riding   HORSE RIDING
(☏2157 3360; www.goldenbayhorseriding.com; 1/1½-hr sunset ride €20/30; ⊙7am-9pm Jun-Sep, 9am-5pm Oct-May) This horse riding centre, signposted from Golden Bay, offers enjoyable one- and two-hour rides on fields overlooking the northwest beaches, for all levels of experience. Advance booking is recommended.

✖ Eating

Your best bet for a meal is to brush the sand of your feet and head to one of the upmarket options at the 10-storey Radisson Blu Resort & Spa (p134).

Essence   MEDITERRANEAN €€€
(☏2356 1111; mains €23-29; ⊙dinner Tue-Sat) Romantic Essence is this area's number one pick for a fancy-pants dinner with beautiful sea views. First courses include lobster linguine with warm sea urchin sauce, followed by beef fillet with enoki mushrooms and polenta. Bookings are recommended.

Mokka Lobby Bar & Terrace   CAFE €€
(☏2356 1000; mains €9-15; ⊙9am-11pm) The fab outdoor terrace of Mokka Lobby Bar & Terrace is perfect for coffee, cake, platters and light meals.

Agliolio   MEDITERRANEAN €€
(☏2356 1000; mains €10-32; ⊙lunch & dinner) Cheery, noisy and aqua-coloured Agliolio has an appealing Med-flavoured menu heavy on pizza, pasta and salads; nab a table outside overlooking the beach.

❶ Getting There & Away

Buses 223 and 224 go from Buġibba to Għajn Tuffieħa Bay (25 minutes, every 10-20 minutes) via St Paul's Bay (10 minutes).

Mġarr & Around

The village of **Mġarr** (mm-*jarr*), 2km to the southeast of Għajn Tuffieħa (not to be confused with Mġarr on Gozo), is dominated by the conspicuous dome of the famous **Egg Church**. The Church of the Assumption was built in the 1930s with money raised by local parishioners, largely from the sale of local eggs. Across the village square from the church is the **Mġarr Shelter** (📞2157 3235; Triq il-Kbira; adult/child €3/1.50; ☺9am-1pm Tue-Sat), used by locals during the WWII bombings of Malta (enter through Il Barri restaurant). You can only imagine the long uncomfortable hours spent down here in the humidity, 12m underground. There are rooms on display that served as classrooms and hospitals, showing how life went on under such tough conditions.

Ta'Ħaġrat Temple (📞2123 9545; Triq San Pietru; adult/child €5/2.50; ☺8am-7pm daily), dating from around 3600 to 3300 BC and the earliest temple building in Malta, is concealed down a side street near the police station (on the road towards Żebbiegħ). It's smaller than other temple sites, but notable for its largely intact doorway, with its huge lintel. The **Skorba Temples** (📞2123 9545; Triq Sant'Anna; adult/child €5/2.50; ☺9am-noon Tue, Thu & Sat), in the neighbouring village of Żebbiegħ, have scant remains, but excavation of the site was important in providing evidence of village habitation on Malta in the period between 4500 and 4100 BC (earlier than the temple-building period), now known as the Skorba Phase.

A minor road leads west from Mġarr past the ornate early-19th-century **Zammitello Palace** – originally a manor house, and now a wedding and function hall – to **Ġnejna Bay**. The gentle red-sand beach is backed by terraced hillsides and has boathouses built into the rocks to one side. The **Lippija Tower** on the northern skyline makes a good target for a short walk.

Il-Barri (📞2157 3235; Triq il-Kbira; mains €6-17; ☺lunch Tue-Sun, dinner daily) is on the village square in Mġarr, close to the Egg Church. From outside it looks like an innocuous pizzeria, so the slick interior is a surprise, with its monochrome styling. It's a favourite local venue for a *fenkata* – whole fresh rabbit served in a casserole, and there are also grilled steaks, lamb chops and king prawns, plus Maltese-as-they-come local favourites such as *aljotta* (fish broth), plus pizzas in the evening. These are some of the hugest portions we have ever seen, so keep that in mind when ordering.

Bus 44 runs from Valletta to Mġarr (50 minutes) about half-hourly daily, via Mosta.

Mellieħa

POP 7900

The sprawling, rapidly developing town of Mellieħa (mell-*ee*-ha) perches picturesquely atop the ridge between St Paul's Bay and Mellieħa Bay. Because of its distance from the beach, Mellieħa escaped the tidal wave of development that blighted Sliema and Buġibba in the early days of Malta's package-holiday boom. There are now several large hotels in town, but Mellieħa retains a certain elegance, and is home to some excellent restaurants. A 15-minute walk leads down the steep hill to **Mellieħa Bay** (also known as Għadira Bay), the longest and most popular sandy beach in the Maltese Islands. It's not especially scenic, as it's backed by a small road, but it's a great place for family fun.

CATCHING THE FERRY

Buses 41 and 42 run between Valletta and Ċirkewwa (one hour 20 minutes, every 10 minutes); X1 operates to/from the airport (55 minutes, hourly) and 221 to/from Buġibba (40 minutes) both calling at Mellieħa (12-20 minutes); and 222 to/from Sliema and St Julian's (one hour, hourly). By car, you can make the trip to/from Valletta in about 45 minutes. A taxi from Malta International Airport to Ċirkewwa costs €32.

Gozo Channel (p113) operates the car ferry that shuttles between Malta's Ċirkewwa and Gozo's Mġarr every 45 minutes from 6am to around 6pm (and roughly every hour and a half throughout the night). You pay on the return journey. For Comino, **United Comino Ferries** (📞9940 6529; www.unitedcomino ferries.com) operates year-round from Ċirkewwa and the Marfa jetty (return €10/5 adult/child; 35 minutes). Services run hourly from 9am to 4pm, with a couple of extra boats daily in summer. **Ebsons Comino Ferries** (📞2155 4991; www.cominoferryservice.com) operates from 8am to 6pm from both Ċirkewwa and Marfa (€10/5 adult/child).

Melieħa

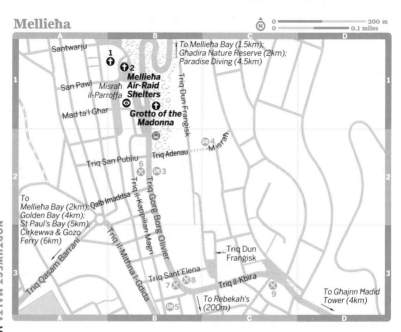

Mellieħa

◉ Sights & Activities

Church of Our Lady of Victory CHURCH

(⊗8am-noon & 5-7pm) The Church of Our Lady of Victory sits prominently on a rocky spur overlooking Mellieħa Bay. Stairs lead down on the eastern side of the church to a little pedestrian plaza beside the Sanctuary of Our Lady of Mellieħa (⊗8am-noon & 5-7pm), which has been a place of pilgrimage since medieval times – it is believed to have been blessed by St Paul himself. Its walls are covered with votive offerings; the fresco of the Madonna above the altar is said to have been painted by St Luke.

Grotto of the Madonna CHURCH

(⊗8am-6pm Sep-May, to 7pm Jun-Aug) Across the main street from the shrine, a gate in the wall and a flight of steps lead down to the Grotto of the Madonna, a shrine dedicated to the Virgin. It is set deep in a cave lit by flickering candles, beside a spring with waters that are reputed to heal sick children. Baby clothes hung on the walls are votive offerings given in thanks for successful cures.

Mellieħa Air-Raid Shelters HISTORIC SITE

(☑7952 1970; Triq il-Madonna tal-Għar; adult/child €2.33/0.58; ⊗9am-3.30pm Mon-Sat) As you approach the sanctuary from the main street, steps to the left lead up to the entrance to the Mellieħa air-raid shelters, dug by hand to shelter the town's population from WWII bombs. It's one of the largest underground shelters in Malta, with a depth of 12m and a length of around 500m, and gives a haunting sense of what it was like to shelter down here – spooky mannequins and some furnishings bring home the cramped, damp environment.

Mellieħa Bay BEACH
The warm, shallow waters of Mellieħa Bay are safe for kids and great for swimming, so the sea gets almost as crowded as the sand. Add the water-skiers, rental canoes, banana rides, parasailing boats and the fact that the reliable northeasterly breeze blowing into the bay in summer makes it ideal for windsurfing, and you begin to realise that Mellieħa Bay is not the place to get away from it all. Still, there are good summertime facilities, including sun beds and umbrellas for rent, windsurfing and kite-surfing gear for hire, and numerous kiosks serving drinks and snacks.

FREE **Għadira Nature Reserve** NATURE RESERVE
(☑2134 7646; www.birdlifemalta.org; admission free, donations welcome; ☺10am-4pm Sat & Sun Nov-May) Ironically, across the road from Malta's busiest beach is the Għadira Nature Reserve. This area of shallow, reedy ponds surrounded by scrub is an important resting area for migrating birds (over 200 species have been recorded at the site). The name, pronounced aa-*dee*-ra, means 'marsh', and this was Malta's first national nature reserve, managed by passionate volunteers of BirdLife Malta on behalf of the government. Volunteers accompany visitors for a walk along a nature trail that leads to a bird-watching hide.

Tunny Net Complex WATERSPORTS
At the southern edge of Mellieħa Bay is the Tunny Net Complex, with restaurants and a few shops, boat trips available, a lido, a watersports operator open from April to October (parasailing, ringo rides on rubber tubes, jet skis for hire, canoes and paddle boats etc) and a diving operator: Meldives Dive School (p22).

Eating & Drinking

Giuseppe's Restaurant & Wine Bar MEDITERRANEAN €€€
(☑2157 4882; cnr Triq Ġorġ Borg Olivier & Triq Sant'Elena; mains €19-21; ☺dinner Mon-Sat) Giuseppe's, run by Malta's favourite TV chef, Michael Diacono, is full of charm. Its walls are hung with paintings, and it has a relaxed atmosphere and a stand-out menu of creative treats – like quail with pistachio and

spinach – that changes regularly according to seasonal produce. The fresh fish is reliably good, and regulars recommend the king prawns. Bookings are advised.

Rebekah's MEDITERRANEAN €€€
(12 Triq It-Tgham; mains €20-25; ☺from 7pm Mon-Sat) Rebekah's is a bit tricky to find, as it's tucked away in Mellieħa's back streets, but it's worth seeking out (head south to the end of Triq Dun Franġisk, then take a right). It has a rustic interior with flagstone walls and a nice little courtyard, and serves up delicious, spectacular food that keeps the punters coming back time and time again. The menu ranges from melt-in-the-mouth scallops to lamb stew cooked slowly, Maltese-style.

Il-Mithna MALTESE €€
(☑2152 0404; 45 Triq il-Kbira; mains €8.50-25; ☺dinner Mon-Sat) This is a lovely place to dine – the restaurant is housed in a 400-year-old windmill, the only survivor of three that once sat atop Mellieħa Ridge. There are outdoor tables in a pretty courtyard, and a menu of local dishes with a twist, like local rabbit stuffed with a chicken and pistachio mousse, wrapped in cured ham, served on an aged port wine reduction. The set menu (€15) served between 6pm and 7.30pm is a bargain.

Arches MEDITERRANEAN €€€
(☑2152 3460; 113 Triq Ġorġ Borg Olivier; mains €25-30; ☺dinner Mon-Sat) This acclaimed restaurant is large, elegant and stately, with dark terracotta-coloured walls; the menu, prices and service all befit the chic decor and formality. The food is accomplished and delicious, with dishes like seared venison fillet with celeriac purée and pear and plum chutney. Book ahead.

Badass Burgers FAST FOOD €€
(☑2755 6633; €9-13; ☺3-10pm Tue-Fri, noon-10pm Sat & Sun, later in summer) Badass' Mellieħa branch has outdoor seating so you can watch the world go past. The decor might look quite plastic – stylish, but not particularly promising – but the burgers are Malta's best, with top-quality meat and a gourmet range, including the 'Tastefully Posh', which includes Stilton and chutney.

Point Break MEDITERRANEAN €€
(☑2152 3190; mains €9-18; ☺lunch & dinner) Inside the sailing centre's Greek Islands–inspired exterior is an alluring cafe-bar. You can enjoy your meal inside the sky-blue

interior or – preferably – alfresco, with water views everywhere you look. The lunchtime menu is small, with a few baguette and burger selections; dinner-time options are greater, with appealing fish and pasta dishes, nachos and an excellent seafood platter.

ⓘ Information

Touchstone (☎2152 0633; 45 cnr Triq Ġorġ Borg Olivier & Triq Sant'Elena; per 30 min €1; ☉9am-1pm & 4-6pm Mon-Sat) is a stylish bookshop, art gallery and cafe with internet access and free wi-fi.

ⓘ Getting There & Away

Buses 37, 41 and 42 from Valletta pass through Mellieħa (one hour). Buses 41 and 42 go on to Ċirkewwa (20 minutes) for the Gozo Ferry. Bus 221 connects with Ċirkewwa too, as well as with Buġibba. Buses 101 and 102 go to Gnejna Bay, calling at Mġarr and Ghajn Tuffieħa en route, and also serve Ċirkewwa .

Around Mellieħa

The crest of Mellieħa Ridge offers some good walking to the southeast and southwest of the town. To the east, the ornate fortress-like **Selmun Palace** which now houses a hotel and restaurant, dominates the skyline above St Paul's Bay. It was built in the 18th century for a charitable order called the Monte di Redenzione degli Schiavi (Mountain of the Redemption of the Slaves), whose business was to ransom Christians who had been taken into slavery on the Barbary Coast.

A right turn just before you get to Selmun Palace leads in just over 1km to the derelict **Fort Campbell**, an abandoned coastal defence built by the British between WWI and WWII. The headland commands a fine view over St Paul's Islands, and you can hike down to the coastal salt pans of Blata il-Bajda and around to Mistra Bay, or westwards along the cliff top to the ruined **Ghajn Ħadid tower** above the little beach at Mġieba Bay.

A left turn at the foot of the hill leading down to Mellieħa Bay puts you on the road to Anchor Bay about 1.5km away on the west coast. Beyond Anchor Bay lies the **Marfa Peninsula**. Some of Malta's most spectacular dive sites lie off this coast, including Marfa Point, Tugboat Rozi and Cirkewwa Arch. Local dive schools with equipment or hire facilities include Meldives Dive School (p22), Dive Deep Blue (p21), Subway Dive Centre (p22) and Buddies Dive Cove (p21).

◎ Sights & Activities

Red Tower   FORTRESS
(☎2121 5222; adult/child €1.50/free; ☉10am-4pm Mon-Sat) The chess piece-like Red Tower was built in 1649 for Grand Master Lascaris, as part of the chain of signal towers that linked Valletta and Gozo; the view from its flat roof is stunning. This simple fortress is one of the more elaborate towers – it once housed a garrison of up to 49 men. The plaque above the entrance indicates that this is not a place of sanctuary, despite containing a chapel.

Sweethaven   AMUSEMENT PARK
(Anchor Bay; ☎2152 4782; www.popeyemalta.com/; adult/child €13.50/10.50, discounts in low season; ☉9.30am-5.30pm Mar-Jul, Sep & Oct, to 7pm Aug, to 4.30pm Nov-Feb) Steep-sided, pretty little Anchor Bay was named after the many Roman anchors that were found on the seabed by divers, some of which can be seen in the Maritime Museum at Vittoriosa.

THE VICTORIA LINES

The Victoria lines were built by the British in the late 19th century, intended to protect the main part of the island from potential invaders landing on the northern beaches, but they never saw any military action. The fortifications were named after Queen Victoria's Diamond Jubilee in 1897.

The lines run about 12km along a steep limestone escarpment that stretches from Fomm ir-Riħ in the west to Baħar iċ-Ċagħaq in the east and are excellent place for a walk, affording magnificent views. If you're interested in doing some independent exploration, try to get hold of *The Victoria Lines*, edited by Ray Cachia Zammit. This guide to the site includes a foldout map and is available in the better bookshops in Valletta. For more information as well as walking routes, see www.victorialinesmalta.com.

Three forts – Madliena Fort, Mosta Fort and Binġemma Fort – are linked by a series of walls, entrenchments and gun batteries. The best-preserved section, the Dwejra Lines, lies north of Mdina.

Driving Tour
Malta's Wildest Corner: The Marfa Peninsula

To explore one of Malta's most atmospheric corners, take a spin around the Marfa Peninsula, the island's final flourish before dipping beneath the waters of the Comino Channel. This trip encompasses a nature reserve, an impressive tower, windswept coastal walks and some favourite local beaches.

Driving onto the peninsula, you'll pass the ❶ **Għadira Nature Reserve** on your left, with ❷ **Mellieħa Bay** on your right. When you reach the next junction, turn left, and aim uphill to the ❸ **Red Tower** and its dizzying views. From here the road gets bumpier. Drive until you reach the wild headland of ❹ **Ras il-Qammieħ**, with more incredible views north to Gozo and south along Malta's western sea cliffs.

Next, return to the main road, following it down towards Ċirkewwa, the Gozo ferry terminal. Take the left before you reach the Paradise Bay Resort Hotel. This lane leads to ❺ **Paradise Bay**, a picturesque but narrow patch of sand backed by cliffs, which is a popular swimming spot.

To access the rest of the peninsula, you'll need to drive back to the main road that runs along its spine. From here you can visit the area's little bays – be mindful that they get packed out at weekends. First stop is ❻ **Ramla Bay**, its small, sandy beach monopolised by the resort of the same name; just east is ❼ **Ramla Tal'Qortin**, which has no sand and is surrounded by an unsightly sprawl of Maltese holiday huts.

Drive back to the main road, and the next two roads lead down to the scrappy sandy beaches at ❽ **Armier Bay**, the most developed beach on the peninsula, with sun loungers, kiosks and a handful of cafes. The fourth road leads to ❾ **White Tower Bay**, which has another seaweed-stained patch of sand and a rash of holiday huts combining to form a small shanty town. A track continues past the tower to the low cliffs of ❿ **Ahrax Point**, from which a pleasant coastal walk leads 1km south to a statue of the Madonna on ⓫ **Dahlet ix-Xilep**. You can also reach the Madonna statue and a small chapel by following the main road east across the Marfa Peninsula.

In 1979 Anchor Bay was transformed into the ramshackle fishing village of Sweethaven and was used as the set for the 1980 Hollywood musical *Popeye,* starring Robin Williams. The vintage set still stands and is a somewhat cheesy and old-fashioned theme park, which younger kids (around four to eight years will get the most out of it) will enjoy. There are animation shows, puppets, small fun park (where you pay extra for rides) and a boat ride.

Getting There & Away

Bus 42 runs through this area to/from Valletta; 221 to/from St Paul's Bay; 222 to/from Sliema/St Julian's; and X1 to/from the Airport. There's also a shuttle bus from the Tunny Net Complex (p75) in Mellieħa.

Xemxija

The small, south-facing village of Xemxija (shem-*shee*-ya), on the north side of St Paul's Bay, takes its name from *xemx,* meaning 'sun' in Malti; it's decked by low-rise custard-coloured apartment blocks that don't do a lot for the view. There are a couple of private lidos along the waterfront, but Pwales Beach at the head of St Paul's Bay is just a narrow strip of gravelly sand.

Sights

FREE Is-Simar Nature Reserve   NATURE RESERVE

(✆2134 7646; www.birdlifemalta.org; admission free, donations welcome; ⏰10am-4pm Sun Nov-May) Is-Simar was opened in 1995 on a marshy patch of neglected land and managed by BirdLife Malta (p28) volunteers on behalf of the government. Over 180 bird species have been recorded at the site. As with the Għadira Nature Reserve (p75), it's wonderful to see this commitment to Malta's natural assets and an area where local and migratory bird life is protected from hunters. The entrance is on the side street Triq Il-Pwales.

Eating

Porto del Sol   MEDITERRANEAN €€

(✆2157 3970; www.portodelsolmalta.com; It Telegħa tax-Xemxija; mains €9-20; ⏰lunch & dinner Mon-Sat) Porto del Sol is a family-run restaurant with views of the bay from its large picture windows. It has the look of an upmarket, British seaside restaurant, but it's popular with locals for its fresh seafood and local dishes.

Buġibba, Qawra & St Paul's Bay

St Paul's Bay is named after the saint who was shipwrecked here in AD 60. The sweep of the bay has unfortunately been marred by unattractive buildings; Buġibba and Qawra, on the eastern side, form the biggest tourist development in Malta.

This is the heartland of the island's cheap-and-cheerful package-holiday trade, and it's mobbed in summer. It's full of hotels, bars and so-so restaurants – fine if you want a week or so of beer-fuelled, sun-filled hedonism, but rather lacking in local charm. Still, there are some points in its favour, number one being that it is affordable.

Sights & Activities

There's not much to see in Buġibba except acres of painted concrete, but it's a lively, cheap-and-cheerful resort and you can often

---

SHARK'S TEETH

The cliffs around the Marfa Peninsula and Ċirkewwa are dotted by fossils. Keep an eye out and you may even spot sharks' teeth, for which Malta is particularly famous. 'Stony tongues' (*glossopetrae*) were collected by visitors to Malta from the earliest times. These were gleamingly polished, triangular objects, and were once thought to be related to the shipwrecking of St Paul in AD 64. According to legend, he was bitten by a snake, and he cursed it, banishing it from the island. The only remnant of the reptile was its petrified tooth.

In the 16th century, the German Conrad Gesner pointed out the similarity of *glossopetrae* to the tooth of the dogfish. In 1666 a Danish doctor, Nikolaus Stensius, dissected a shark that had washed up locally and was able to prove the real origin of the stony tongues. It's now forbidden to collect fossils, but if you don't spot any on the cliffs, you can see the impressive teeth at either Malta or Gozo's Natural History Museums.

pick up amazingly inexpensive package deals to stay here. The main activities available are strolling along the spruced-up promenade, browsing the tourist-trap shops, swimming or taking a boat trip. There are various diving and boating operators based here, and a number of private lidos lining the waterfront, many offering sun lounges, watersports, swimming pools and cafe-bars, but the man-made sandy beach is best avoided. However, the new €15.6 million Malta National Aquarium (www.aquarium.com.mt), close to Qawra Tower, promises to be a splendid state-of-the-art wonder and a great new focus for family fun.

Malta Classic Car Collection   MUSEUM
(☑2157 8885; www.classiccarsmalta.com; Triq it-Turisti; adult/child €7/4.50; ⊙9.30am-6pm Mon-Fri, 9.30am-1.30pm Sat & Sun) On the ground floor of an apartment complex, the Malta Classic Car Collection a temple to one man's love of cars. The privately owned collection of mint-condition vehicles (cars and motorbikes) includes plenty of 1950s and '60s British- and Italian-made classics, plus a collection of photos from these eras that give an idea of Malta's past.

Wignacourt Tower   FORTRESS
(☑2122 5222; Triq it-Torri; adult/child €2/free; ⊙10am-1pm Mon-Wed, Fri & Sat) Built in 1609, the Wignacourt Tower was the first of the towers built by Grand Master Wignacourt. It guards the point to the west of the church, and houses a tiny museum with exhibits on local fortress history, including a small selection of guns and armour. There are great views from here.

Church of St Paul's Bonfire   CHURCH
The old fishing village of St Paul's Bay, now merged with Buġibba, has retained something of its traditional Maltese character and has a few historical sights. The 17th-century Church of St Paul's Bonfire stands on the waterfront to the south of Plajja Tal'Bognor, supposedly on the spot where the saint first scrambled ashore. A bonfire is lit outside the church during the festival of St Paul's Shipwreck (10 February).

Għajn Rasul   FOUNTAIN
Further west, near the fishing-boat harbour at the head of the bay, is Għajn Rasul (Apostle's Fountain), where St Paul is said to have baptised the first Maltese convert to Christianity.

Boat Trips & Water Sports
Plenty of smaller operators offer tours from the jetty at Plajja Tal'Bognor. As well as shorter trips around St Paul's Bay, some operators offer trips from to Comino for around €15. Head down to the jetty area to see what's available.

Captain Morgan Cruises   BOAT TOUR
(☑2346 3333; www.captainmorgan.com.mt) Most Captain Morgan Cruises operate out of Sliema, but there are Buġibba departures for an hour-long 'underwater safari' in a glass-bottomed boat exploring the marine life around St Paul's Islands. Underwater safaris depart from Plajja Tal'Bognor three times daily Monday to Saturday June to September, and Monday to Friday April, May and October (€15/11 adult/child).

Yellow Fun Watersports   WATERSPORTS
(☑2355 2570; www.yellowfunwatersports.com; Dawret il-Gżejjer) Offers powerboat trips to the Blue Lagoon on Comino. Trips leave daily at 10.30am returning at 3.30pm; the cost is €18 per person. Yellow Fun can also arrange boat charter, sea-taxi service, fishing trips and showers of watersports fun, such as water-skiing, jet skiing, canoeing, windsurfing and paragliding.

Diving
There are several dive operators in Buġibba that can help you explore the excellent nearby dive sites or sites around the Maltese Islands. These include:
» Buddies Dive Cove (p21)
» Dive Deep Blue (p21)
» Subway Dive Centre (p22)

✖ Eating
Buġibba is awash with cheap eating places, many offering 'full English breakfast' or named 'Mr Kebab'. But there's a selection of other cuisines and a few good Maltese places, too.

Tarragon   MEDITERRANEAN €€€
(☑2157 3759; Triq il-Knisja; mains €20-30; ⊙dinner Mon-Sat, lunch Sun) Tucked above the harbour at St Paul's Bay, Tarragon is a haven of wood-panelled sophistication with a Mediterranean/fusion menu that pulls in food-lovers from all over Malta. The speciality is fresh fish (landed earlier that day at the quay below the restaurant) baked in salt (or cooked whichever way you want).

Buġibba

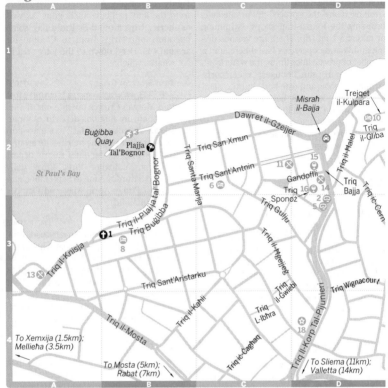

NORTHWEST MALTA BUĠIBBA, QAWRA & ST PAUL'S BAY

Venus
MEDITERRANEAN €€

(☎2157 1604; cnr Triq Bajja & Gandoffli; mains €15-22; ☺Wed-Mon) Venus is an oasis of class on Buġibba's food scene. There's a bright and sophisticated interior and the modern fusion menu adds an imaginative twist to traditional ingredients – try calamari in soy and lime leaves or Thai fish cakes, followed by herb-encrusted New Zealand lamb with a rosemary jus, or or tender steak. The three-course set menu is splendid value at €20.

Ta'Pawla
MALTESE €€

(☎2157 6039; Triq it-Turisti; mains €6-15; ☺dinner) You can get a taste of good, authentic Maltese cuisine in the cute gingham-clad interior of this busy little place, which is fronted by a small glass-covered terrace. A set three-course Maltese menu is only €13.80. The menu includes local classics like rabbit in

garlic and octopus stew, but there's also an assortment of stock-standard pizza, pasta and steak.

Capuvino
MEDITERRANEAN €

(www.capuvino.com; Triq Sant Antnin; mains €3-10; ☺10am-late Wed-Mon) Capuvino is near Buġibba's centre but feels slightly removed; the restaurant is shaded by tall palms and features chequered tablecloths and a few outside tables on a pedestrianised section of street. Food includes *ftira* (Maltese bread) sandwiches, pasta and Maltese platters.

Malét
MALTESE €€

(☎2758 1023; Triq San Xmun; mains €10-20; ☺from 6pm) This popular traditional Maltese restaurant, just off the promenade, has an intimate feel, white linen tablecloths, and rabbit on the menu as well as fillet of beef.

♟ Drinking

Take your pick from the dozens of bars along Triq it-Turisti and the streets around Misraħ il-Bajja (particularly Triq Sant'Antnin), mainly traditional British-style pubs or buzzing bars-to-get-sloshed-in.

Simon's Pub　　　　　　　THEME PUB
(☏2157 7566; simonselvisbar.com/; Triq it-Turisti) Simon is clearly a huge fan of the King – and so are we, so we love this place, which is a two-room shrine to Elvis. There's live entertainment every night – stop in on Monday or Friday for the highlight, the Elvis tribute. Cheesy fun, thankyouverymuch.

Fat Harry's　　　　　　　　　　PUB
(☏2158 1298; Triq Bajja) Fat Harry's is an English-style pub that offers all-day traditional pub grub like fish and chips, and offering plenty of draught beer, out-door tables for people-watching and, inside, live sports on the big screen or live entertainment.

Rookies Sports Bar & Grill　　SPORTS BAR
(☏2157 4550; www.rookiesmalta.net; Triq Sponoż) Giant screens televise international sports at this large and popular American-style sports bar. There are also regular live bands and a bevy of international beers (and meals) to get you going.

☆ Entertainment

Fuego　　　　　　　　　　　　CLUB
(☏2138 6746; Dawret il-Qawra) The sister salsa bar to Fuego (p67) in Paceville is perfect for a boozy night out, with DJs playing pure and commercial Latin music, free entry, Wednesday 'foam' parties, tequila specials and open terraces (covered and heated in winter).

Amazonia CLUB

(☎2355 2410; Dawret il-Gżejjer) This pumping summer club, at the lido opposite the Dolmen Resort Hotel, is popular with tourists and locals happy to carry on all night to cool tunes in a lush waterfront setting.

Empire Cinema Complex CINEMA

(☎2158 1787; www.empirecinema.com.mt; Triq il-Korp Tal-Pijunieri) The Empire features seven-screen multiplex showing first-run movies. Tickets cost €6/3.50 adult/child (€5 for adults before 5pm weekdays).

ⓘ Information

Emergency
Police Station (☎2157 6737, 2157 1174; Triq it-Turisti)

Money
HSBC Bank (Misraħ il-Bajja)

ⓘ Getting There & Away

There is a central taxi rank on Misraħ il-Bajja in Buġibba.

Buġibba bus station is on Triq it-Turisti near the Dolmen Resort Hotel. Bus 12 runs to/from Valletta (every 12 minutes, one hour), via Sliema (20 minutes) and St Julian's (35 minutes). Bus 31 also runs between Buġibba and Valletta (every 10-20 minutes), via Naxxar (18 minutes) and Mosta (37 minutes). Buses 223 and 224 go from Buġibba to Għajn Tuffieħa Bay (25 minutes, every 10-20 minutes) via St Paul's Bay (10 minutes). Bus 221 heads to Ċirkewwa for ferries to Gozo (40 minutes), via Mellieħa (20 minutes) and St Paul's Bay (10 minutes).

Baħar iċ-Ċagħaq

Baħar iċ-Ċagħaq (*ba*-har eetch *cha*-ag; also known as White Rocks) lies halfway between Sliema and Buġibba. It has a scruffy rock beach and a couple of hugely popular family-friendly attractions.

◉ Sights

Splash & Fun Park THEME PARK

(☎2137 4283; www.splashandfun.com.mt; adult/child €20/12, €14/8 after 3pm Jul–mid-Sep, after 1pm low season; advance family ticket €48; ⏱9.30am-6pm late May–Jun & late Sep–early Oct, 9am-9pm Jul–early Sep) This huge wave park is a fun place for a day out, and kids will love it, although it could do with a facelift and some TLC. That said, the wave pool constantly pumps 1.5m artificial waves; there are plenty of tunnels and spray jets; fibreglass waterslides; the 'Black Hole'; and a 240m-long 'lazy river' you can coast down

ST PAUL IN MALTA

The Bible (Acts 27–8) tells how St Paul was shipwrecked on Malta (most likely around AD 60) on his voyage from Caesarea to stand trial in Rome. The ship full of prisoners was caught in a storm and drifted for 14 days before breaking up on the shore of an unknown island. All aboard swam safely to shore, '...and when they were escaped, then they knew that the island was called Melita'.

The local people received the shipwrecked strangers with kindness and built a bonfire to warm them. Paul, while adding a bundle of sticks to the fire, was bitten by a venomous snake – a scene portrayed in several religious paintings on the island – but suffered no ill effects. The Melitans took this as a sign that he was no ordinary man.

Act 28 goes on to say that Paul and his companions met with 'the chief man of the island, whose name was Publius; who received them, and lodged them three days courteously', during which time Paul healed Publius' sick father. The castaways remained on Melita for three months before continuing their journey to Rome, where Paul was imprisoned and sentenced to death.

According to Maltese tradition, Paul laid the foundations of a Christian community during his brief stay on the island. Publius, who was later canonised, was converted to Christianity and became the bishop of Malta and later of Athens. The site of the shipwreck is traditionally taken to be St Paul's Islands. The house where Publius received the shipwrecked party may have occupied the site of the 17th-century church of San Pawl Milqi (St Paul Welcomed) on the hillside above Burmarrad, 2km south of Buġibba, where excavations have revealed the remains of a large Roman villa and farm. The site can be visited by appointment with Heritage Malta (p45).

on a rubber tube. Note that food can't be brought into the park.

Mediterraneo Marine Park THEME PARK
(☎2137 2218; www.mediterraneopark.com/; adult/child €15.90/9.90; ☺10am-5pm) The marine park is home to a group of dolphins, mostly imported from the Black Sea and Cuba, who go through their routine at 1.30pm and 4.30pm daily, and swimming with dolphins is also on offer (€120 per person for 30 minutes, including park admission; over 8's only; bookings recommended). The dolphins are preceded by a sea-lion show (11.30am and 3.30pm) and a performing parrot show (10.15am and 2.30pm). Other kid-friendly attractions include a seal enclosure, a reptile house and a playground and kiddies' amusement rides.

Qalet Marku Tower FORTRESS
Qalet Marku Tower, on Qrejten Point, west of Baħar iċ-Ċagħaq Bay, was built in a frenzy of fortified development ordered by Grand Master de Redin, which saw 12 such watchtowers constructed in a year along this coastline.

❶ Getting There & Away

To get to Baħar iċ-Ċagħaq, take bus 12 from Valletta (45 minutes, every 12-20 minutes), which travels via Sliema (20 minutes) and St Julian's (25 minutes).

Central Malta

Includes »

Best Places to Eat

» De Mondion (p90)
» Bobbyland Restaurant (p94)
» The Cliffs (p94)
» Café Luna (p95)

Best Places to Stay

» Xara Palace (p135)
» Point de Vue Guesthouse & Restaurants (p135)

Why Go?

This is one of Malta's most fascinating regions. You can explore Mdina, Malta's ancient walled capital, visit remarkable medieval frescoes in ancient underground catacombs, marvel at one of Europe's largest church domes, then spend the night worshipping the dance gods at Gianpula, a huge open-air nightclub. Natural attractions include stark cliffs (the perfect place to watch a sunset), a scenic bay ideal for swimming (if only you can find it) and the only decent patch of greenery on this rather barren island. There are sleeping and eating options ranging from luxurious five-star hotels to rustic village restaurants where locals come for their weekend feasts of rabbit.

If you're after traditional Maltese traditional culture and a tranquil holiday that's a little off the well-worn path, this is the perfect base.

When to Go

Spring (April to June), and Autumn (September and October) are the best times to visit this region. If you're coming in early spring, you can see the pageantry of Holy Week and catch the Mdina Medieval Festival in mid-April.

Rabat & Mdina

MDINA

POP 241

The golden-stone walled city of Mdina is historic Malta at its most fairytale-like. Its hidden lanes offer exquisite architectural detail and respite from the day-tripping crowds, who largely stick to the main street.

The citadel of Mdina was fortified from as long ago as 1000 BC when the Phoenicians built a protective wall here and called their settlement Malet, meaning 'place of shelter'. The Romans built a large town here and called it Melita. It was given its present name when the Arabs arrived in the 9th century – *medina* is Arabic for 'walled city'. They built strong walls and dug a deep moat between Mdina and its surrounding suburbs (*rabat* in Arabic).

In medieval times Mdina was called Città Notabile – the Noble City. It was the favoured residence of the Maltese aristocracy and the seat of the *universitá* (governing council). The Knights of St John, who were largely a sea-based force, made Grand Harbour and Valletta their centre of activity, and Mdina sank into the background as a holiday destination for the nobility. Today, with its massive walls and peaceful, shady streets, it is often referred to as the Silent City, a nickname that's particularly appropriate after dark.

You can hire a DiscoverMdina (www.mdinatoursmalta.com) audioguide to explore the city. The guides are available in six languages and narrated by the fictional Baron Phillippe Caxaro d'Antonio Murina della Verga; they're available from Vilhena Palace just behind Mdina's main gate.

◉ Sights

TOP CHOICE **St Paul's Cathedral** CHURCH
(Pjazza San Pawl; adult/child €5/free incl Cathedral Museum; ⊙9.30-4.45pm Mon-Sat, 3-4.45pm Sun) The cathedral is said to be built on the site of the villa belonging to Publius, the Roman governor of Malta who welcomed St Paul in AD 60.

The original Norman church was destroyed by an earthquake, and the restrained baroque edifice you see today was built between 1697 and 1702 by Lorenzo Gafa, who was influenced by the Italian master Borromini. Note the fire and serpent motifs atop the twin bell-towers, symbolising the saint's first miracle in Malta.

Echoing St John's Co-Cathedral in Valletta, the floor of St Paul's is covered in polychrome marble tombstones of Maltese nobles and important clergymen, while the vault is painted with scenes from the life of St Paul. The altar painting *The Conversion of St Paul* by Mattia Preti survived the earthquake; so too did the beautifully carved oak doors to the sacristy on the north side, and the apse above the altar, featuring with the fresco *St Paul's Shipwreck*.

There are free guided tours on Wednesday and Friday (English at noon, German at 10.30am).

Palazzo Falson HISTORIC BUILDING
(☏2145 4512; www.palazzofalson.com; Triq Villegaignon; adult/child €10/free; ⊙10am-5pm Tue-Sun, last admission 4pm) If you see only one museum in Mdina, make it the magnificent Palazzo Falson, a beautifully preserved medieval mansion. Formerly the home of artist and philanthropist Olof Gollcher (1889–1962), the

CENTRAL MALTA RABAT & MDINA

THE MDINA UPRISING

After the French invasion of Malta in June 1798, Napoleon stayed on the island for only six days before continuing his journey to Egypt, where his fleet was defeated by the British Navy at Aboukir. He left behind a garrison of only 4000 troops.

The French retreated to the safety of Valletta, where the Maltese, under the command of Canon Caruana of St Paul's Cathedral, besieged them. Having learned of Napoleon's misfortune in Egypt, the Maltese asked for help from the British, who imposed a naval blockade on Malta. The Maltese forces suffered two hard years of skirmishing and stand-off until the French finally capitulated on 5 September 1800.

With revolutionary fervour, the French tried to impose their ideas on Maltese society. They abolished the nobility, defaced their escutcheons, persecuted the clergy and looted the churches. But on 2 September 1798, when they attempted – on a Sunday – to auction off the treasures of Mdina's Carmelite Church, the Maltese decided that enough was enough. In a spontaneous uprising, they massacred the French garrison at Mdina, throwing its commander, Capitaine Masson, off a balcony to his death.

Central Malta Highlights

1 Enjoying the haunting silence of beautiful **Mdina** (p85) after dark

2 Going underground to admire the frescoes of **St Agatha's Catacombs** (p91) in Rabat

3 Lunching among the locals at **Bobbyland Restaurant** (p94), followed by a stroll along the top of the **Dingli Cliffs** (p94)

4 Finding your way to and chilling out at the remote bay of **Fomm ir-Riħ** (p92)

5 Questioning divine intervention while marvelling at the unexploded bomb in the **Mosta Dome** (p95)

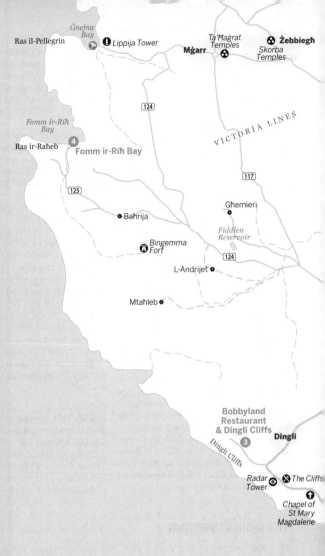

Ras il-Pellegrin

Għejna Bay

1 Lippija Tower

Ta'Ħaġrat Temples

Mġarr

Żebbieġ

Skorba Temples

Fomm ir-Riħ Bay

Ras ir-Raħeb

4 Fomm ir-Riħ Bay

VICTORIA LINES

124

117

125

• Baħrija

Għemieri

Fiddien Reservoir

Bingemma Fort

124

L-Andrijet •

Mtaħleb •

Bobbyland Restaurant & Dingli Cliffs

3

Dingli

Dingli Cliffs

Radar Tower

The Cliffs

Chapel of St Mary Magdalene

MEDITERRANEAN SEA

0   2 km
0   1 mile

Rabat & Mdina

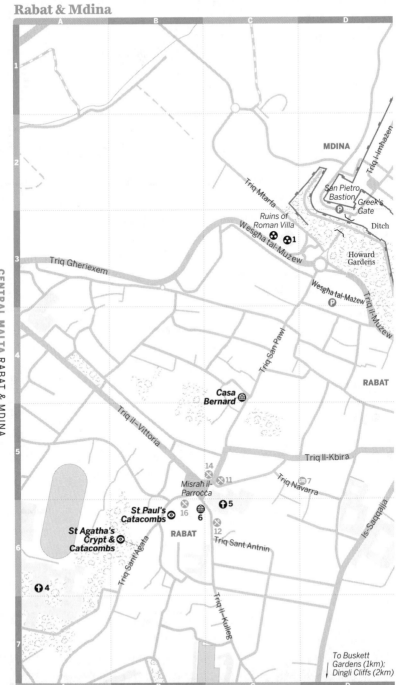

MDINA

Triq l-Imħażen

Triq Mtarfa

San Pietro Bastion

Greek's Gate

Ruins of Roman Villa

Wesgħa tal-Mużew

Ditch

Howard Gardens

Triq Gheriexem

Wesgħa tal-Mażew

Triq il-Mużew

Triq San Pawl

RABAT

Casa Bernard

Triq il-Vittoria

Triq il-Kbira

Triq Navarra

14

Misraħ il-Parrocca

11

7

St Paul's Catacombs

16

6

5

St Agatha's Crypt & Catacombs

12

RABAT

Triq Sant Antnin

Triq Sant Agata

4

Is-Saqqajja

Triq il-Kulleg

To Buskett
Gardens (1km);
Dingli Cliffs (2km)

palace offers a rare glimpse into the sumptuous private world behind Mdina's anonymous aristocratic walls. A self-guided audio tour leads you from the beautiful stone courtyard through Gollcher's kitchen, studio, 4500-volume library, bedroom and chapel – all decorated with his impressive collections of art, documents, silver, weapons and rare rugs from Azerbaijan and Kazakhstan.

Cathedral Museum   MUSEUM
(☎2145 4697; Pjazza San Pawl; adult/child €5/free incl St Paul's Cathedral; ⊘9.30am-4.30pm Mon-Fri, to 3.30pm Sat) The Cathedral Museum's outstanding highlight is a series of woodcut and copperplate prints and lithographs by the German Renaissance artist Albrecht Dürer. However, there are other items of interest, including Egyptian amulets dating from the 5th century BC, and a remarkable coin collection, which includes Carthaginian and Romana-Maltese examples. The museum is housed in a baroque 18th-century palace originally used as a seminary.

Carmelite Priory   CHURCH
(☎2702 0404; www.carmeleiteprioymuseum.com; Triq Villegaignon; €4/free adult/child, with audioguide €5/free; ⊘10am-5pm Apr-Sep, 10am-4pm Tue-Sun Oct-Mar) One of Mdina's most beguiling sights, this baroque building allows a glimpse into the lives of cloistered Carmelite friars. It's the only priory in Malta open to the public, and is still functioning; the Carmelite friars live upstairs. The highlight is the dramatic refectory, where, until the 1960s, monks used to eat in silence as scriptures were read to them from the pulpit. There are free concerts on Saturdays from noon, and there's a frescoed cafe (accessible even if you don't visit the priory). It's not worth getting the audioguide, as the same text is given in each room.

National Museum of
Natural History   MUSEUM
(☎2145 5951; Pjazza San Publiju; adult/child €5/2.50; ⊘9am-5pm) Housed in the elegant Palazzo de Vilhena is an interesting – if old-school fusty – array of displays. Of particular note is the geology section, which explains the origins of Malta's landscape and displays the wide range of local fossils. The tooth belonging to the ancient shark *Carcharodon megalodon* is food for thought – measuring 18cm on the edge, it belonged to a 25m monster that prowled the Miocene seas 30 million years ago. The skeletal anatomy room is also interesting, including the delicate filigree bones

CENTRAL MALTA RABAT & MDINA

Rabat & Mdina

of a snake. Incongruously tucked away on the first floor is a 4000-year-old mummified crocodile from Egypt.

Mdina Experience AUDIOVISUAL ATTRACTION
(☑2145 4322; www.themdinaexperience.com; Misraħ Mesquita; adult/child €6/3; ⊙10am-4.30pm daily) This film about Mdina's history of siege and embattlement brings the town's past vividly to life. The show begins roughly every half-hour.

✗ Eating

TOP CHOICE De Mondion MEDITERRANEAN €€€
(☑2145 0560; www.xarapalace.com.mt; Xara Palace, Misraħ il-Kunsill; mains €32-39; ⊙dinner Mon-Sat) This sumptuous gourmet restaurant, voted Malta's finest by respected guide Restaurantsmalta.com, is set on the 17th-century rooftop of one of the island's loveliest hotels. The menu is seasonal, but expect esoteric delights like foie gras and truffles.

Fontanella Tea Gardens CAFE €
(☑2145 4264; Triq is-Sur; mains €2-15; ⊙10am-6pm Mon-Fri, 10am-10pm winter, to 11pm summer) Fontanella – a Maltese institution – has a wonderful setting atop the city walls, with sweeping views. It serves delicious home-baked cakes, sandwiches, pizzas and light meals, including particularly tasty *ftira* (traditional Maltese bread sandwiches).

Medina MEDITERRANEAN €€€
(☑2145 4004; 7 Triq is-Salib Imqaddes; mains €19-26; ⊙dinner Mon-Sat) Medina is a pretty-as-a-

picture romantic venue – a medieval townhouse with vaulted ceilings and fireplaces, and a leafy garden-courtyard for alfresco dining. The menu offers a mix of Maltese, Italian and French dishes, with good vegetarian selections.

Ciapetti MEDITERRANEAN €€
(☑2145 9987; 5 Wesgħa Ta'Sant'Agata; mains €14-22; ⊙closed dinner Sun) Ciapetti attracts a mix of locals and tourists with its Mediterranean menu that ranges from traditional rabbit stew to pan-fried calamari with marjoram and lemon thyme (from the restaurant's own herb garden). You can eat in the art-filled dining room, the small vine-draped courtyards or out on the terrace atop the city walls.

Point de Vue Guesthouse & Restaurants MEDITERRANEAN, AFRICAN €€
(☑2145 4117; www.pointdevuemalta.com; 5 Is-Saqqajja; mains €7-26; ⊙lunch & dinner; 🐾) Point de Vue, just outside Mdina's city walls, overlooks Mdina's car park from its simple Java Lounge & Terrace, which is popular with locals for its tasty pizzas and traditional dishes. At the rear, the more formal Butcher's Grill prepares a steak-heavy mix of African and continental dishes, and has a rather better 'point of view' across the local countryside.

RABAT
POP 11,410

Rabat, sprawled to the south of Mdina, is an attractive town in its own right, with narrow streets and wooden balconies. It's full of interesting sights, and has a splendidly traditional feel, particularly in the evening, when the day trippers have ebbed away.

◉ Sights

St Agatha's Crypt
& Catacombs
CATACOMBS

(📞2145 4503; Triq Sant'Agata; adult/child €5/2; ☺10am-6pm Mon-Fri, to 2pm Sat Apr-Oct, 9am-4.30pm Mon-Fri, to 12.30pm Sat Nov-Mar) These catacombs contain a series of remarkable frescoes dating from the 12th to the 15th centuries AD. According to legend, this was the hiding place of St Agatha when she fled Sicily. Back at ground level is a quirky little museum containing everything from fossils and minerals to coins, church vestments and Etruscan, Roman and Egyptian artefacts. Regular tours are available of the crypt and catacombs.

St Paul's Catacombs
CATACOMBS

(📞2145 4562; Triq Sant'Agata; adult/child €5/2.50; ☺9am-5pm) St Paul's Catacombs (so-named for their proximity to the church) date from the 3rd century AD and were used for burial for around 500 years. Worship took place here in the Middle Ages, but later the complex was used as an agricultural store. It's an atmospheric labyrinth of rock-cut tombs, narrow stairs and passages. On either side of the entry stairs you'll find *loculi*, small niches used for the burial of children, indicating the high infant mortality rate. Admission includes a self-guided, 45-minute audio tour available in various languages, and at 11.30am daily there's a free tour in English.

FREE Casa Bernard
HISTORIC BUILDING

(📞2145 1888; 46 Triq San Pawl; admission €8; ☺10am-4pm Mon-Sat) You'll be personally guided through this privately owned 16th-century palace by one of the home's charming owners, who will explain the history of the mansion and the impressive personal collection of art, objets d'art, furniture, silver and china. Tours take around 50 minutes, and take place on the hour, with the last at 4pm.

Domus Romana
ARCHAEOLOGICAL SITE

(📞2145 4125; Wesgħa tal-Mużew; adult/child €6/3; ☺9am-5pm) The Roman House was built in the 1920s to incorporate the excavated remains of a large 1st century BC townhouse. There's a small but fascinating museum, which includes Roman glass perfume bottles and bone hairpins, as well

as a display on the 11th-century Islamic cemetery that overlaid the villa. There are also some beautiful mosaics. At the centre of the original peristyle court, there is a depiction of the *Drinking Doves of Sosos*, a fashionable Roman motif.

FREE St Paul's Church
& the Grotto of St Paul
CHURCH

(Misraħ il-Parroċċa; admission free, donations welcome; ☺9.30am-5pm Mon-Sat) St Paul's Church was built in 1675. Beside it, stairs lead down into the mystical Grotto of St Paul, a cave where the saint is said to have preached during his stay in Malta. The statue of St Paul was gifted by the Knights in 1748, while the silver ship to its left was added in 1960 to commemorate the 1900th anniversary of the saint's shipwreck. Come in the early morning or late afternoon to avoid the tour groups that congest the narrow space.

Wignacourt Museum
MUSEUM

(📞2145 1060; Triq il-Kulleġ) This is a gloriously hotchpotch collection that encompasses 4th-century Christian catacombs, a WWII air-raid shelter, a baroque chapel, religious icons and vestments, and changing art exhibitions. Undergoing refurbishment at the time of research, it should be open by the time you read this.

✖ Eating

There are some authentic hole-in-the-wall cafe-bars at the top of Triq San Pawl, where you can pick up a fresh-from-the-oven *pastizza* (ricotta- or pea-filled flaky pastry).

THE TRAGEDY OF ST AGATHA

St Agatha was a 3rd-century Christian martyr from Sicily – Catania and Palermo both claim to be her birthplace – who fled to Malta to escape the amorous advances of a Sicilian governor. On returning to Sicily she was imprisoned and tortured, and her breasts were cut off with shears – a horrific punishment gruesomely depicted in many paintings and statues in Malta. She was then burnt at the stake. In Rabat there's a church, **St Agatha's Chapel**, dedicated to her, near the catacombs (p91) that are said to have been her hiding place in Malta.

Cosmana Navarra
ITALIAN €€

(📞2145 0638; Triq San Pawl; mains €7-20; ☺lunch & dinner) Cosmana Navarra was the Maltese aristocrat who paid for St Paul's Church – and this restaurant is housed in her former home. It's a lovely old building that preserves many original features, and has been brightened with colourful tiles and modern lamps. It's a good family choice, predominantly serving pizza and pasta. The pick of the desserts is the *imqarets* (fried date pastries) with icecream.

Grotto Tavern
MEDITERRANEAN €€

(📞2145 5138; Misrah il Parroċċa; mains €5-26; ☺lunch daily, dinner Thu-Sat) Grotto Tavern, run by a French-Maltese couple, offers French-influenced wining and dining in a cavern on Rabat's main square. The menu encompasses Maltese and French dishes, for example the *lapin a la Maltaise* (Maltese-style rabbit) and *canard au cognac et fruits rouges* (duck with cognac and red fruits), plus pasta and pizza. Save room for desserts like *tarte aux pommes* (apple tart).

Parruċċan Confectionery
SWEETS €

(Misrah il-Parroċċa; sweets from €1; ☺9.30am-5pm) Here you can pick up samples of Maltese specialities like nougat, delicious nut brittle and fig rolls.

Falzon Bakery
BAKERY €

(Triq il-Kulleg; bread from around €0.60; ☺24 hours) This timeless hole-in-the-wall bakery operates around the clock, but always has a queue. The punters keep coming for fresh crusty bread and brightly iced buns.

ℹ Information

Just inside Mdina's main gate is a helpful **Tourist Information Centre** (📞2145 4480; Torre dello Standardo; ☺9am-5.30pm Mon-Sat 9am-1pm Sun, 10am-4pm Oct-Mar).

You'll find banks and ATMs in Rabat opposite the bus stop, and an ATM on Pjazza tas-Sur. There are public toilets outside the Main Gate. Point de Vue (p90) has internet access and wi-fi.

A ride in a *karrozin* (traditional horse-drawn carriage), departing from Mdina's main gate, costs €35 for 35 minutes; you'll soak up far more atmosphere on foot.

ℹ Getting There & Away

The local bus terminus is in Rabat is on Is-Saqqajja, 200m south of Mdina's Main Gate.

From Valletta, take buses 50, 51, 52 or 53 (30 minutes, every 10 minutes). Bus 52 goes on to Dingli. Buses 202 and 203 travel to/from Sliema (50 minutes, half-hourly) and St Julian's

(one hour), with the 202 also going on to Dingli. The X3 express bus travels between here and Buġibba (25 minutes, half-hourly) as well as the airport (55 minutes).

Around Rabat & Mdina

Ta'Qali Crafts Village
CRAFT VILLAGE

(☺7.15am-4.15pm Mon-Fri, 9am-1pm Sat) The scruffy arts-and-crafts workshops at Ta'Qali are housed in the old Nissen huts on this WWII RAF airfield. It looks more shanty town than a village. However, the workshops here are well worth a look. You can watch glass-blowers at work, and shop for gold, silver and filigree jewellery, paintings by local artists, leather goods, Maltese lace, furniture, ceramics and ornamental glass.

Bus 205 connects Ta'Qali with Naxxar (15 minutes), Mosta (10 minutes) and Rabat (5 minutes). It's about 2km from the bus terminus in Rabat to the village.

Malta Aviation Museum
MUSEUM

(📞2141 6095; www.maltaaviationmuseum.com; adult/child €6/2; ☺9am-5pm) This is a real enthusiast's museum, with bits of engines, airframes and instruments lying around, and numerous restoration projects underway – including a De Havilland Tiger Moth. You can watch locals working on the aircraft and other exhibits. Stars of the show here are a WWII Spitfire MkIX and a Hawker Hurricane IIa, salvaged in 1995 after 54 years at the bottom of the sea off Malta's southwest coast; other aircraft on display include a vintage Flying Flea, a De Havilland Vampire T11, a Fiat G91R and a battered old Douglas Dakota DC-3. To visit, catch bus 205 (from Mosta, Naxxar or Rabat) or circular bus 106, which calls at Attard; there's also a CitySightseeing Malta (p176) open-top bus tour stop (north route) outside the museum.

Fomm ir-Riħ & Around

Fomm ir-Riħ (meaning 'mouth of the wind') is Malta's most remote and difficult-to-reach bay. During rough weather, the grey clay slopes and limestone crags merging with the grey clouds and the wave-muddied waters. But on a calm summer's day it's a beautiful spot, with good swimming and snorkelling in the clear blue waters off the southern cliffs, and few other people to disturb the peace.

Fomm ir-Riḣ Bay

`124` Żebbiegħ

`17`

Mosta

`11` **END**

`125`

`117`

`16`

National Stadium

Birkirkara

Bahrija

`124`

Ghemieri

Ghain Qajjied

Attard

`7`

HAMRUN

L-Andrijet

`10`

Mdina `7`

`21`

QORMI

Mtahleb

`9` **Rabat**

Hal Bajjada

`133`

Żebbuġ

`16`

Dingli

`8`

`5`

`7`

`4`

`3`

`117`

Siġġiewi

Tás Salvatur

`6`

MEDITERRANEAN

SEA

Ta'Żuta (253m)

Tal Bajjada

Tal Providenza

Mqabba

N

Ghar Lapsi

`2` **START**

Qrendi

Ḣaġar Qim `1`

Żurrieq

Driving Tour
Temples, Seacliffs & Gardens

❯ In this remarkably small area you can experience some of Malta's finest prehistoric temples, some breathtaking stretches of coast, grand palaces and mysterious cart ruts, on this trip around the island's most traditional region.

Start your tour at the megalithic temples of ① **Ḣaġar Qim & Mnajdra**. From here, drive towards ② **Ghar Lapsi**, a particularly beautiful stretch of coastline. From Ghar Lapsi, take the road inland through the Girgenti valley, then veer towards the coast again, along the southern end edge of Dingli Cliffs. After about a kilometre, turn inland to visit the ③ **Cart Ruts** – mysterious prehistoric tracks scored into the rock – at Clapham Junction.

From here it's a short drive to ④ **Buskett Gardens** (from the Italian *boschetto*, meaning 'little wood'), the only extensive woodland area in Malta. The gardens were planted by the Knights as a hunting ground; today they are a hugely popular outing for the Maltese, and the groves of Aleppo pine, oak, olive and orange trees provide shady picnic sites in summer and orange-scented walks in winter.

Close by is ⑤ **Verdala Palace**, which was built in 1586 as a summer residence for Grand Master Hugues Loubeux de Verdalle. It was designed by Gerolamo Cassar in the form of a square castle with towers at each corner, but only for show. The British used Verdala Palace as the Governor of Malta's summer residence and today it's the summer residence of the Maltese president.

Next, double back to the cliffs to rejoin the panoramic road, passing the ⑥ **Chapel of Mary Magdalene** on the way. You'll see the outlandish ⑦ **Radar Tower** perched on the edge of the cliffs. From here you can drive onwards, stopping at ⑧ **Bobbyland Restaurant** for a drink or some lunch.

After lunch, drive inland to ⑨ **Rabat**, from where you can take Triq Ghajn Qajjet eastwards towards the village of ⑩ **Baħrija**, which has several good local restaurants. Where the village's road splits, take the right-hand fork and follow the road towards the coast. When the road forks, turn right; this will lead you down to a viewpoint over the bay of ⑪ **Fomm ir-Riħ**.

Locals will marvel at any nonlocals who manage to find it! You'll need your own transport. Head to Baħrija, and after passing through the village, take the right fork next to the children's playground.

About 1.2km from Baħrija's town square the road drops down to the left into a valley; drive down the road until you reach a junction with 'RTO' (reservato) painted on the wall. Turn right and follow this road down to a small parking area.

To reach the head of the bay, you need to follow a precarious footpath across a stream bed and along a ledge in the cliffs. Locals say that former Maltese Prime Minister Dom Mintoff used to ride his horse along this path – today posts have been cemented in place to prevent horses and bicycles using it.

From here, you can hike north to the wild cape of Ras il-Pellegrin and down to Ġnejna Bay, or west to Ras ir-Raħeb and south along the top of the coastal cliffs to the tiny village of Mtaħleb and back into Rabat. Be aware that this area is a favourite haunt of birdhunters – you'll spy their stone shacks all over the countryside.

BAĦRIJA

The village of Baħrija is perfect if you're looking for somewhere off the trail in which to participate in the true Maltese Sunday lunch ritual, dining with the locals on authentic dishes (including horse meat and rabbit). There are a handful of unassuming options on the village square, including Ta'Gaġin (2145 0825; Misrah Patri Martin Caruana) and North Country Bar & Restaurant (2145 6688; Triq Is-Sajf Ta' San Martin).

Dingli Cliffs

Dingli, named after the famous Maltese architect Tommaso Dingli (1591–1666) – or possibly his 16th-century English namesake Sir Thomas Dingley, who lived nearby – is an unremarkable little village. But less than a kilometre to the southwest the land falls away at the spectacular 220m-high Dingli Cliffs. A potholed tarmac road runs along the top of the cliffs, and it's well worth heading here for some great walks south, past the incongruous radar tower to the lonely little Chapel of St Mary Magdalene, built in the 17th century, and onwards to Ta'Żuta (253m), the highest point on the Maltese Islands. Here you'll enjoy excellent views along the coast to the tiny island of Filfla.

FOMM IR-RIĦ BY BOAT

If you don't have a car, or the directions to Fomm ir-Riħ sound far too complicated, you can view the bay from the water, on a boat trip out of Golden Bay with Charlie's Discovery Speedboat Trips (p72)

✕ Eating

Bobbyland Restaurant MALTESE €€
(2145 2895; mains €9-18; ⊘lunch Tue-Sun Oct-May, lunch Tue-Sun, dinner Tue-Sat Jun-Sep) At the northwest end of the Dingli Cliffs you'll find Bobbyland Restaurant, where you can chow down with the locals before walking off your meal with a postprandial cliff-top stroll. This friendly, rustic former Nissen hut is 500m from the Dingli junction; on Sundays in particular the indoor and outdoor tables are crowded with diners munching contentedly on house specialities like spaghetti with rabbit sauce. They also serve pizza.

The Cliffs MALTESE €€
(7927 3747; www.thecliffs.com.mt; ⊘10.30am-6.30pm Wed-Mon) This new venture, close to Dingli's radar tower, is run by two local brothers. It combines interpretation centre (there are boards up about the area and books on wildlife and walking for sale) with an attractive contemporary brasserie-style restaurant specialising in local food, for example using wild asparagus and wild garlic, local cheeses and honey, and Maltese wines. They also sell quince, chutney and jam.

ⓘ Getting There & Away

Bus 52 runs from Valletta (45 minutes; at least hourly). Bus 201 connects Dingli with Rabat (15 minutes; hourly), and, in the other direction, runs along the coast to Ħaġar Qim (20 minutes), the Blue Grotto and the Airport (45 minutes). Bus 202 runs between Dingli, Rabat, Mosta (35 minutes; hourly), Sliema (1 hour 10 minutes) and St Julian's.

CLAPHAM JUNCTION

Continue past the entrance to Buskett Gardens and follow the signs to reach a rough track signposted 'Cart Tracks'. To the right (west) of this track is a large area of sloping limestone pavement, scored with several sets of intersecting prehistoric 'cart ruts'. The ruts are about 1.5m apart and up to 50cm deep. The name Clapham Junction – a notoriously complicated railway junction in London – was given to the site by British visitors.

Mosta

POP 19.115

Mosta is a busy and prosperous town spread across a level plateau, famous for its splendid church. It's an ideal starting point for exploring the Victoria Lines.

◉ Sights

FREE Mosta Dome   CHURCH
(☑2143 3826; Pjazza Rotunda; admission free, donations welcome; ☺9.15-11.30am & 3-5pm) The Parish Church of Santa Maria, better known as the Rotunda or Mosta Dome, was designed by the Maltese architect Giorgio Grognet de Vassé and built between 1833 and 1860 using funds raised by the local people. It has a stunning blue, gold and white interior, where you can also see the bomb that fell through it in 1942. Be sure to dress appropriately for a place of worship.

The church's circular design with a six-columned portico was closely based on the Pantheon in Rome, and the great dome – a prominent landmark (its external height is 61m) is visible from most parts of Malta. With a diameter of 39.6m, it's one of the world's largest domes, though dome comparison is a tricky business: the parishioners of Xewkija on Gozo claim that their church has a bigger dome than Mosta's – although the Gozitan Rotunda has a smaller diameter (25m), it is higher and has a larger volumetric capacity. So there!

✗ Eating

Ta'Marija Restaurant   MALTESE €€
(☑2143 4444; www.tamarija.com; Triq il-Kostituzzjoni; mains €8.50-30; ☺dinner daily, lunch Tue-Sun) Ta'Marija Restaurant is a worthwhile option if you're keen on traditional Maltese cuisine and don't mind a bit of (dare we say?) cheesy entertainment with your meal. The food is highly rated by locals, and there is folkloric entertainment on Wednesday and Friday, traditional Maltese folk music on Saturday, and a Maltese buffet on Sunday.

Pjazza Café   CAFE €
(☑2141 3379; Pjazza Rotunda, 1st level; mains €6-17; ☺breakfast, lunch & dinner) At the elevated Pjazza Café you can enjoy good views of the dome from a table by the window, while downing a light lunch or snack, pizza or pasta.

ⓘ Getting There & Away

Numerous buses pass through Mosta. From Valletta take buses 41, 42 or 44 (30 minutes). Bus 41 goes on to St Paul's Bay (25 minutes), Mellieha (40 minutes and then Cirkewwa (for Gozo; 55 minutes). Bus 31 connects with Buġibba, and buses 21 and 23 with Sliema. Buses stop by the Rotonda.

Naxxar

POP 12,350

Naxxar, a couple of kilometres northeast of Mosta (and more or less joined by the urban sprawl), is another bustling town with an important few historic sights.

◉ Sights

Palazzo Parisio   HISTORIC BUILDING
(☑2141 2461; www.palazzoparisio.com; Pjazza Vittorja; adult/child €12/7 incl audioguide; ☺9am-6pm daily) The glorious Palazzo Parisio was originally built in 1733 by Grand Master Antonio Manoel de Vilhena, and later acquired and refurbished by a Maltese noble family in the late 19th century. The magnificent interior and baroque gardens have been described as a 'miniature Versailles'.

Parish Church of Our Lady   CHURCH
The Parish Church of Our Lady is one of the tallest baroque edifices on Malta. Construction was started in the early years of the 16th century according to the designs of Vittorio Cassar (son of the more famous Gerolamo Cassar, who designed Verdala Palace).

✗ Eating

Café Luna   CAFE €€
(☑2141 2461; Pjazza Vittorja; mains €12-29; ☺9am-6pm, afternoon tea 3-5.45pm) In the gardens of Palazzo Parisio you'll find the excellent Café Luna, patrolled by gracious, white-clad

---

THE MIRACLE OF MOSTA

On 9 June 1942, during WWII, while around 300 parishioners waited to hear Mass, three enemy bombs struck the Mosta Dome. Two bounced off and landed in the square without exploding. The third pierced the dome, smashed off a wall and rolled across the floor of the church. Miraculously, no one was hurt and the bomb failed to detonate. A replica of the bomb can be seen in the church sacristy, to the left of the altar.

staff serving superb coffee, luscious cakes, and a menu of tempting lunch specials and elegant afternoon teas. There's also a children's menu.

⚠ Getting There & Away

To get to Naxxar, take bus 55 or 56 from Valletta, or bus 65 from Sliema.

The Three Villages

The main road from Valletta to Mosta passes through the town of Birkirkara (population 22,000), one of the biggest population centres on the island and part of the huge conurbation that encircles Valletta and the Three Cities. Birkirkara's Church of St Helen is probably the most ornate of Malta's churches, a late flowering of baroque exuberance built in the mid-18th century. On the strength of his performance here, the designer, Domenico Cachia, was given the job of remodelling the facade of the Auberge de Castile in Valletta.

Just west of Birkirkara is an upmarket suburban area known as the Three Villages, centred on the medieval settlements of Attard, Balzan and Lija. Although modern development has fused the three into a continuous urban sprawl, the old village centres still retain their parish churches and narrow streets, and there are some interesting historical sites here.

Triq il-Mdina, the main road that skirts the southern edge of Attard, follows the line of the Wignacourt Aqueduct, built between 1610 and 1614 to improve the water supply to Valletta. Substantial lengths of the ancient structure still stand beside the road.

◎ Sights

San Anton Palace & Gardens   GARDENS
(☉dawn-dusk) The main attraction in the Three Villages area is the San Anton Palace & Gardens, in Attard. The palace (closed to the public) was built in the early 17th century as the country mansion of Grand Master Antoine de Paule. It later served as the official residence of the British Governor of Malta, and is now the official residence of the Maltese president. The lovely walled gardens stretch between the palace and the main entrance on Triq Birkirkara; they contain groves of citrus and avocado, as well as a bird aviary. The Eagle Fountain, just inside the main gate, dates from the 1620s.

Church of St Mary   CHURCH
(Pjazza Tommaso Dingli) The Church of St Mary in Attard, designed by Tommaso Dingli and

THE RIDDLE OF THE RUTS

One of the biggest mysteries of Malta's prehistoric period is the abundance of so-called 'cart ruts' throughout the islands. In places where bare limestone is exposed, it is often scored with a series of deep parallel grooves, looking for all the world like ruts worn by cartwheels. But the spacing of the ruts varies, and their depth – up to 60cm – means that wheeled carts would probably get jammed if they tried to use them.

A more likely explanation is that the grooves were created by a travois – a sort of sled formed from two parallel poles joined by a frame and dragged behind a beast of burden, similar to that used by the Plains Indians of North America. The occurrence of the ruts correlates quite closely to the distribution of Bronze Age villages in Malta.

This still leaves the question of what was being transported. Suggestions have included salt and building stone, but it has been argued that whatever the cargo was, it must have been abundant, heavy and well worth the effort involved in moving it. The best suggestion to date is that the mystery substance was topsoil – it was carted from low-lying areas to hillside terraces to increase the area of cultivable land, and so provide food for a growing population.

In some places the ruts are seen to disappear into the sea on one side of a bay, only to re-emerge on the far side. In other spots they seem to disappear off the edge of a cliff. These instances have given rise to all sorts of weird theories, but they are most convincingly explained as the results of long-term erosion and sea-level changes due to earthquakes – the central Mediterranean is a seismically active area and Malta is riddled with geological faults.

Good places to see the ruts and come up with your own theories include Clapham Junction near Buskett Gardens and the top of the Ta'Ċenċ cliffs on Gozo.

built between 1610 and 1614, is one of the finest Renaissance churches in Malta.

Church of St Saviour CHURCH
(Misrah it-Trasfigurazzjoni) Lija's Church of St Saviour, designed in 1694, is the focus of the Feast of the Transfiguration of Our Lord, a lively festa (feast day), famed for its spectacular fireworks, held on 6 August.

✖ Eating

A good dining option for the evening is to frock up a little and visit one of the highly regarded restaurants at the gracious Cor-inthia Palace Hotel in Attard – the elegant Corinthia Room (☺dinner nightly) for fine dining; Rickshaw (☺dinner Mon-Sat) offering pan-Asian cuisine; and Pizza, Pasta e Basta (☺dinner nightly May-Oct), a seasonal alfresco pizza and pasta eatery. There's also an all-day cafe in the hotel's lobby.

❶ Getting There & Away

Bus 54 travels betwen Valletta and Attard, via Birkirkara (30 minutes). Birkirkara is also accessible on bus 41 or 43 from Valletta (20 minutes).

Southeast Malta

Includes »

Best Places to Eat

» Tartarun (p99)

» Ir-Rizzu (p99)

» La Campanna (p102)

» La Favorita (p103)

Best Places to Stay

» Duncan Guesthouse (p136)

» Summer Nights Guesthouse (p136)

Why Go?

Several of Malta's most significant historical sites lie in the less-visited southeast of the country, including two impressive temples (Ħaġar Qim and Mnajdra) dating back over 5000 years, and the Għar Dalam cave, full of fossilised remains of prehistoric animals. There's splendid coastal scenery, too, boat trips available to visit grottoes, and enticing swimming spots well off the tourist trail. A highlight is the old fishing village of Marsaxlokk, with a photogenic harbour full of colourful boats and a waterfront lined with restaurants specialising in fresh fish, patronised by discerning locals and camera-toting day-trippers.

It's also the base of much of the country's heavy industry, which means tourism is less developed. Although Maltese will travel to Marsaxlokk and Marsaskala to lunch on fresh fish, and the Marsaxlokk Sunday market is thronged by tourist buses, there aren't many accommodation options, and few holiday-makers choose to base themselves here.

When to Go

It's worth timing your visit to this part of the island to coincide with the summer solstice. You can take part in seasonal guided tours of Ħaġar Qim and Mnajdra. Late spring and early autumn (May, June and September) are ideal months to be in this part of the country, while high summer will see the area at its busiest. Avoid the Blue Grotto and Għar Lapsi on public holidays as they'll be packed.

Marsaxlokk

POP 3300

Despite the encroachment of modern industry, the ancient fishing village of Marsaxlokk (marsa-shlock; from *marsa sirocco,* meaning 'southeasterly harbour') at the head of Marsaxlokk Bay remains resolutely a slice of real Maltese life.

Old low-rise houses ring the waterfront, and a photogenic fleet of brightly coloured *luzzu* (fishing boats) dance in the harbour. Men with weathered faces sit by the waterside mending nets and grumbling about the tax on diesel, while others scrape, paint and saw as they ready their boats for the sea. The town is home to around 70% of the Maltese fishing fleet, and is – not surprisingly – renowned for its top-notch seafood restaurants, making it a magnet for long-lunching locals and busloads of day-trippers.

It makes a relaxed place to base yourself. If you're after nightlife into the wee small hours you'll be disappointed, but if you're looking to chill out (and regularly tuck into all manner of fishy morsels), you'll be happy. Once the lunchtime tourist buses depart, it'll just be you and the locals.

History

Marsaxlokk Bay is Malta's second natural harbour. It was here that the Turkish fleet was moored during the Great Siege of 1565, and Napoleon's army landed here during the French invasion of 1798. In the 1930s the calm waters of the bay were used as a staging post by the huge, four-engined Short C-Class flying boats of Britain's Imperial Airways as they pioneered long-distance air travel to the far-flung corners of the Empire. During WWII Marsaxlokk Bay was the base for the Fleet Air Arm, and in 1989 the famous summit meeting between Soviet and US Presidents Mikhail Gorbachev and George Bush (senior) was held on board a warship anchored in the bay. Today the harbour is framed by the fuel tanks and chimney of a power station and the huge cranes of the Kalafrana Container Terminal – eyesores that are likely to prevent any serious tourist development.

☉ Sights & Activities

Sunday Fish Market   MARKET

At Marsaxlokk's colourful, packed-to-the-gills Sunday Fish Market, you can admire the riches of the Med before they're whisked off to Malta's top hotels and restaurants (rest assured: you'll find the tourist tat here, too). The market starts early in the morning and the best stuff is long gone by afternoon.

Delimara Point
& St Peter's Pool   COASTLINE

Delimara Point, southeast of Marsaxlokk, is blighted by a huge power station whose chimney can be seen for miles around, but there are a few good swimming places on the eastern side of the peninsula, where the power station isn't in view. St Peter's Pool is the best, a natural lido in the rocks with large areas of flat slab for sunbathing between swims. Follow the narrow, potholed road out towards Delimara Lighthouse until you are just past the power station chimney (about 1.5km from the main road), and you'll see a low building on the left with 'Peter's Pool' signposted on it. A rough track leads down to a parking area. Don't leave anything in your car – this is a favourite spot for thieves.

Waterfront Market   MARKET

The daily market mainly sells kitsch aimed at tour groups visiting the town, but it's a scenic place to browse.

✕ Eating

It's all about the seafood in Marsaxlokk. Restaurants ranging from casual to smart line the harbour, most offering alfresco dining. This is a favourite location for the Maltese to enjoy a long Sunday lunch among family and friends – if you wish to join them in this weekly ritual, booking is advised.

TOP CHOICE Tartarun   SEAFOOD €€

(☑2165 8089; www.tartarun.com; Xatt is-Sajjieda; mains €12.50-25; ⊙lunch Tue-Sun, dinner Tue-Sat) This highly rated restaurant is the most up-market dining option on the strip, and offers a more sophisticated take on all things fishy. Dishes such as sea bream, roasted prawn and cherry tomatoes are perfectly executed. There are a few outside tables, though they're somewhat traffic-plagued on Sunday.

Ir-Rizzu   SEAFOOD €€

(☑2165 1569; 52 Xatt is-Sajjieda; mains €7-21; ⊙lunch & dinner) Ir-Rizzu has a large and bustling dining room devoid of airs and graces, and only a couple of outside tables. The fish do the talking here – check out the mind-boggling list of local piscatorial specimens, everything from *lampuka* (dolphin fish) and delicious octopus salad to king prawns or a hearty bowl of *aljotta* (Maltese fish soup). Lots of locals trust Ir-Rizzu for its quality.

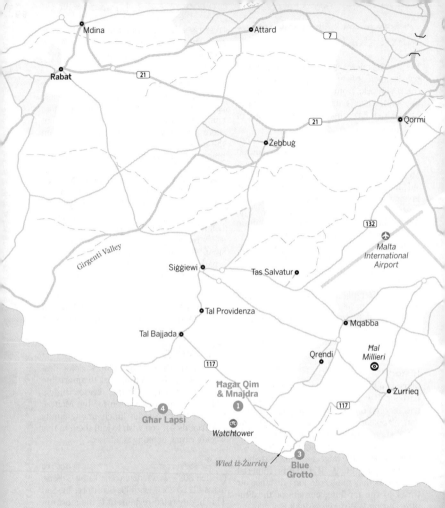

Southeast Malta Highlights

1 Questioning who, when, how and why, and drinking in the scenery at the mysterious **Ħaġar Qim** and **Mnajdra** temples (p105)

2 Devouring local seafood specialities with a view of colourful, bobbing fishing boats in **Marsaxlokk** (p99)

3 Taking a midmorning boat trip to marvel at the **Blue Grotto** (p103)

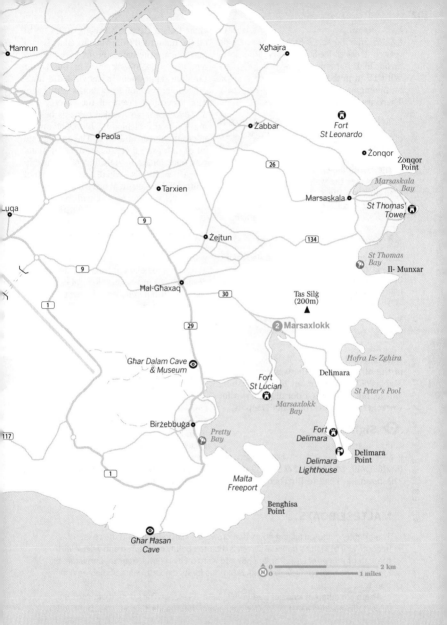

Hamrun

Xgħajra

Paola

Żabbar

Fort
St Leonardo

Żonqor

Żonqor
Point

26

Marsaskala
Bay

Tarxien

Marsaskala

St Thomas'
Tower

Luqa

9

Żejtun

134

St Thomas
Bay

Il- Munxar

9

Ħal-Għaxaq

30

Tas Silġ
(200m)
▲

1

29

② Marsaxlokk

Hofra Iż- Żghira

Għar Dalam Cave
& Museum

Fort
St Lucian

Delimara

St Peter's Pool

Birżebbuġa

Marsaxlokk
Bay

117

Pretty
Bay

Fort
Delimara

Delimara
Point

1

Delimara
Lighthouse

Malta
Freeport

Benghisa
Point

Għar Ħasan
Cave

0 ———————— 2 km
Ⓝ 0 ———————— 1 miles

④ Sunning yourself,
snorkelling and enjoying a
seafood lunch at **Għar Lapsi**
(p106)

La Campanna   SEAFOOD €€
(☎2165 7755; 60 Xatt is-Sajjieda; mains €9-20; ⊘lunch & dinner Tue-Sun) This little local favourite is famous for its delicious fish. With TV in in the corner and great seafood on the menu, it gets packed out with locals. There are only two outside tables.

Ix-Xlukkajr   SEAFOOD €€
(☎2165 2109; 47 Xatt is-Sajjieda; mains €9-29; ⊘lunch & dinner Tue-Sun) Xlukkajr (Malti for 'a person from Marsaxlokk') is a village favourite, with tables spilling onto the little piazza beside the waterfront. It serves fresh seafood from the display outside the door, including locally caught octopus, prawns, mussels, clams and many other shellfish.

⊕ Getting There & Away

Buses 81 and 85 run from Valletta to Marsaxlokk every 20 minutes daily (40 minutes), via Paola. Bus 206 also runs here from Paola (25 minutes, hourly). Several buses, including the hourly 119, serve Marsaskala (20 minutes).

Birżebbuġa

POP 9405

Birżebbuġa (beer-zeb-*boo*-ja, meaning 'well of the olives') lies on the western shore of Marsaxlokk Bay. It began life as a fishing village, but today it's a dormitory town for workers from the nearby Malta Freeport.

◉ Sights

Għar Dalam Cave & Museum   ARCHAEOLOGICAL SITE
(☎2165 7419; adult/child €5/2.50; ⊘9am-5pm) The reason to head to Birżebbuġa is to see

Għar Dalam Cave & Museum, 500m north on the main road from Valletta. Għar Dalam (aar-da-lam; the name means 'cave of darkness') is a 145m-long cave in the Lower Coralline Limestone. It has yielded a magnificent harvest of fossil bones and teeth. The lowermost layers of the cavern, over 500,000 years old, yielded remains belonging to dwarf elephants, hippopotamuses, micro-mammals and birds. The animals are all of European type, suggesting that Malta was once joined to Italy, but not to northern Africa. It's also where the first signs of human habitation on Malta, some 7400 years ago, have been discovered, with remains including pottery dating back to 5200BC and neanderthal teeth found in the top layer.

The museum at the entrance contains an exhibition hall with displays on how the cave was formed and how the remains of such animals came to be found here, plus about their development in response to local conditions, evolving in different ways to such creatures elsewhere. In the older part of the museum are display cases mounted with thousands and thousands of bones and teeth. Beyond the museum a path leads down through gardens to the mouth of the cave, where a walkway leads 50m into the cavern. A pillar of sediment has been left in the middle of the excavated floor to show the stratigraphic sequence.

Għar Ħasan Cave   CAVE
Għar Ħasan Cave lies within the cliff-bound coastline south of Birżebbuġa. From Birżebbuġa follow the road towards Żurrieq, then turn left on the minor road at the top of the hill to reach a cliff-top parking area just before an industrial estate; the cave entrance

---

MALTESE BOATS

The brightly coloured fishing boats that crowd the harbours around the coast have become one of Malta's national symbols. Painted boldly in blue, red and yellow, with the watchful 'Eyes of Osiris' on the bows to ward off evil spirits, they are unmistakably Maltese. The harbour at Marsaxlokk is famous for its colourful vista of moored fishing boats.

There are different kinds of traditional Maltese vessels. The *luzzu* (*loots*-zoo) is a large double-ended fishing boat (for nonsailors, that means it's pointed at both ends). The *kajjik* (*ka*-yik) is similar in appearance, but has a square transom (it's pointed at the front end only). The *dgħajsa* (*dye*-sa) is a smaller and racier-looking boat, with a very high stem and stern-posts – a bit like a Maltese gondola. These are not solid, seaworthy fishing boats, but sleek water taxis. A small flotilla of *dgħajsas* is now carrying tourists back and forth between Valletta and the Three Cities. They were once all powered by oars, but today's *dgħajsas* generally carry an outboard engine. Local enthusiasts maintain – and race – a small fleet of oar-driven vessels. The waterfront at Vittoriosa and Senglea is the best place to admire these classic boats.

is down some steps in the cliff-face to the left. (At the time of research, the access to the cave was fenced off for safety reasons – check with the tourist office in Valletta to see if it has reopened.) The 'Cave of Ħasan' is supposed to have been used as a hide-out by a 12th-century Saracen rebel. With a torch you can follow a passage off to the right to a 'window' in the cliff-face.

ⓘ Getting There & Away

To get to Għar Dalam and Birżebbuġa, take bus 85 from Valletta (35 minutes, every 20 minutes), which runs via Paola.The cave museum is on the right-hand side of the road at a small, semicircular parking area 500m short of Birżebbuġa – look out for it, as it's not well signposted. There is no public transport to Għar Ħasan – it's a 2.5km walk south of Birżebbuġa.

Marsaskala

POP 9850

Marsaskala (also spelt Marsascala), gathered around the head of a long, narrow bay, was originally a Sicilian fishing community: the name means 'Sicilian Harbour'. Today it is an increasingly popular residential area and seaside resort among the Maltese. It's not a place to head for sights and is not particularly picturesque, but appeals because of its great restaurants, bustling little harbour, and local feel – few tourists make it here.

◉ Sights & Activities

The main things to do here are hanging out in cafes and bars along the waterfront, strolling along the promontory and fishing in the harbour.

St Thomas Bay   BEACH
St Thomas Bay is a deeply indented bay to the south of Marsaskala, lined with concrete-block huts and a potholed road, and surrounded by newly developed apartments. It has a slightly desolate feel, but a sandy beach of sorts, and the place is popular with local people and windsurfers. It's about a 10-minute walk from Marsaskala along Triq Tal-Gardiel. From St Thomas Bay you can continue walking along the coast to Marsaxlokk (about 4km).

St Thomas' Tower   FORTRESS
This small 17th-century fortress lies at the northern point of St Thomas Bay. It was built by the Knights of St John after a Turkish raiding party landed in Marsaskala Bay in 1614 and plundered the nearby village of Żejtun.

✖ Eating & Drinking

Locals travel across Malta to enjoy the many restaurants of Marsaskala. The town is particularly famed for its seafood.

La Favorita   SEAFOOD €€
(☑21634113; Triq Tal-Gardiel; mains €7-20; ☺Tue-Sun lunch, Mon-Sat dinner) This long-standing family-run restaurant is popular with locals for its delicious fresh fish. Head here for a long lazy lunch or dinner. It's simply decorated with large plate-glass windows fronting the room facing the street.

Tal-Familja   SEAFOOD €€
(☑2163 2161; Triq Tal-Gardiel; mains €7-19; ☺lunch & dinner Tue-Sun) A particular local favourite is the friendly and relaxed Tal-Familja, away from the town centre (about 300m past the cinema). You'll need some time to choose from the huge menu and daily specials, at the heart of which are fresh seafood and classic Maltese cuisine (kids and vegetarians are well looked after, too). The excellent service and massive portions will have you heading home well sated.

ⓘ Getting There & Away

Buses 91 and 92 run regularly from Valletta to Marsaskala (every 20-35 minutes); bus 135 runs to the airport hourly; and nightbus N91 connects with St Julian's. The bus terminus is on Triq Sant'Antnin at the southern end of the waterfront promenade.

Żurrieq

POP 10,040

The village of Żurrieq sprawls across a hillside on the south coast, in a sort of no-man's-land to the south of the airport. This part of Malta feels cut off from the rest of the island, and, although it's only 10km from Valletta as the crow flies, it seems much further. Signage from Żurrieq to neighbouring towns is poor, but this region is small and it shouldn't take long to find the direction you need (ask locals for guidance if you get stuck).

◉ Sights & Activities

Wied iż-Żurrieq   BOAT TOUR
(☑9945 5347, 2164 0058; adult/child €7/3.50) About 2km west of Żurrieq lies the tiny harbour of Wied iż-Żurrieq, set in a narrow inlet in the cliffs and guarded by a watchtower. Here, boats depart for enjoyable 30-minute cruises to the Blue Grotto, a huge natural arch in the sea cliffs 400m to the east.

MEGA-ATTRACTIONS

The megalithic temples of Malta, which date mainly from the period 3600 to 3000 BC, are among the oldest freestanding stone structures in the world. They predate the pyramids of Egypt by more than 500 years.

The oldest surviving temples are thought to be those of Ta'Ħġrat and Skorba near the village of Mġarr on Malta. Ġgantija on Gozo and Ħaġar Qim and Mnajdra on Malta are among the best preserved. Tarxien is the most developed, its last phase dating from 3000 to 2500 BC. The subterranean tombs of the Hypogeum date from the same period as the temples and mimic many of their architectural features below ground.

The purpose of these mysterious structures is the subject of much debate. They all share certain features in common – a site on a southeasterly slope, near to caves, a spring and fertile farmland; a trefoil or cloverleaf plan with three or five rounded chambers (apses) opening off the central axis, which usually faces between south and east; megalithic construction, using blocks of stone weighing up to 20 tonnes; and holes and sockets drilled into the stones, perhaps to hold wooden doors or curtains made from animal hide. Most temple sites have also revealed spherical stones, about the size of cannonballs – it has been suggested that these were used like ball bearings to move the heavy megaliths more easily over the ground.

No burials have been found in any of the temples, but most have yielded statues and figurines of so-called 'fat ladies' – possibly fertility goddesses. Most have some form of decoration on the stone, ranging from simple pitting to the elaborate spirals and carved animals seen at Tarxien. There are also 'oracle holes' – small apertures in the chamber walls which may have been used by priests or priestesses to issue divinations. The temples' southeasterly orientation has suggested a relationship to the winter solstice sunrise, and one amateur investigator has put forward a convincing theory of solar alignment (see www.weathermalta.net/websites/mariovassallo/3/).

The boat trips take in about seven caves, including the Honeymoon Cave, Reflection Cave and Cat's Cave. The best time is before midmorning, when the sun is shining into the grotto. Small boats (carrying up to eight passengers) depart from 9am to around 5pm daily, weather permitting (trips are less likely to run from December to February). If there is any doubt about the weather or sea conditions, call to check.

You can see the Blue Grotto without a boat from a viewing platform beside the main road, east of the turn-off to Wied iż-Żurrieq.

Parish Church of St Catherine CHURCH
The Parish Church of St Catherine was built in the 1630s and houses a fine altarpiece of St Catherine – painted by Mattia Preti in 1675, when the artist took refuge here during a plague epidemic – and there are several 17th- and 18th-century windmills dotted about the village.

Chapel of the Annunciation CHURCH
(☑2122 5952; www.dinlarthelwa.org) On a minor road between Żurrieq and Mqabba is the Chapel of the Annunciation in the deserted medieval settlement of Ħal Millieri. This tiny church, set in a pretty garden, dates from the mid-15th century and contains important 15th-century frescoes – the only surviving examples of medieval religious art in Malta. Both church and garden are normally locked, but are open to the public from 9am to noon on the first Sunday of each month.

✗ Eating & Drinking

Step In SEAFOOD €€
(☑2168 3104; Triq Wied Hoxt; mains €7-16.50; ⊙lunch daily, dinner Jun-Aug) There is a cluster of restaurants around the launching point for Blue Grotto trips, but they are not particularly inspiring. This is the pick of the bunch, however, with a fantastic terrace offering views out to sea and over to the little island of Filfa. It's very informal and a great place for a drink-with-a-view.

ℹ Getting There & Away

Bus 102 runs hourly Monday to Saturday from Rabat to Wied iż-Żurrieq via Dingli Cliffs and Ħaġar Qim, and goes on to the Airport, via Żurrieq. Buses 71 and 73 connect Żurrieq (which is about 1.5km from the Blue Grotto harbour) with Valletta about hourly, daily. The Blue Grotto harbour is also a stop on the south route of the CitySightseeing Malta (p180) hop-on, hop-off bus.

Ħaġar Qim & Mnajdra

The megalithic temples of Ħaġar Qim (*adge-ar eem*; 'standing stones') and Mnajdra (*mm-nigh*-dra) are the best preserved and most evocative of Malta's prehistoric sites, and have an unparalleled location atop sea cliffs, looking over to the islet of Filfa. They're believed to have been specially constructed to align with movements of the sun. It's worth the effort to take a tour, especially around the summer (21 June) and winter (21 December) solstices at some of the supposed solar alignments, when Heritage Malta (p45) organises special guided tours (€15 per person; book well in advance).

Tentlike canopies have been erected over the temples to protect them from the elements. There's also an informative visitors centre with some nice hands-on exhibits to help explain how and why the structures may have been built, and some way-marked nature trails in the area surrounding the temples, which allow for splendid views out to sea.

Ħaġar Qim is the first temple you reach after the visitors' centre. The facade, with its trilithon entrance, has been restored, and gives an idea of what it may once have looked like. The temples were originally roofed over, probably with corbelled stone vaults, but these have long since collapsed.

Before going in, look round the corner to the right – the megalith here is the largest in the temple, weighing over 20 tonnes. The temple consists of a series of interconnected, oval chambers with no uniform arrangement, and differs from other Maltese temples in lacking a regular trefoil plan. In the first chamber on the left is a little altar post decorated with plant motifs, and in the second there are a couple of pedestal altars. The 'fat lady' statuettes and the so-called Venus de Malta figurine that were found here are on display in the National Museum of Archaeology in Valletta.

Mnajdra, a 700m walk downhill from Ħaġar Qim, is more elaborate. There are three temples side by side, each with a trefoil plan and a different orientation. The oldest temple is the small one on the right, aligned towards the southwest and Filfla Island. The central temple, pointing towards the southeast, is the youngest. All date from between 3600 and 3000 BC.

It has been claimed that the southern temple is full of significant solar alignments. At sunrise during the winter solstice, a beam of sunlight illuminates the altar to the right of the inner doorway. At sunrise during the summer solstice, a sunbeam penetrates the window in the back of the left-hand apse to the pedestal altar in the left rear chamber.

Ħaġar Qim Temple

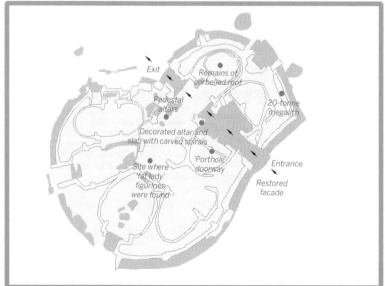

In the right-hand apse there is a separate chamber entered through a small doorway, with a so-called 'oracle hole' to its left. The function of this is unknown.

On the cliff top to the southeast of Mnajdra is a 17th-century watchtower and a memorial to Sir Walter Congreve (Governor of Malta 1924–27), who was buried at sea off this point. You can hike west along the cliffs to Għar Lapsi. The tiny uninhabited island Filfla, 5km offshore, is clearly visible. It suffered the ignominy of being used for target practice by the British armed forces until it was declared a nature reserve in 1970. It supports important breeding colonies of seabirds, including an estimated 10,000 pairs of storm-petrels, and a unique species of lizard. Landing on the island is forbidden.

Eating

Ħaġar Qim Restaurant MALTESE €€
(☎2142 4116; mains €6-20; ☺lunch daily, dinner Mon-Sat) This pleasingly spacious restaurant, just above the Ħaġar Qim & Mnajdra car park, has a large open-air terrace shaded by a bamboo-slatted canopy, a cheesy music soundtrack, some classical statuary, and serves the usual suspects (pizza and pasta), plus excellent beef, rabbit and fish dishes.

ℹ Getting There & Away

Bus 102 runs hourly Monday to Saturday from Rabat to Ħaġar Qim via Dingli Cliffs and Wied iż-Żurrieq, going on to the Airport. Ħaġar Qim is also a stop on the south route of the CitySightseeing Malta (p180) hop on, hop off bus.

Għar Lapsi

On the road west of the Ħaġar Qim & Mnajdra temples is a turn-off (signposted) to Għar Lapsi. The name means 'Cave of the Ascension', and there was once a fishermen's shrine here. The road winds steeply to the coast and ends at a car park beside a couple of restaurants and boathouses. The main attraction here is the swimming – a little cove in the low limestone cliffs has been converted into a natural lido, with stone steps and iron ladders giving access to the limpid blue water. It's a popular spot for bathing and picnicking among locals, and is well frequented by divers and fishermen.

Eating & Drinking

If swimming has given you an appetite, try one of the two contrasting restaurants above the cove.

Lapsi View MALTESE €€
(☎2164 0608; mains €6-19; ☺lunch & dinner Tue-Sun) This 1950s-style restaurant has the look of a 1950s municipal swimming pool, with a slightly crumbling exterior fronted by trestle tables, but inside is a taste of retro-Malta, an echoing place with high ceilings. As you'd expect, old-fashioned home-cooking is the order of the day, with burgers, sandwiches and pizzas, plus rabbit, steak, *lampuki* and stewed octopus.

Blue Creek MEDITERRANEAN €€
(☎2146 2786; mains €8-25; ☺lunch & dinner Wed-Mon) Blue Creek has an appealing primary-coloured interior, although its best tables are the hotly contested ones on the sunny outdoor terrace (directly above the water). The menu has something for all: snacks, sandwiches, pasta or seafood, including octopus stewed in red wine, and a shellfish platter of steamed mussels, clams, razor clams and prawns. Come for lunch rather than dinner, and enjoy the setting.

Carmen's BAR
(☺9am-2am Fri-Sun, daily in summer) This tiny bar is set among the fishing boats, just above the Għar Lapsi swimming hole. It's a splendid, if basic, place to sit and have a drink.

ℹ Getting There & Away

For hikers, there is a footpath along the 3km stretch of cliff top between Għar Lapsi and Ħaġar Qim. In summer, bus 71 runs from Valletta (one hour, hourly Mon-Sat), calling at the Blue Grotto (20 minutes) and Ħaġar Qim (10 minutes), and bus 109 operates from Rabat (45 minutes, hourly).

Gozo & Comino

Includes »

Best Places to Eat

- » Rew Rew (p115)
- » Ta'Frenċ (p120)
- » Ta'Rikardu (p113)
- » Patrick's (p113)

Best Places to Stay

- » Gozitan farmhouses
- » Ta'Ċenċ (p136)
- » Thirtyseven (p138)
- » Kempinski Hotel (p138)

Why Go?

Gozo, called Għawdex (*aow*-desh) in Malti, moves at a much slower pace than its bigger, busier neighbour. Although it is more than one-third the size of Malta, it has less than one-tenth of the population – only about 30,000 Gozitans live here (and they are Gozitans first, Maltese second). There's much more fertile land here, and much more space and greenery: the scenery is fantastical.

This is a lovely place to kick back, with a superb coastal landscape and excellent scuba diving and snorkelling, plus history in the form of megalithic temples and medieval citadels. There's so much to see and do, and so many opportunities for relaxation, it's worth scheduling at least a few days here; or, indeed, making Gozo the primary focus of your trip.

When to Go

Gozo and Comino are at their loveliest in spring and autumn, when the crowds have ebbed away. If you want to visit Comino's famous Blue Lagoon, it's much easier to enjoy its charms outside the summer months – in July and August it's mobbed by tourists and holidaying locals. Still, high summer is a great time for clubbing at the island's Ibiza-style clubs, and it's worthwhile being here during Carnival and Easter to bask in local colour.

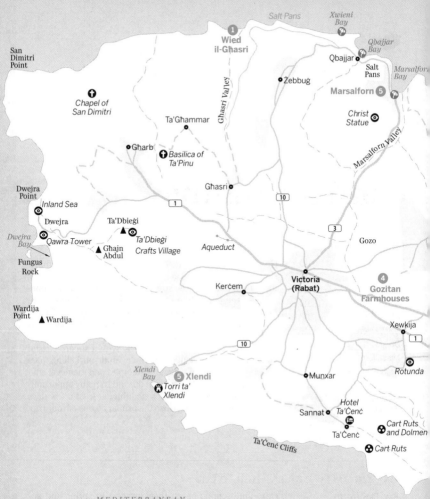

Gozo & Comino Highlights

1 Swimming in azure coves like **Wied il-Għasri** (p120)

2 Getting red sand in your shorts at lovely **San Blas Bay** (p125)

3 Taking in the incredible 360-degree views from tiny **Comino** (p126)

4 Renting a **converted farmhouse** (p137) in a Gozitan village

5 Learning to dive with the experts in **Xlendi** or **Marsalforn** (p22)

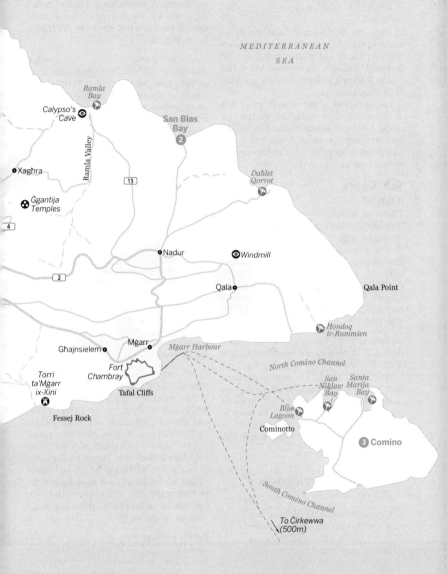

MEDITERRANEAN

SEA

Ramla
Bay

Calypso's
Cave

Ramla Valley

Xaghra

Ġgantija
Temples

San Blas
Bay
2

Dahlet
Qorrot

15

4

2

Nadur

Windmill

Qala

Qala Point

Hondoq
ir-Rummien

Ghajnsielem

Mġarr

Mġarr Harbour

North Comino Channel

San
Niklaw
Bay

Santa
Marija
Bay

Torri
ta'Mġarr
ix-Xini

Fort
Chambray

Tafal Cliffs

Blue
Lagoon

Fessej Rock

Cominotto

3 Comino

South Comino Channel

To Ċirkewwa
(500m)

0   2 km
0   1 mile

GOZO

Victoria (Rabat)

POP 6290

Victoria, the chief town of Gozo, sits in the centre of the island, 6km from the ferry terminal at Mġarr and 3.5km from the resort town of Marsalforn. It's crowned by the tiny citadel Il-Kastell, which appears to grow out of its rocky outcrop.

Gozo's capital is the island's main hub of shops and services. Named for the Diamond Jubilee of Queen Victoria in 1897, it was originally known as Rabat, and is still called that by many of the islanders (and on several road signs).

◉ Sights

Il-Kastell

While the walls surrounding Il-Kastell date from the 15th century, there have been fortifications atop this flat-topped hill since the Bronze Age: it developed under the Phoenicians and later became a Roman town. After some terrible raids on Gozo by the Turks, it became customary for all the island's families to stay within Il-Kastell overnight, a practice that lasted into the 17th century.

Cathedral of the Assumption   CHURCH

(Map p112; Misraħ il-Katidral; adult/child €3/free; ☺9am-5pm Mon-Sat) The cathedral was built between 1697 and 1711 to replace a church that had been destroyed by an earthquake in 1693. The earthquake had struck in southern Italy yet caused damage as far away as Malta. The replacement was designed by Lorenzo Gafa, who was also responsible

VISITING VICTORIA'S MUSEUMS

Museum afficionados can purchase a ticket to two of Victoria's museums (€5/2.50 per adult/child, excluding the Cathedral Museum). For the really dedicated there's the Citadel Day Ticket (€8/4 per adult/child) allowing entry to all four. If you have a Malta Pass (maltapass.com.mt), of course, all entry is covered; otherwise passes can be purchased at each museum.

for St Paul's Cathedral (p85) at Mdina. The elegant facade is adorned with the escutcheons of Grand Master Ramon de Perellos and Bishop Palmieri. Due to a lack of money the dome was never finished, but a clever trompe l'oeil painting gives the impression of completion.

Cathedral Museum   MUSEUM

(Map p112; ☑2155 6087; Triq il- Fossos; admission in cathedral ticket price; ☺9am-5pm Mon-Sat) This jumble of objects within the Cathedral Museum includes church gold and silver, some religious art (including a disturbing 19th-century painting depicting the martyrdom of St Agatha), a 19th-century bishop's carriage and an altar with a wax model of the Last Supper.

Archaeology Museum   MUSEUM

(Map p112; ☑2155 6144; Triq Bieb il-Mdina; adult/child €5/2.50 incl two museums; ☺9am-5pm) Victoria's Archaeology Museum is small, but contains some incredible finds. The highlights are the delicate artworks found at the Ġgantija temples and Xagħra, including two voluptuous figures sitting cosily on a couch, and a series of stick figurines with faces, thought possibly to be a family group. All are around 3000 to 4000 years old. There are also Roman anchors, and some fascinating amulets in the form of the Eye of Osiris – an ancient link to the symbols seen on Maltese fishing boats of today.

Old Prison   HISTORIC BUILDING

(Map p112; ☑2156 5988; Triq il-Kwartier; €5/2.50 incl two museums; ☺9am-5pm) The Old Prison served as a jail from the late 1500s to 1904, and proved particularly useful for locking up hot-tempered knights until they cooled off. For a few months the cells here once held Jean Parisot de la Valette for the crime of 'aggressive behaviour', before he became Grand Master. Particularly fascinating is the historic graffiti etched into the walls by the inmates, including crosses, ships, hands and the cross of the Knights.

Folklore Museum   MUSEUM

(Map p112; ☑2156 2034; Triq Bernardo de Opuo; €5/2.50 incl two museums; ☺9am-5pm) The Folklore Museum is a maze of stairs, rooms and courtyards: the fine rambling old building itself, dating to 1500, is more interesting than the large collection of domestic, trade and farming implements that give an insight into rural life on Gozo.

Victoria

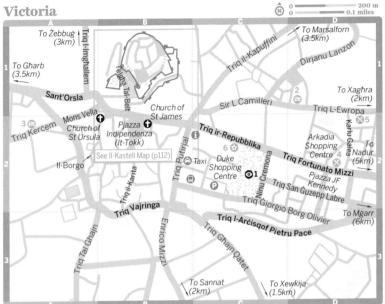

Natural Science Museum MUSEUM

(Map p112; ☏2155 6153; Triq il-Kwartier; €5/2.50 incl two museums; ⊗9am-5pm) This gracious old building houses a series of low-key exhibits explaining the geology of the island and its water supply. There are some interesting fossils downstairs, including huge Megatholon shark teeth.

Basilica of St George CHURCH

(Map p112; Pjazza San Ġorġ) The original parish church of Rabat dates from 1678, and the lavish interior contains a fine altarpiece of *St George and the Dragon* by Mattia Preti.

Gozo 360° AUDIOVISUAL ATTRACTION

(Map p112; ☏2155 9955; entrance on Telgha Tal-Belt; adult/child €6/3; ⊗every 30 minutes, 10.30am-4pm Mon-Sat) Gozo 360°, at the Citadel Cinema, is a 30-minute audiovisual show that gives a good, basic introduction to the island's history and sights before veering off into tourist board–style fluff. Commentary is available in eight languages.

Other Sights

Pjazza Indipendenza PIAZZA

(Map p112) Victoria's main square hosts a daily market (from around 6.30am to 2pm), which is known throughout the island as It-Tokk (the meeting place). The semicircular

Victoria

◎ Sights

1 Rundle Gardens C2

🛏 Sleeping

2 Downtown Hotel D1
3 The Gardens A2

✗ Eating

4 Arkadia Supermarket...........................D2
5 Patrick's D2

☺ Entertainment

6 Aurora Opera House C2

baroque building at the western end of the square is the **Banca Giuratale** (Map p112; Pjazza Indipendenza), built in 1733 to house the city council; today it contains government offices.

Il-Borgo OLD TOWN

The old town, known as Il-Borgo, is a maze of narrow, meandering alleys around Pjazza San Ġorġ. It's a beguiling place to wander.

Rundle Gardens GARDEN

(Map p111; ⊗6am-8pm summer, 7am-6pm winter) Rundle Gardens, south of Triq ir-Repubblika, were laid out by General Sir Leslie Rundle (Governor of Malta 1909–15) in around 1914.

Il-Kastell

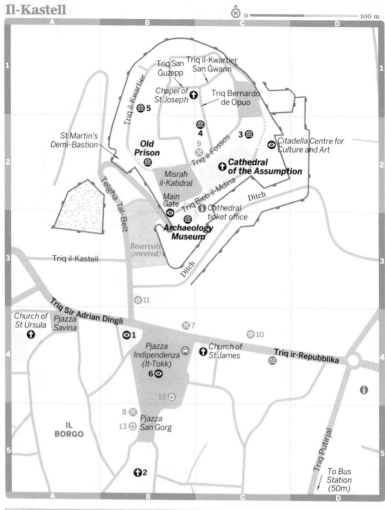

N
0   100 m

Il-Kastell

✕ Eating & Drinking

TOP CHOICE Ta'Rikardu   MALTESE €
(Map p112; ☑2155 5953; 4 Triq il-Fossos; mains €5-12.50; ⊙9am-6pm) An institution in Victoria and the only place to eat in Il-Kastell, Ta'Rikardu sells excellent local produce – honey, cheese and wine – along with souvenirs and paintings. Take a seat and order a cheap, delicious platter (€10.75) which includes cheese, bread, local tomatoes, sundried tomatoes, capers and olives. Veggie soup or homemade ravioli is also available; wash it all down with Gozitan wine.

Patrick's   MEDITERRANEAN €€
(Map p111; ☑2156 6667; www.patrickstmun.com; Triq I-Ewropa; mains €8.50-23; ⊙dinner Mon-Sat, lunch Sun; ☜) Patrick's (named after and run by the son of the restauranteurs at Tmun Mġarr ,(p115), is polished and professional, from the linen-covered tables to the extensive wine list and menu of fusion dishes. Asian influences, New Zealand beef, fresh local fish and creative pasta options come together wonderfully in a nautical yet elegant blue and white dining room. There's a lounge and a bar available for nightcaps and chilling out, too. This place regularly wins local awards; it's worth booking ahead.

Grapes Wine Bar   WINE BAR €
(Map p112; ☑7947 3503; Pjazza San Ġorġ; mains €4-14; ⊙lunch & dinner) For a memorable Gozitan experience, sit at the old sewing-machine tables with views of the basilica, choose a good local –or international – wine, and graze on a platter of regional cheese/sausage/seafood, *ftira* (traditional Maltese bread), a serve of rabbit or a pizza. But be ready to spend some time doing so – service can be slow.

Café Jubilee   CAFE €
(Map p112; ☑2155 8921; Pjazza Indipendenza; mains €4-8; ⊙8am-midnight, to 2am Fri & Sat; ☜) This old-fashioned cafe has a classy interior featuring a marble counter, brass rails, lots of dark wood and waiters in black waistcoats, and has some outside tables on the square. In the evening it becomes a popular wine bar and serves good local drops.

Arkadia Supermarket   SELF CATERING
(Map p111; Triq Fortunato Mizzi; ⊙8am-8pm daily) Gozo's best supermarket.

☆ Entertainment

Despite its diminutive size, Victoria has two theatres to Valletta's one.

Aurora Opera House   THEATRE
(Map p111; ☑2156 2974; www.teatruaurora.com; Triq ir-Repubblika) The Aurora Opera House stages opera, ballet, comedy, drama, cabaret, pantomime, celebrity concerts and exhibitions.

Astra Theatre   THEATRE
(Map p112; ☑2155 0985; www.teatruastra.com; Triq ir-Repubblika) Astra Theatre is the 19th-century home of Soċjetà Filarmonika La Stella, and stages predominantly opera, music and ballet.

Citadel Cinema   CINEMA
(Map p112; ☑2155 9955; www.citadelcinema.com; Telgħa Tal-Belt; ticket per adult/child €4.50/3.50.) The two-screen Citadel Cinema shows mainstream films and Gozo 360° (p111).

🛍 Shopping

Bottega del Sole e della Luna   FOODSTUFFS
(Map p112; ☑7961 8718; 31 Pjazza San Ġorġ; ⊙9.30am-7pm Mon-Fri, 9.30am-2.30pm Sat) A small shop selling locally grown organic produce and stocking a range of fine food and drink from Malta and Italy. This is a great place to pick up wildflower honey or prickly pear jam.

Organika   FOODSTUFFS
(Map p112; ☑27013548; 13 Pjazza San Ġorġ; ⊙10am-6pm Mon-Fri, 10am-4pm Sat) Locally grown organic produce.

ℹ Information

Emergency
Gozo's main police station (p171) is located in Victoria, near the corner of Triq ir-Rebubblika and Triq Putirjal.

Internet Access
There's free wi-fi at Pjazza San Ġorġ, though it's not always working. Alternatively, there are a few computers in the foyer of the opera house.

Medical Services
General Hospital (Craig Hospital; ☑2156 1600; Triq I-Arċisqof Pietru Pace)

Post
Post Office (Triq ir-Repubblika; ⊙8.15am-4.30pm Mon-Fri, 8.15am-12.30pm Sat)

Tourist Information
Tourist Information Office (☑2156 1419; Tigrija Palazz, cnr Triq ir-Repubblika & Triq Putirjal; ⊙9am-5.30pm Mon-Sat, 9am-1pm Sun & public holidays) A helpful office with maps and brochures.

ℹ Getting There & Away

Gozo Channel (☑2155 6114; www.gozo channel.com) runs the car and foot passenger ferry connecting Ċirkewwa in Malta and Gozo's Mġarr (every 45 minutes from 6am to around 6pm, and roughly every 1½ hours overnight). You pay your ticket in Mġarr on the return trip, not on the way out.

Harbour Air (2122 8302; www.harbourair malta.com) operates a floatplane service between Valletta Waterfront and Mġarr Harbourm, with two 10-minute flights daily (weather and sea conditions permitting), costing approximately €150 return. At the time of writing flights were grounded for maintenance work, but will have recommenced by the time you're reading this. The floatplane terminal is on Triq Martino Garces, on the north side of Mġarr Harbour.

❶ Getting Around

BUS

Since the new Arriva bus service arrived in 2011, Gozo's bus network has been transformed, with much more regular services. Buses tend to run daily, about hourly, and most pass through Victoria. You can buy your ticket aboard the bus, or at the ticket machines or ticket booth at the Victoria bus station, which is close to the town centre. A single day ticket costs €2.20/2.60.

CAR & BICYCLE

If you want to see as much of the island as possible, then it makes sense to rent a car. It's also quite cheap – even cheaper than in Malta. You'll find too that the quieter roads and shorter distances make cycling a much more attractive option on Gozo than on Malta.

Victoria Garage (2155 6414; www.victoria garagegozo.com; Triq Putirjal) opposite the bus station, rents out bicycles (€6 per day, or €4 per day for longer rentals) and cars (daily rate of around €30, or €25 for longer periods).

Mayjo Car Rentals (p178) has a large range of car at good rates (from €20/25 per day in the low/high season for the smallest vehicle – for rentals of a week or longer). Prices vary with length of rental, size of car and time of year.

TAXI

Approximate taxi fares from Victoria include: to Marsalforn €5; to Mġarr €15; to Xagħra €10; and to Xlendi €10. To book a taxi, call Belmont Garage (p180) or **Mario's Taxis** (2155 7242). Otherwise, there's a taxi rank near Victoria's bus station and at Pjazza Indipendenza.

SOUTHERN GOZO

Mġarr

Mġarr is Gozo's main harbour and the point of arrival for ferries from Malta. The ferry terminal houses an underground car park, waiting rooms, a cafe and public toilets.

❖ Sights & Activities

Church of Our Lady of Lourdes   CHURCH
(Triq Lourdes) This 20th-century neo-Gothic church appears almost to hang over the

---

GOZO AGRITOURISM

The nonprofit **Ager Foundation** (www.agerfoundation.com) organises the Gozo Experience, a project with the noble aims of promoting responsible, sustainable tourism on Gozo and safeguarding the natural environment. It offers visitors (locals and tourists alike) the chance to get back to nature – milk a goat, go fishing, cook up a traditional feast – alongside Gozitans and according to Gozitan traditions. Options for one-day outings include:

» experiencing the life of a local shepherd, and being shown how *gbejniet,* the traditional cheese, is made

» preparing and tasting natural Gozitan food

» fishing from the shore or from a boat with a local fisherman

» learning about local wine-making practices

» birdwatching with local birders

» exploring Gozo's archaeology and heritage

The experiences are designed with families in mind (especially parents who'd like their kids to have some understanding of where supermarket produce comes from) and are a hit with city slickers enamoured with the romance of rural life. Groups are kept small (maximum eight participants) and costs are very reasonable (eg a day spent meeting a local shepherd, with the chance to milk a sheep and make cheese, costs adult/child €18.50/9.25, including lunch).

village. Begun in 1924, lack of funds meant that its construction was not completed until the 1970s. The hilltop above it is capped by the ramparts of **Fort Chambray**, which was built by the Knights of St John in the early 18th century. It was originally intended to supplant Victoria's citadel as Gozo's main fortified town, and the area within the walls was laid out with a grid of streets similar to that of Valletta. But with the decline of the Order in the late 18th century, the plan came to naught. Instead, the fort served as a garrison and later as a mental hospital. Part of the complex has been converted into luxury apartments, with more to come.

Viewpoint   VIEWPOINT
Triq iż-Żewwiega leads to a stunning viewpoint just south of Qala. It's worth the effort to get here – 1.8km uphill from the harbour; once here you can enjoy the magnificent panorama over Gozo and out to sea.

Belvedere   VIEWPOINT
A right turn at the top of the harbour hill leads to a belvedere with a grand view over the harbour to Comino and northern Malta.

Boat Trips
Traders selling boat rides to Comino sit by the kerb of the main road through **town**. The going rate is €8 to €10 return, and boats generally leave Mġarr hourly from around 10am to 4pm. For a small supplement most offer a quick trip to view some of Comino's caves.

Xlendi Pleasure Cruises   BOAT TOUR
(☑2155 9967; www.xlendicruises.com) This outfit offers half- and full-day boat trips around Gozo and/or Comino from April to October. A 5½ hour trip taking in Gozo and Comino costs €22.50/11.25 per adult/child; a buffet lunch costs €8.50/4.25. A 3½ hour trip around Comino and the Blue Lagoon costs €25/12.50 (€19.50 without lunch). A four-hour fishing trip costs €45/22.50. Trips depart from Mġarr harbour, but transfers can be arranged. You can book trips through most travel agents in the resort towns on Gozo.

🍴 Eating & Drinking
Mġarr has become something of a foodie paradise in recent years, with some excellent restaurants within a short walk of the ferry terminal.

Porto Vecchio   MEDITERRANEAN €€
(☑2156 3317; Triq Martino Garces; mains €11-21; ⊙lunch & dinner Thu-Tue) Porto Vecchio gets top marks for location – a fantastic marina-side terrace – as well as for its friendly, knowledgeable service. The menu is mostly seafood and Italian, with dishes like *filleto di cernia al limoncello* (grouper with lemon liqueur), though you can also dine on quail and steak.

Tmun Mġarr   MEDITERRANEAN €€
(☑2156 6276; Triq Martino Garces; mains €11-22; ⊙lunch & dinner Wed-Mon; ☑) Family-run Tmun Mġarr is a local favourite, with a menu is rich in dishes like bouillabaisse and fresh-from-the-sea fish. There are good vegetarian choices, too, and the desserts are delicious.

Sicilia Bella   ITALIAN €€
(☑2156 3588; 1 Triq Manuel de Vilhena; mains €9-17; ⊙dinner Tue-Sun, lunch Sat & Sun) This recommended portside eatery offers seafood cooked with a Sicilian slant. It does what Italians do best: taking the finest fresh ingredients and cooking them with simple brilliance.

Bugeja Fish Market   SELF-CATERING €
(⊙8.30am-12.30pm & 4.30-7pm Mon-Sat) Head to Bugeja, just outside Mġarr, to purchase your fresh fish for the BBQ. It has a great range of local fish and seafood, and attracts queues of locals.

Gleneagles Bar   PUB
(☑2155 6543; Triq ix-Xatt) This is the social hub of the village – if not the island – and the place to head for a sundowner, with views over the harbour. It fills up in the early evening with a lively mix of locals, fishermen, yachties and tourists looking for some Gozitan colour.

Mġarr ix-Xini

The narrow, cliff-bound inlet of Mġarr ix-Xini (Port of the Galleys) was once used by the Knights of St John as their main harbour on Gozo. One of their watchtowers, **Torri ta' Mġarr ix-Xini**, still guards the entrance. The Turkish admiral Dragut Reis also found it handy, using it when he raided Gozo in 1551 and took most of the island's population into slavery.

There's a tiny shingle beach at the head of the inlet, and a paved area where tourists and locals stake out their sunbathing territories. It's a gorgeous place to swim and snorkel. It's home to a classic Gozo restaurant, the marvellous **Rew Rew** (mains around €20; ⊙11am-5pm daily Mar-Nov). This simple-looking

EDWARD LEAR ON GOZO

Edward Lear (1812–88), an English landscape painter and nonsense poet (he popularised the limerick as a form of comic verse), spent much of his life travelling around the Mediterranean. Lear visited Gozo in 1866, and described the scenery as 'pomskizillious and gromphiberous, being as no words can describe its magnificence'.

place has a few chairs and tables next to a little cabin on the beach, and serves up fresh, delicious seafood to hungry punters. It's the perfect place for a long, lazy lunch looking out to sea. Book ahead.

Mġarr ix-Xini can be tricky to find, and the road from Sannat and Xewkija down to it is quite steep and narrow, but it's perfectly accessible in a normal car, and worth the effort.

Xewkija

POP 3105

The village of Xewkija – and most of southern Gozo – is dominated by the vast dome of the Parish Church of St John the Baptist, better known as the Rotunda (☑2155 6793; ⊙6am-noon & 3-8pm). Work on the church began in 1951 and was completed in 1971; it was built mainly with the volunteer labour of the parishioners, and paid for by local donations. Its extraordinary size – the 75m dome is higher than St Paul's Cathedral in London, and the nave can seat 4000 people – is said to be due to rivalry with Mosta in Malta, whose rotunda was also funded by the local people.

It was built around the old 17th-century church, which was too small for the community's needs. There's no such risk with the rotunda, which can seat around three times the village's population. The interior is plain, but impresses through sheer size. Paintings of scenes from the life of St John the Baptist adorn the six side-chapels. To the left of the altar is a museum displaying baroque sculptures and other relics salvaged from the old church. The wooden statue of St John was fashioned in 1845 by Maltese sculptor Paul Azzopardi. A small lift takes visitors up to the gallery surrounding the dome, for great panoramas.

Ta'Ċenċ

The quiet village of Sannat, once famed for its lace-making, lies 2km south of Victoria, and gives access to the Ta'Ċenċ plateau. Signs from the village square point the way to Hotel Ta'Ċenċ (p136), one of Gozo's finest, whose bar is a great place for a sundowner. The track to the left of the entrance to the walled hotel grounds leads to the high plateau of Ta'Ċenċ – the views north to Victoria, Xewkija and Xagħra are good, especially towards sunset. Wander off to the left of the track, near the edge of the limestone crag, and you will find a prehistoric dolmen – a large slab propped up on three smaller stones like a table. Keep your eyes peeled – the dolmen is not signposted and is a little tricky to spot.

The best walking is off to the right, along the top of the huge Ta'Ċenċ sea cliffs. These spectacular limestone crags, more than 130m high, were once the breeding ground of the Maltese peregrine falcon. Near the cliff top you can see traces of prehistoric 'cart ruts', origins unknown.

Bus 305 runs between Victoria and Ta'Ċenċ (12 minutes), going on to Gharb and San Lawrenz.

Xlendi

Development has turned the sometime fishing village of Xlendi into a popular resort town. Although the cluster of buildings won't win any architectural awards, the bay still enjoys an attractive setting. It's a favourite place for weekending Maltese and tourists to chill out by the sea, with good swimming, snorkelling and diving, and plenty of rocks for sunbathing. In the 19th century, this was known as 'women's harbour', as it was reserved for women-only bathing.

By the bus stop and car park, a block back from the waterfront, is an ATM, currency exchange machine and internet cafe.

◉ Sights & Activities

At the head of the bay, steps lead over the cliff above the little fishing-boat harbour to a tiny cove in the rocks where you can swim. Alternatively, you can keep walking up the hillside above and then hike over to Wardija Point and Dwejra Bay. On the south side of Xlendi Bay, a footpath winds around to the 17th-century watchtower, Torri ta'Xlendi, on

Ras il-Bajjada. From here you can hike east to the Sanap cliffs, and on towards Ta'Ċenċ.

Boat Trips

Xlendi Pleasure Cruises BOAT TOUR

(☎2155 9967; www.xlendicruises.com) Waterside Xlendi Pleasure Cruises offers motorboats, canoes and paddleboats for hire, as well as fishing trips, water-skiing, snorkelling and cave tours. The company also has a menu of cruises leaving from Mġarr Harbour and will provide transfers.

Diving

Moby Dives (p22) and St Andrews Divers Cove (p22) can help you explore the excellent nearby dive sites, offering 'taster' dives, beginners' courses and excursions for those who already know what they're doing.

Eating

Boat House MEDITERRANEAN €€

(☎2156 9153; €6-20; ⊙noon-10.30pm) This is a highly rated restaurant where you can eat fresh fish with the sea almost lapping at your toes – there's a seafront, tented terrace. Seafood is the obvious choice, prices are reasonable, and it's a great choice for families.

Ta' Karolina MEDITERRANEAN €€

(☎2155 9675; Triq Marina; ⊙lunch & dinner Tue-Sun) This long-running seafront restaurant is a local favourite. It's named after historic local character Karolina Cauchi, who raised money to have the steps cut into the cliffs at Xlendi in the 19th century. These days it features a covered terrace, and a great range of soups, pasta and Gozitan specialities. You have to walk through two other restaurants to reach it.

Iċ-Ċima Restaurant GOZITAN, ITALIAN €€

(☎2155 8407; Triq San Xmun; mains €12-20; ⊙lunch & dinner Wed-Mon) This friendly restaurant is situated high up over the village, away from the waterfront hubbub, with an outstanding view over the bay and the coastal cliffs from its rooftop garden. It's an excellent choice, with the emphasis on seafood, plus dishes like *coniglio alla nonna* (rabbit grandma's way), but there's also a variety of inexpensive pizzas to choose from.

Gelateria Granola ICE CREAM €

(☎2155 6634; Xlendi; ice cream from €1.50) The marvellous Gelateria Granola place serves up delicious ice cream with a wide range of flavours.

Entertainment

La Grotta NIGHTCLUB

(www.lagrottaleisure.com; Triq ix-Xlendi; admission varies; ⊙10pm-dawn Fri & Sat May-Oct) On the road to Victoria about 600m east of Xlendi is the best nightclub in the Maltese Islands, in a unique, lovely setting with amazing views. It's housed in a limestone cave in the cliffs above the valley, with two large dance areas (indoors and out) and hosts big-party nights, DJs and live music.

Ku Club NIGHTCLUB

(Triq Mro Giuseppe Giardini Vella; ⊙10pm-late) Gozo's biggest Ibiza-style club hauls in lots of international names, and is where to head for hands-in-the-air trance, house etc and to worship before godlike DJs.

Getting There & Away

Bus 306 runs between Xlendi and Victoria (10 minutes), and Marsalforn (20 minutes). By car, follow signs from the roundabout at the southern end of Triq Putirjal in Victoria. Or, it's a 3km walk from Victoria bus station.

NORTHERN GOZO

Għarb & Around

POP 1070

The village of Għarb (pronounced aarb, meaning 'west') in the northwest of Gozo has one of the most beautiful churches on the Maltese Islands.

Sights

Basilica of Ta'Pinu CHURCH

(www.tapinu.org; Triq ta'Pinu; ⊙6.45am-7pm Mon-Sat, 5.45am-12.15pm & 1.30-7pm Sun) The Basilica of Ta'Pinu, accessible via a short, scenic walk from Għarb, is an extraordinary sight – a huge, lone church on a Gozitan hillock, towering over the countryside. Malta's national shrine to the Virgin Mary is an important centre of pilgrimage. It was built

WALKING ON GOZO

Gozo is so small that you could walk from Mġarr to Marsalforn in two hours. Away from the relatively busy road between Mġarr and Victoria the roads are quiet and you'll find the landscape gorgeous for hiking in.

in the 1920s on the site of a chapel where a local woman, Carmela Grima, heard the Virgin speak to her in 1883. Thereafter, numerous miracles were attributed to the intercession of Our Lady of Pinu, and it was decided to replace the old church with a grand new one. Built in a Romanesque style, with an Italianate campanile, it has a tranquil interior of pale golden stone. Part of the original chapel, with Carmela Grima's tomb, is incorporated behind the altar. The rooms to either side of the altar are filled with votive offerings, including children's clothes and a letter from an American who worked in the Twin Towers. The basilica's name comes from Filippino Gauci, who used to tend the old church – Pinu is the Malti diminutive for Filippino. Visitors should dress appropriately.

The track leading to the top of the hill of Ta'Ghammar opposite the church is punctuated by marble statues marking the Stations of the Cross.

Għarb Folklore Museum   MUSEUM
(☑2156 1929; Triq il-Knisja; adult/child €5/free; ☺10am-3pm Mon-Sat, 10am-noon Sun) This 18th-century house has 28 rooms crammed with a fascinating and charming private collection of folk artefacts. The exhibits, assembled by the owner over the past 20 years, include a child's hearse, farming implements, fishing gear and jam-making equipment.

Church of the Visitation   CHURCH
Għarb's baroque Church of the Visitation was built between 1699 and 1729, with an elegant curved facade and twin bell towers.

Three female figures adorn the front: Faith, above the door; Hope, with her anchor, to the right; and Charity. Inside, there is an altarpiece, *The Visitation of Our Lady to St Elizabeth,* which was gifted to the church by Grand Master de Vilhena.

Chapel of San Dimitri   CHURCH
A drive or pleasant walk of about 30 minutes (just over 2km) from Għarb leads to the tiny Chapel of San Dimitri (signposted on the road to the left of the church). This small, square church with its baroque cupola dates originally from the 15th century, though it was rebuilt in the 1730s. It stands in splendid isolation amid terraced fields. You can continue the walk down to the coast, and return via the Basilica of Ta'Pinu.

Eating

Jeffrey's Restaurant   GOZITAN €€
(☑2156 1006; 10 Triq il-Għarb; mains €13-25; ☺dinner Mon-Sat Apr-Oct) Where the road to Għarb from Victoria forks (400m after the turning to Ta'Pinu) you'll find Jeffrey's Restaurant. Set in a converted farmhouse with a rustic interior and pretty courtyard, Jeffrey's offers homestyle cooking that makes good use of local produce, and you can sample Gozitan specialities including the highly rated rabbit in wine and garlic.

ℹ Getting There & Away

Bus 305 connects Għarb with San Lawrenz (6 minutes) and Victoria (10 minutes, hourly), while the 308 runs between Victoria and Ta' Pinu (12 minutes, hourly).

DWEJRA GEOLOGY

Dwejra is formed of marine tertiary sedimentary rocks deposited around 24 million years ago. Besides blue clay, lower Coraline limestone is prevalent, mainly exposed in the sheer cliffs on the coastline and in the crust of the Inland Sea. Gobigerina limestone is also found in this area, which is widely used in the building industry; all Gozo's major soft-stone quarries are located nearby. The way that marine erosion has worn these layers of material has resulted in a remarkable sequence of sea caves, tunnels, arches, stacks and reefs, and the area is listed as a Unesco World Heritage Site. In 2012, part of the Azure Window collapsed, weakened by a long-term fissure.

San Lawrenz

POP 590

The charming village of San Lawrenz is where novelist Nicholas Monsarrat (1910–79) lived and worked for four years in the early 1970s. His love for the Maltese Islands is reflected in his novel *The Kappillan of Malta.*

Between San Lawrenz and Santa Lucija is the **Ta'Dbieġi Crafts Village** selling handicrafts, lace, glass and pottery. The stalls have variable hours, generally from around 10am to 4pm, but it's best to go in the morning.

🍴 Eating

Tatita's   MEDITERANEAN €€
(☑2156 6482; Pjazza San Lawrenz; mains €12-35; ☺lunch & dinner Apr-Oct) Tatita's occupies what was once San Lawrenz police station;

FUNGUS ROCK

Fungus Rock is known in Malti as Il-Ġebla tal-Ġeneral (the General's Rock). Both its names derive from the fact that the Knights of St John used to collect a rare plant from the rock's summit. The plant (Cynomorium coccineus) is dark brown and club-shaped, and grows to about 18cm in height. It is parasitic and has no green leaves, which is why it was called a fungus or, in Malti, għerq tal-Ġeneral (the General's root). It's native to North Africa, and Fungus Rock is the only place in Europe where it's found.

During the time of the Knights, extracts from the plant were believed to have powerful pharmaceutical qualities, and were said to stem bleeding and prevent infection when used to dress wounds. The miracle plant was also said to cure dysentery and ulcers, and was used to treat apoplexy and venereal diseases. It was long known to the Arabs as 'the treasure among drugs', and when a general of the Knights of St John discovered it growing on a rock on Gozo, he knew he had struck gold. A rope was strung between the mainland and the rock, and harvesters were shuttled back and forth in a tiny, one-man cable car. In 1637 the Knights built the fortress of Qawra Tower from which to guard the precious resource. As well as being much in demand in the Knights' hospitals, it was sold at a high price to the various courts of Europe.

GOZO & COMINO DWEJRA

when it's warm you can dine alfresco on the postcard-perfect square. It's very welcoming – and family friendly, too, despite the formal look and snow-white tablecloths. The kitchen prepares local treats like grilled quail with Calvados and mushroom sauce; and calamari and king prawns.

🛈 Getting There & Away

Bus 305 connects San Lawrenz with Għarb (six minutes, hourly) and Victoria (15 minutes).

Dwejra

Geology and the sea have conspired to produce some of Gozo's most spectacular coastal scenery at Dwejra on the west coast. Two vast, underground caverns in the limestone have collapsed to create two circular depressions now occupied by Dwejra Bay and the Inland Sea.

⊙ Sights & Activities

The Blue Hole & the Azure Window   DIVE SITE
The Azure Window, a huge natural arch in the sea cliffs, is a breathtaking Gozitan view. In the rocks in front of it is another geological freak called the Blue Hole – a vertical chimney in the limestone, about 10m in diameter and 25m deep, that connects with the open sea through an underwater arch about 8m down. Understandably, it's a very popular dive site and the snorkelling here is excellent, too. Moby Dives (p22) and St Andrews Divers Cove (p22), both located in Xlendi, are available for lessons and equipment hire.

The Inland Sea   LAGOON
The Inland Sea is a cliff-bound lagoon connected to the open sea by a tunnel that runs for 100m through the headland of Dwejra Point. The tunnel is big enough for small boats to sail through in calm weather, and the Inland Sea has been used as a fishermen's haven for centuries. Today, the fishermen supplement their income by taking tourists on boat trips (per person €3.50, 15 min) through the tunnel, and to Fungus Rock (€7 per person, 30 minutes).

Dwejra Bay & Dwejra Point   COASTLINE
The collapsed cavern of Dwejra Bay has been invaded by the sea, and is guarded by the brooding bulk of Fungus Rock. Qawra Tower (p119), overlooking the bay, affords spectacular coastal views. A path below the tower leads to a flight of stairs cut into the rock, leading down to a little slipway on the edge of the bay. There is good swimming and sunbathing here, away from the crowds of day-trippers who throng the rocks around the Azure Window. For even more peace you can hike right around to the cliff top on the far side of the bay, for a view encompassing Fungus Rock and Dwejra Point and, between them, Crocodile Rock (seen from near Qawra Tower it looks like a crocodile's head).

The broad horizontal shelf of rock to the south of Dwejra Point has been eroded along the geological boundary between the Globigerina Limestone and the Lower Coralline Limestone – the boundary is marked by a layer of many thousands of fossilised scallop shells and sand dollars (a kind of flattened, disc-shaped sea urchin).

Chapel of St Anne CHURCH
Between the Inland Sea and the Azure Window is the little Chapel of St Anne, built in 1963 on the site of a much older church.

 Getting There & Away
Bus 302 runs between Victoria and Dwejra (16 minutes, hourly). Alternatively, catch bus 305 to San Lawrenz and walk the 1.5km down to the bay.

Marsalforn

Former fishing village Marsalforn (the name is possibly derived from the Arabic for 'bay of ships') is Gozo's main holiday resort. It's small-scale and has a pleasant feel; the promenade (with its handful of restaurants) has been nicely updated, though the developments of low-rise hotels and apartments are somewhat straggly and sprawling.

At the head of Marsalforn's bay is a tiny scrap of sand, but better swimming and sunbathing can be found on the rocks out to the west. You could also hike eastward over the hill a couple of kilometres to Calypso's Cave (p123) and Ramla Bay (p125).

Sights & Activities

Wied il-Għasri BEACH
A 5km hike west along the coast from Marsalforn is the narrow, cliff-bound inlet of Wied il-Għasri. Here a narrow staircase cut into the rock leads down to a tiny shingle beach at the head of the inlet. It's a gorgeously picturesque place and there is good swimming and snorkelling when the sea is calm, but it's best avoided in rough weather when the waves come crashing up the narrow defile. You can also drive or walk to Wied il-Għasri from the village of Għasri, about 2km south, but it's a bit tricky to find – you'll need a decent map if you're

DIVING

A number of Marsalforn dive operators can help you explore Gozo's great dive sites, including:
» Atlantis (p22)
» Calypso Diving Centre (p22)
» Nautic Team (p22)

coming from this direction. If you're coming from Marsalforn, there is an unsigned turn-off about 300m after the coast road heads inland, where a rough track drops down to the right and leads to a rocky parking area (4WD recommended!).

Beaches & Salt Pans COASTLINE
If you walk west from town along the nicely updated promenade (with a handful of restaurants en route), you'll reach the tiny sand beaches at Qbajjar Bay (now heavily developed) and the more scenic Xwieni Bay, separated by a headland with a small fort. Beyond Xwieni, a newly made road runs along a rocky shore that has been carved into an impressive patchwork of salt pans, which are still worked in summer.

Christ Statue CHRISTIAN
As you enter Marsalforn from Victoria, you'll see the figure of Christ on a hill. The statue was erected in the 1970s, replacing earlier statues and a wooden cross from around the 1900s; the 96m-high hill is known as Tas-Salvatur (the Redeemer).

Eating & Drinking

The majority of restaurants in Marsalforn have reduced hours in winter – call ahead to check somewhere is open before setting off.

TOP CHOICE Restaurant
Ta'Frenċ MEDITERRANEAN €€€
(2155 3888; www.tafrencrestaurant.com; Triq ir-Rabat; mains €28-35; ⊙lunch & dinner Wed-Mon;) Treat yourself and head to this très élégant restaurant, about 1.5km south of Marsalforn on the road to Victoria. It's in a beautiful setting (a 200-year-old converted farmhouse surrounded by garden) and has an impressive menu of French, Italian and Maltese dishes, created from fresh local ingredients: bread is baked in-house and salt comes from local salt pans. Vegetarians are catered to, as are children, surprisingly. There's also an extensive, award-winning wine list – take a taxi home. Bookings advised.

Otters Bistro MALTESE, ITALIAN €€
(2156 2473; Triq Santa Marija; mains €9-20; ⊙lunch & dinner Feb-Oct, lunch Nov-Jan) Waterfront Otters has a glorious shady outdoor terrace overlooking the bay. The menu has some great Gozitan choices, including braised lamb shank with fig and orange sauce, or spaghetti Gozitana (tossed with Maltese sausage, olives, capers, tomatoes and chilli).

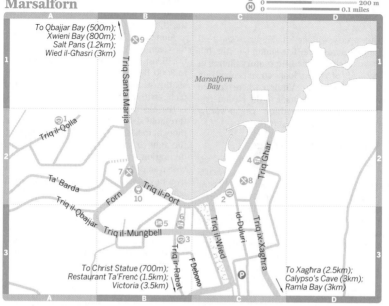

Marsalforn

Activities, Courses & Tours

Sleeping

Eating

Drinking

Il-Kartell MEDITERRANEAN €€

(2155 6918; Triq il-Port; mains €7-17; lunch daily, dinner Sat & Sun winter, lunch & dinner summer) This bustling place was a former boathouse; you can eat in the rustic dining rooms or by the waters edge. The menu includes pasta dishes, including penne Gozitana (pasta with local sausage, sun-dried tomatoes, garlic, herbs and white wine), as well as fresh fish, traditional dishes and daily specials chalked up on the blackboard.

La Trattoria MEDITERRANEAN €€

(2155 9173; Triq il-Port; mains €7-22; lunch & dinner) This welcoming family-run place has a small, arched interior and a cute little wooden terrace overlooking the town's tiny beach, The house speciality is *lampuka en paupiette* (rolled fillets of *lampuka* – dolphin fish – stuffed with prawns in a cream sauce), but the menu extends to pasta, risotto and a choice of pork and beef dishes.

+39 Village WINE BAR

(Triq il-Port;) This small lounge bar on the waterfront has a sleek interior and a couple of outside tables. It also serves decent pizzas (€5 to €8).

Information

You can change money at the **Bank of Valletta** on the promenade, which has an ATM and a 24-hour money-changing machine.

Getting There & Away

Bus 306 runs between Marsalforn and Victoria (10 minutes, hourly), and on to Xlendi (30 minutes). Bus 322 travels to/from Mġarr (38 minutes, every 1½ hours) via Ramla Bay (15 minutes) and Xagħra (25 minutes).

Xagħra

POP 4015

The pretty village of Xagħra (*shaa*-ra) spreads across the flat summit of the hill east of Victoria. The 19th-century Church of Our Lady of Victory looks down benignly on the tree-lined Pjazza Vittorja, where old men sit and chat in the shade of the oleanders – there's always something gossip-worthy going on in the village square.

⊙ Sights & Activities

Ġgantija Temples   ARCHAEOLOGICAL SITE
(☑2155 3194; access from Triq I-Imqades; adult/child €5/2.50 incl admission to Ta'Kola Windmill; ⊙9am-5pm) Perched on the crest of the hill to the south of Xagħra, the megalithic Ġgantija Temples command a splendid view over most of southern Gozo and beyond to Comino and Malta. As the name implies (*ġgantija* – dje-gant-ee-ya – means 'giantess'), these are the largest of the megalithic temples found on the Maltese Islands – the walls stand over 6m high, and the two temples together span over 40m.

Along with Ta'Ħaġrat and Skorba in Malta, the Ġgantija Temples are thought to be Malta's oldest, dating from the period 3600 BC to 3000 BC. Both temples face towards the southeast, and both have five semicircular niches within. The south temple (on the left) is the older, and is entered across a huge threshold slab with four holes at each side, thought to be for libations. The first niche on the right contains an altar with some spiral decoration – there was once a pillar here with a snake carved on it, but the pillar now lives in Victoria's Archaeology Museum. The left-hand niche in the inner chamber has a well-preserved trilithon altar; on the right is a circular hearth stone and a bench altar.

The outer wall of the later north temple complex is particularly impressive in scale. The largest of the megaliths measures 6m by 4m and weighs around 57 tonnes, and the

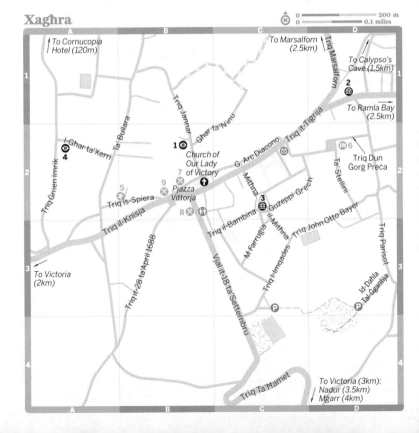

Xagħra

wall may originally have stood up to 16m tall – it's incredible to contemplate how these huge stones were put in place. The exterior walls were built of harder-wearing coralline limestone, while the interiors were built of the lighter globigerina limestone – brought here from around a kilometre away.

Heritage Malta has set up a small 'info pod' giving a short audio narration on the temples in a half-dozen different languages. Tours are also available in English, Italian and Malti.

Xerri's Grotto & Ninu's Cave CAVE
In the back streets to the north of the village square lie **Xerri's Grotto** (☑2156 0572; l'Għar ta'Xerri; adult/child €2.50/1; ☺9am-4pm daily, to 6pm Jun-Aug) and **Ninu's Cave** (Triq Jannar; admission €2). These fun underground caverns, complete with stalactites and stalagmites, are unusual in that they are both entered through private houses. Having discovered the caves beneath their homes, the owners decided to cash in on the tourist potential. Xerri's Grotto was discovered in 1923 when Antonio Xerri was digging a well. It's the bigger, deeper and more interesting of the two.

Pomskizillious Museum of Toys MUSEUM
(☑2156 2489; Triq Ġnien Xibla; adult/child €2.80/1.50; ☺10.30am-1pm Thu-Sat Apr & Oct-Nov, 10.30am-1pm Mon-Sat May, 10.30am-1pm & 4-6pm daily Jun-Sep, 10.30am-1pm Sat Oct-Mar) This small labour of love has an impressive array of 19th-century and 1930s doll's houses, toy soldiers, and creepy-looking china dolls, mostly in glass cases. There's a display case

---

Xaghra

◉ Sights

---

devoted to nonsense poet Edward Lear, who coined the word 'pomskizillious' to describe Gozitan scenery.

Ta'Kola Windmill HISTORIC BUILDING
(☑2156 1071; Triq il-Bambina; adult/child €5/2.50 incl admission to Ġgantija Temples; ☺9am-5pm) Built in 1725 at the instigation of the Knights who built many such windmills to encourage the production of flour (this is one of the few left standing), it now houses a museum of country life, with exhibits of woodworking tools, farm equipment and period bedroom and living quarters. Climb up the narrow stairs to see the original milling gear, complete with millstones.

Calypso's Cave CAVE
Signposts near the Pomskizillious Museum of Toys point the way through the maze of minor roads east of Xaghra down to Calypso's Cave, overlooking the sandy beach of Ramla Bay (p125) – it's a 30-minute walk from the village square. The cave itself is hardly worth the hike – it's just a hollow under an overhang at the top of the cliff – but the view is lovely. On a calm day visitors can usually see the remains of an artificial reef extending into the sea off the eastern headland of the bay. This was part of the defences built by the Knights of St John to prevent attackers landing on the beach. In theory, the enemy ships would run aground on the reef, where they would be attacked using primitive mortarlike weapons.

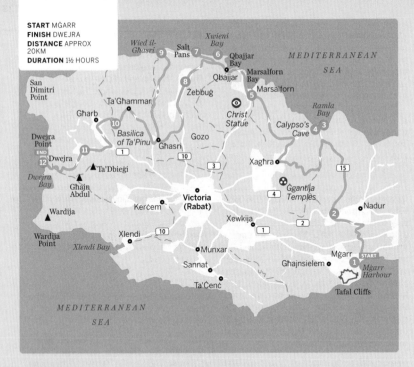

START MĠARR	
FINISH DWEJRA	
DISTANCE APPROX 20KM	
DURATION 1½ HOURS	

Driving Tour
Northern Gozo

❭ This drive takes in some of Gozo's loveliest scenery. Begin at the port of ① **Mġarr**, then take Triq Sant Antnin uphill towards ② **Nadur**, perched on a hilltop and with great views from its modified watchtower. From Nadur, take the road through lovely countryside towards ③ **Ramla Bay**. When you reach the bay, stop for a look and perhaps a paddle, then on leaving take the first right-hand-turn. You'll drive through a landscape of terraced fields and copper-coloured walls. On reaching the next junction, if you take the right-hand fork, you can drive round to ④ **Calypso's Cave** for a great view over the bay. Next, double back the way you came, taking the second right turn into Triq Tal-Masri, which will lead you down to Gozo's largest (yet still low-key) resort, ⑤ **Marsalforn**. Drive along the seafront and then take the coastal road. This will lead you to ⑥ **Xwieni Bay**, which is overlooked by the scooped-out, photogenic ⑦ **salt pans**. From here, take the road inland to the village of ⑧ **Żebbuġ** (the name means 'olives'), which is famous for

the onyx found locally (check out the decoration of the Parish church) and for lacemaking. Next drive around to visit the breathtaking gorge and bay of ⑨ **Wied Il-Għasri**. Head back at Għasri village and take Triq il Fanal towards the dramatically isolated pilgrim age ⑩ **Basilica of Ta'Pinu**. From here, take the road towards the pretty village of ⑪ **St Lawrenz** before finishing your drive at ⑫ **Dwejra**, an area featuring some of Gozo's most stunning coastal formations.

Lino's Stables HORSE RIDING
(☎2156 2477; www.linostables.com; 16 Triq is-Spiera) These stables offer one-/two-hour horse rides to Marsalforn for €15/30 for both beginners and more experienced riders. Children over 10 may ride their own horse, but younger children can ride with their accompanying adult or in a gig.

✖ Eating

Oleander MALTESE €€
(☎2155 7230; Pjazza Vittorja; mains €14-18; ⊙lunch & dinner Tue-Sun) The much-loved Oleander, located on the pretty village square, has reopened under its original management and has a new menu specialising in Maltese cooking, with dishes including rabbit cooked in various ways, homemade ravioli with Gozitan cheese, and fresh fish of the day.

D-Venue MEDITERRANEAN €€
(☎7955 7230; www.dvenuerestaurant.com; Pjazza Vittorja; €11-17.50; ⊙lunch & dinner Tue-Sun) D-Venue has a contemporary look and a great glass-covered terrace on the first floor. Food is equally stylish, with choices like spaghetti with prawns and rocket, calamari and rabbit.

M&M SELF CATERING
(Vjal it-18 Ta'Settembru; ⊙6am-7pm Mon-Sat) For those who prefer to picnic or self-cater, there's a handy minimarket just south of the square.

❶ Getting There & Away

Bus 307 runs between Victoria and Xagħra (10 minutes, hourly). Bus 322 connects the town with Marsalforn (13 minutes, every 1½ hours), Ramla Bay (10 minutes) and Mġarr (25 minutes).

Nadur

POP 4200

Nadur is Gozo's 'second city', spreading along a high ridge to the east of Victoria. In Malti, Nadur means 'lookout', and a 17th-century watchtower overlooks the Comino sea lanes from the western end of the ridge.

◎ Sights

Church of Saints Peter & Paul CHURCH
(Pjazza San Pietru u San Pawl) Nadur's ornate Church of Saints Peter & Paul was built in the late 18th century – the entrance is framed by white statues of the two saints, giving the church its local nickname of *iż-Żewġ* (the pair). The interior is richly deco-rated with marble sculptures, and the vault is covered with 150 paintings.

Kelinu Grima Maritime Museum MUSEUM
(☎2156 5226; Triq il-Kappillan; adult/child €2.50/1.25; ⊙9am-4.45pm Mon-Sat) Kelinu Grima Maritime Museum is a charming and worthwhile private collection of ship models, relics and maritime memorabilia.

✖ Eating

Nadur is famous for its delicious *ftira* (Maltese bread) and pizza, sold at the fantastic **Mekrens** (☎21552342; Triq Hanaq; pizza from €3.50) and **Maxokk** (☎21550014; maxokkbakery. com; Triq San Ġakbu; pizza from €3.50; ⊙10am-7pm Mon-Sat, from 1pm Sun) bakeries. Meals are sold as takeaways, so it's best to call around 30 minutes' ahead to order.

❶ Getting There & Away

To get to Nadur, take bus 322, which runs from Mġarr (seven minutes), and goes on to Ramla (eight minutes), Xagħra (18 minutes) and Marsalforn (21 minutes).

Ramla Bay, San Blas Bay & Daħlet Qorrot

◎ Sights

Ramla Bay BEACH
(Ir-Ramla) Ramla Bay is the biggest and best sandy beach on Gozo, and one of the prettiest on the islands – the strand of reddish-gold contrasts picturesquely with the blue of the sea and white statue of the Virgin Mary. As such, it is usually heaving with people in summer, when cafes, souvenir stalls and watersports facilities abound. It is much quieter and more pleasant in spring and autumn, and in winter you can have the place almost to your (goose-pimpled) self. The minimal remains of a Roman villa are hidden among the bamboo behind the beach, and Calypso's Cave (p123) looks down from the hilltop to the west. Ramla Bay is also easily accessed (on foot or by car) from Xagħra.

Bus 322 travels to Ramla Bay from Mġarr (38 minutes, every 1½ hours) and on to Marsalforn (15 minutes) and Xagħra (25 minutes).

San Blas Bay BEACH
San Blas, a tiny, rock-strewn bay with some patches of coarse, rust-coloured sand, is backed by steep, terraced fields with prickly-pear hedges. It's a lovely place to take a picnic

lunch and a good book, and perhaps a mask and fins for snorkelling – the water is quite shallow and very clear. There are no facilities here, and there's parking space for only a handful of cars at the beginning of the very narrow track above the bay – it's a steep walk down to it.

You can walk to San Blas from Nadur in about 30 minutes; it's just over 2.5km from town (take Triq San Blas off Triq it-Tiġrija, two blocks north of Nadur's church).

Daħlet Qorrot
BEACH

Attractive Daħlet Qorrot is popular with local weekenders. There's a tiny gravel beach, but most of the swimming is off the rocks beside the rows of little boathouses (carved out of the rock, and with brightly painted doors); there's usually plenty of space to park. A turn-off en route to San Blas leads to

Daħlet Qorrot is within walking distance of Nadur: from Triq it-Tiġrija, head north for about 300m on Triq San Blas, then take the Triq Daħlet Qorrot turnoff; the bay is just over 2km away.

Qala

The village of Qala (a-la) has little to see except for a couple of 18th-century windmills. The road east of the village square (Triq il-Kunċizzjoni) leads down to the coast at Ħondoq ir-Rummien, a popular swimming cove with a scrap of sand, bathing ladders on the rocks and benches with a view across the water to Comino. There are toilets here and a kiosk catering to sunbathers.

COMINO

POP 4

Comino (Kemmuna in Malti) is a small, barren chunk of limestone wedged smack-bang between Malta and Gozo. It was once reportedly the hideout of pirates and smugglers, and its remoteness saw it used as a place of isolation for cholera and plague victims in the early 19th century. The almost empty island – there's just one hotel here – is a breathtakingly beautiful place, ringed by caves and sea cliffs. It's home to the Blue Lagoon, one of Malta's loveliest but also most-visited natural attractions. In summer, hordes of day-trippers descend from Malta

and Gozo, but in spring, autumn and winter, you have a better chance of enjoying the turquoise waters.

Comino is only 2.5km by 1.5km. It's a nature reserve and bird sanctuary, and free of cars; away from the hotel and the Blue Lagoon the island is peaceful and unspoilt. A walk along the rough tracks affords some great views of northern Malta and of Gozo. It's impossible to get lost here.

The main part of the Comino Hotel is on San Niklaw Bay, and the Comino Hotel Bungalows are on Santa Marija Bay, 500m to the east. Triq Congreve, a rough track lined with oleander trees, runs from Santa Marija Bay south to St Mary's Tower. Side tracks lead to the Blue Lagoon and San Niklaw Bay.

The only buildings of note are the stark little Chapel of Our Lady's Return from Egypt, built in 1618, at Santa Marija Bay and the fortified St Mary's Tower (☑2122 5222; admisson €2.50), built by the Knights in the same year. It was once part of the chain of signal towers between Gozo and Mdina. At the time of research, St Mary's Tower was being restored and was closed to the public; you can still climb the steps and enjoy the views.

◉ Sights

Blue Lagoon
LAGOON

Comino's biggest attraction is the Blue Lagoon, a sheltered cove between the western end of the island and the uninhabited islet of Cominotto (Kemmunett in Malti). It's incredibly beautiful and inviting: a white-sand seabed and clear waters. The blue is so intense it's as if you've stepped into an over-saturated postcard. The southern end of the lagoon is roped off to keep boats out; there is top-notch swimming and snorkelling here, plus you can swim over to Cominotto.

However, in summer the bay's charms are almost obscured, such as the numbers of people, and the constant stream of boats. It's busiest daily between around 10am and 4pm; if you're staying at the hotel, of course, you can enjoy the lagoon in relative peace in the early morning and late afternoon.

Take care in the unrelenting summer heat – there is no shade here, and most sunbathing is done on the exposed rocky ledges surrounding the cove. There are public toilets and a few kiosks selling cool drinks, ice creams and snacks (eg burgers, hot dogs and sandwiches). Deckchairs (per day €3) and umbrellas (€5) can be hired for extended luxurious lazing about.

ℹ Getting There & Away

Numerous companies operate trips to Comino from Mġarr on Gozo. Return tickets for adults are €8 to €12 and for children €4 to €5 – the more expensive rate includes a quick whizz around the island's caves.

Independent water taxis also operate regularly to the island from the ports Mġarr and Ċirkewwa – from Mġarr it's usually €8 to €10 return, and from Ċirkewwa it's €10 to €12 return. Sightseeing trips operate to the Blue Lagoon from tourist areas like Sliema, Buġibba and Golden Bay in Malta, and Xlendi and Marsalforn in Gozo.

If you'd like to visit the Blue Lagoon from Malta without the crowds, take advantage of the trip leaving at 4pm from Golden Bay with Charlie's Discovery Speedboat Trips (p72).

Accommodation

Includes »

Best Places to Stay

» Palazzo Vittoriosa (p131)
» Hotel Juliani (p133)
» Xara Palace (p135)
» Hotel Ta'Ċenċ (p136)

Best Atmospheric Apartments

» Palazzo San Pawl (p130)
» Valletta Suites (p130)
» Indulgence Divine (p132)
» Valletta G-House (p130)

Best Rural Escapes

» Thirtyseven (p137)
» Hotel Ta'Ċenċ (p136)
» Kempinski Hotel (San Lawrenz; p138)
» Comino Hotels (p139)

Where to Stay

There has long been a wealth of accommodation on the Maltese Islands, but it's now increasing in variety, particularly in and around the capital Valletta, which has lately gained some inviting boutique apartments and hotels. Birgu (Vittoriosa), across the harbour from the capital, is also an extremely attractive base and has several new handsome, characterful options.

If you're after a beach holiday, you'll probably want to aim for the main resort towns on the northern coast, such as St Julian's, Buġibba and Mellieħa. These predominantly tourist-oriented towns are crammed with fairly uniform resort hotels and apartments, but places are often well appointed, sometimes with great sea views, and there are some budget gems.

Another option is to stay inland, where you'll feel more in touch with Maltese culture, in the atmospheric towns of Mdina, Rabat or Naxxar.

The islands are so small that wherever you base yourself you'll be in relatively easy reach of destinations all over the island. This is particularly true if you hire a car, though the new Arriva bus network is also extremely efficient. The only fly in the transportation ointment is the traffic, which can be heavy.

Great alternatives to hotels, especially for families, are self-catering converted apartments or houses, and there are various options dotted all over Malta. On Gozo it's highly recommended that you rent a farmhouse for the duration of your stay.

Pricing

The price indicators in this book refer to the cost of a double room in high season, including private bathroom and breakfast unless otherwise noted.

CATEGORY	COST
€ Budget	less than €60
€€ Midrange	€60 to €140
€€€ Top End	more than €140

Camping

There is only one camping ground in Malta, on the Marfa Peninsula in northwest Malta, but it suffers from shadeless grounds. You'll need your own transport to get to this remote location.

Guesthouses

Guesthouses in Malta are usually small, simple, family-run places and are good value at around €20 to €30 per person. Most rooms will have a washbasin, but showers and toilets are often shared. A simple breakfast is normally included in the price. Facilities will usually not include air-con or a swimming pool, but there are a few exceptions. Bear in mind that some guesthouses in resort areas close in the low season (but guesthouses in Valletta open year-round).

Hostels

The National Student Travel Service (p50) is an associate member of Hostelling International (HI), and operates the well-located Hibernia Residence & Hostel (Malta's only true hostel), in Sliema.

Hotels

Hotels in Malta range from quaint, homely guesthouses to modern gilt-and-chrome five-star palaces overlooking private marinas on the coast. The majority (especially somewhere like Buġibba) are bland, faceless, tourist hotels, block-booked by package tour companies in summer, and closed or eerily quiet in winter. However, there is an increasing number of places to stay in Malta that have real character and style, such as Palazzo Vittoriosa, Indulgence Divine, Palazzo San Pawl, Xara Palace; and Thirtyseven, Kempinski Hotel San Lawrenz and Hotel Ta'Ċenċ on Gozo.

Most of the large four- and five-star places offer the kind of holiday where you may not need to leave the hotel's grounds – they're fully equipped with cafes, bars and restaurants (most hotels include breakfast in their rates, and some offer half-board and full-board arrangements). At these places you'll usually find indoor and outdoor pools; a gym and/or sporting facilities; a program of children's activities; and quite possibly a health spa, a dive company and perhaps a beachside lido offering a pool and watersports, including water-skiing, boat trips, canoe or boat hire and ringo rides (large rubber rings towed by speedboats).

Three-star hotels can feel a little like going back in time, but usually offer rooms with bathroom and air-conditioning, and, increasingly, free wifi.

Loads of internet sites offer information on hotels and other accommodation options in Malta, including Holiday Malta (www.holiday-malta.com) and Malta Hotels (www.malta-hotels.com).

Rental Accommodation

The most atmospheric way to stay in self-catering accommodation on the islands is to rent a farmhouse on Gozo. These are usually several hundred years old and are often beautiful rental properties with swimming pools and garden courtyards. However, although they are usually called 'farmhouses', they are often town houses, where livestock were once kept in the basement or outhouses – so don't expect them necessarily to be in the open countryside. For more information see the boxed text, p137. You can also occasionally find characterful self-catering townhouses or apartments on Malta – search sites such as www.ownersdirect.co.uk to find what's available.

However, it must be said that there are also hundreds of self-catering apartments with little to choose between them. Most have a private bathroom, a balcony and a kitchen area with fridge, sink and two-ring electric cooker. Though lacking a little in charm, they are often good value at under €30 per person, even in high season.

High & Low Seasons

The cost of accommodation in Malta can vary considerably according to the time of year, and low-season rates can be a bargain – often around half the high-season price. Low season is almost always November to March. High season generally refers to the period April to October, but some accommodation providers have a 'shoulder' or 'mid' season covering from April, May and October, with high-season prices restricted to July and August (plus Easter and Christmas). The high- and low-season prices quoted are generally the maximum and minimum rates for each establishment. Some cheaper places don't vary their prices much across the year.

Bear in mind that certain places (small guesthouses and cheaper hotels) in some resort areas close in the low season – as does Comino Hotels, making a stay on Comino impossible from November to March.

ACCOMMODATION

BOOK YOUR STAY ONLINE

For more accommodation reviews by Lonely Planet authors, check out hotels.lonelyplanet.com/malta. You'll find independent reviews, as well as recommendations on the best places to stay. Best of all, you can book online.

VALLETTA & AROUND

There is an increasing number of atmospheric places to stay, both in Valletta and across the water in Vittoriosa/Birgu. This is the best place in Malta to be based if you're more interested in history and culture than a beach holiday. The main museums and attractions are within easy walking distance, and buses depart from Valletta terminus to all parts of the island.

Many places offer discounts on stays of seven days or longer – it's always worth asking. Some also offer half-board and full-board options: these are usually reasonable value, but you're better off with the freedom to eat wherever you like.

Valletta

TOP CHOICE **Valletta G-House** APARTMENT €€
(Map p40; ☑7981 5145; www.vallettahouse.com; Triq it-Tramuntana; apt for two €89-95, min 7 nights; 🐾)
You'll need to book early to snare time at this sumptuous apartment (no children). The artistic owner has restored a 16th-century, character-filled town house to offer wonderfully romantic self-catering accommodation within its limestone walls. The entrance area doubles as a small sitting room, with TV and DVD (classic movies provided). Downstairs is a rustic, low-ceilinged cellar kitchen and a small, modern bathroom. On the first level is the apartment's pièce de résistance – the large and luxurious bedroom, which includes a sitting area, traditional Maltese enclosed balcony and striking floor tiles. Books, CDs, artwork, tapestries, fresh flowers and fine linen round out the picture beautifully. Prices include airport transfers and a welcome basket of local produce.

TOP CHOICE **Palazzo San Pawl** APARTMENT €€
(Map p40; ☑9942 3110; www.livinginvalletta.com; 318 Triq San Pawl; d €80-90; 🐾) Palazzo San Pawl is housed in a beautifully restored 17th-century mansion, and offers three graceful suites – 'Hompesch', 'Pinto' (with a traditional Maltese balcony) and ground-floor 'del Monte'. They give on to the courtyard in the main building, and each has a sitting room and kitchenette. Decor is elegant, ceilings are high, and there's a lift to take you up to the roof terrace for stunning views across the Valletta rooftops and the harbour – sunbeds and BBQ facilities are supplied. There's also another suite in the building next door, 'Vilhena', with three 12 sq m rooms atop each other (which could be stuffy in summer). Other treats include LCD TV and DVD, cable TV, bathrobes, a welcome pack and an open fireplace. In the basement is a newly converted cellar suite, a cool if somewhat underground place to stay, which can be rented for a bargain €50 per night.

Valletta Suites APARTMENT €€
(☑7948 8047; www.vallettasuites.com; apt per night €98, min 3-4 nights) These are two beautifully designed, boutique one-bedroom apartments with all mod cons. Maison La Vallette is handy for both central Valletta and the ferry to Sliema; Valletta Nobile is in the further flung northeastern part of town. Both are in 400-year-old stone buildings with original wooden beams and a scattering of antique furniture – and Nobile has a balcony with a view along Triq il-Merkanti. Both also come with modern fitted kitchens, iPod-compatible sound systems and flatscreen TVs.

Valletta Suites - Lucia Nova APARTMENT €€
(Map p40; ☑7948 8047; www.lucianova.com; 88 Triq Santa Luċija; 2-4 people €98-125, min 3 nights) Lucia Nova offers a large apartment, with two double bedrooms, sitting room and roof terrace. Each room is atop the other, and all are connected by the traditional Maltese spiral stone staircase. The decor is a thrilling mix of distressed original wall coverings, Philippe Starck chairs and silk Venetian headboards.

Asti Guesthouse GUESTHOUSE €
(Map p40; ☑2123 9506; http://mol.net.mt/asti; 18 Triq Sant'Orsla; r per person with shared bathroom from €20) You'll get a taste of old-school Valletta charm here plus some of the best-value accommodation in town. This classy, 350-year-old town house features huge, airy guest rooms and gleaming shared bathrooms. It's run by a lovely lady and has a simple elegance – breakfast is served in a cheery, plant-filled room with a vaulted ceiling and

chandelier. Up the stairs on various levels are eight large rooms, each with two or three beds, fuss-free wooden furniture and a washbasin. Plants, wall hangings and ornaments adorn the halls, lending a warm and homely feel. Book well ahead.

Grand Hotel Excelsior
HOTEL €€

(off Map p40; ☑2125 0520; www.excelsior.com.mt; Triq I-Assedju I-Kbir; r from €120; ✳@☎☁) The Grand lies outside the city walls, tucked beneath the northwestern bastions. It's a curvaceous concrete block; sea-front rooms have balconies with fabulous views over Marsamxett Harbour; the less expensive rooms overlook the gardens or hotel plaza. Rooms are decorated in plush beiges calculated not to offend, and the hotel's five-star rating is particularly evident through its staff, service and food.

Osborne Hotel
HOTEL €€

(Map p40; ☑2124 3656; www.osbornehotel.com; 50 Triq Nofs in-Nhar; s/d low season €48/65, high season €60/90; ✳@☎) The Osborne fills a notable lower-midrange accommodation gap in Valletta. It has a smart, red-shuttered exterior. The lower-level 'superior' rooms feature pale, streamlined furnishings and decent storage space, plus flatscreen TVs as a mark of modernity. As you move up the building, the furniture grows darker and the fittings more dated. Soundproofing can be an issue, but there's cable TV and rooms with views are available. On the 6th floor there's a roof terrace with city views and a tiny splash pool.

Castille Hotel
HOTEL €€

(Map p40; ☑2124 3678; www.hotelcastillemalta.com; Pjazza Kastilja; s/tw low season €45/90, high season €65/130; ✳☁) Castille has a number of points in its favour – not least its cheerful front-desk staff and its grand position in an old palazzo next to the ornate 16th-century Auberge de Castile. The hotel's small lobby and lounge make a good first impression, while guestrooms have a more faded charm and feature heavy Italianate furnishings. Decent-sized single rooms are available for solo travellers. Request a room at the front of the building for better light and views of the square. There's a fun pizzeria, La Cave, in the basement, and the rooftop restaurant for breakfast or dinner with a view over Grand Harbour.

British Hotel
HOTEL €€

(Map p40; ☑2122 4730; www.britishhotel.com; 40 Triq il-Batterija; s/d €40/70, d with sea view €80-

90; ✳@☎☁) Large parts of the 2005 movie *Munich* were filmed in Malta, and when location scouts wanted a 1970s-styled hotel, they chose the British – and barely needed to do a thing to it. The decor in the foyer, the TV room and the bar is so dated it has a retro-cool feel. The hotel has its pros and cons – on the plus side it's affordable, welcoming and well located; it enjoys great views over the harbour and the Three Cities; and the rooms have been refreshed and smartened up. The minuses: said rooms are basic; it's a real rabbit warren; and air-con costs €7 per day. It's worth paying extra for a view.

Valletta Apartments
APARTMENT €

(Map p40; ☑7766 7777; Flat 6, 51 Triq I-Ifran; 4-5 person apt €50-70) This place consists of three basic apartments in central Valletta. If you're travelling in a group, this is an inexpensive and spacious – if somewhat gloomy – choice. Facilities include a self-catering kitchen, a lounge and left luggage, and reception is open 9am to 10pm. By the time you read this, it may also offer dorm accommodation.

Floriana

Phoenicia Hotel
HOTEL €€€

(Map p52; ☑2122 5241; www.phoeniciamalta.com; Il-Mall; r from €140; ✳✳☁) Just outside Valletta's main gate, this grand old dame feels like a relic from another era – the kind of place Miss Marple might stay if she were in town, with its potted palms and piano bar. Built in the late 1940s and retaining many original art-deco features, it is one of Malta's most historic hotels – in 1949, Princess Elizabeth (soon to be queen) and Prince Philip danced in the ballroom here. Some rooms are refurbished, some somewhat faded; a worthwhile higher rate gets you views of Marsamxett Harbour or Valletta's city walls. Facilities include 24-hour room service, free car parking, a business centre, lush 7-acre gardens, a heated outdoor pool, a bar, a brasserie and a restaurant.

Vittoriosa

TOP CHOICE / Palazzo Vittoriosa
BOUTIQUE HOTEL €€€

(Map p54; ☑9984 1163; www.palazzovittoriosa.com; 54-56 Triq Hilda Tabone; d from €350; ✳☎☁) There's no other hotel like this on Malta. The Dutch owners have renovated an ancient

ACCOMMODATION FLORIANA

auberge to create a designer three-suite place (the largest suite is 150 sq m), centred on a courtyard, with one-off chandeliers, natural-fibre mattresses imported specially from Greece, an in-room iPad, and a rooftop infinity pool with glorious views over to Valletta. Staff plan to run cooking courses from the rooftop kitchen-with-a-view. There are several sitting rooms and terraces.

TOP CHOICE Indulgence Divine — APARTMENT €€

(Map p54; ☑+44 781 3988827; www.indulgence divine.com; Triq Allesandru VII; apt €95-109, min 5 nights; ☎) This sumptuous and historic self-catering apartment (no children) is a romantic base, and you get lots of space for your money. It's a 16th-century town house for two, tucked away in a Birgu backstreet, that's been decorated with flamboyant shots of colour. It comprises a funky white-and-orange kitchen, a dining area with a pale blue Murano glass chandelier, a coolly minimalist living room, and a sunny roof terrace with chairs and table. The en suite has a double shower, the bed is king-size and overhung by a grand tapestry canopy, and you can also make the most of the flat-screen TV, iPod dock and a welcome pack.

Knight's Quarter — HOUSE €

(Map p54; ☑2137 0830; 8 Triq Gilormu; per week €400; ☎) This lovely little house in Birgu's most photographed street is a bargain to rent, with two bedrooms, a living room (with TV, internet, DVD player, books, board games, DVDs), a dining room with kitchenette and a roof terrace (sun beds, chairs, tables and BBQ) with a sea view. There's underfloor heating, a washing machine and a tumble dryer, and the walls are decked with original artworks from local artists or international artists with a Maltese theme. Prices include wifi and all bills. You'll need to book well ahead.

SLIEMA, ST JULIAN'S & PACEVILLE

Most of the accommodation here is pitched for the package-holiday and luxury-hotel market; there are some bargains to be had during the low season. Only the most upmarket places tend to offer parking for guests; enquire at your hotel about local parking opportunities.

Sliema

Palace Hotel — HOTEL €€

(Map p62; ☑2133 3444; www.thepalacemalta.com; Triq Il-Kbira; r from €125; ☀@☎☷) If this modern boutique-style hotel's stylish designer bedrooms with all the trimmings aren't good enough for you, try the sumptuous 'concept suites' – six suites each designed around a different theme, including a 'Music Suite' complete with functioning drum kit and other instruments (yes, it's soundproofed!). Facilities include a luxurious spa with indoor pool, and a roof terrace with outdoor pool that commands a superb view across the Sliema rooftops to the bastions of Valletta. There are also five old palace–style 'palazzo' suites, housed in the 200-year-old Palazzo Capua, four of which are duplex.

Waterfront Hotel — HOTEL €€

(Map p62; ☑2133 3434; www.waterfronthotel malta.com; Triq ix-Xatt; r from €100; ☀☎☷) The bright and breezy Waterfront, circa 2000, has a nautically themed lobby, blue-and-white rooms and a rooftop pool and terrace with excellent panoramas across the harbour. Plus it's in a nice location on the Sliema waterfront. It's worth paying the €10 or so extra for a sea-view room.

Victoria Hotel — HOTEL €€

(Map p62; ☑2133 4711; www.victoriahotel.com; Triq Ġorġ Borg Olivier; r from €90; ☀@☎☷) This neo-Victorian hotel's lobby and bar are full of dark wood and leather club sofas – it's not exactly Victorian, but the thought is there. Some rooms are equipped with mahogany furniture, some with pale blue painted wood. The hotel is in a quiet location away from the seafront, and features a rooftop pool, plus a small indoor pool on the seventh floor.

Imperial Hotel — HOTEL €€

(Map p62; ☑2134 4093; www.imperialhotelmalta. com; Triq Rudolfu; s low/high season €30/70, d €40/110; ☀☎☷) Things move rather slowly at the Imperial, in keeping with the old-world interior (it dates from 1865) and vintage patrons. It's tucked away in the heart of residential Sliema, and inside you'll be impressed by the lobby's chandelier and grand sweeping staircase. The rooms don't quite live up to the expectations raised by downstairs, but they're comfortable and well equipped (you'll pay more for a garden/pool view and a balcony). Facilities include a courtyard garden and restaurant. There's access for guests with disabilities. Pay a bit extra for a view.

NSTS Hibernia Residence & Hostel

HOSTEL €

(Map p62; ☎2558 6000; www.nsts.org; Triq Mons G Depiro; dm €8-13, tw studio €42-76; @) Malta's only true hostel, the Hibernia proffers quality budget accommodation and a ready-made crowd (it's popular with English-language students). As well as a comprehensive roll-call of facilities inside this modern, seven-storey building (laundry, internet cafe, breakfast room/cafeteria, TV lounge, rooftop sun terrace, good security), there's a choice of sleeping options. Shoestringers can camp out in the single-sex dorm sections, where three to four bedrooms (each with six to eight beds) share bathrooms and a generous kitchen-dining area. Long-stayers or travellers after more privacy can choose a B&B studio or apartment in the 'residence'. These sleep up to four and have their own kitchenette and en suite.

Pebbles ApartHotel

APARTMENTS €€

(Map p62; ☎2131 1889; www.pebblesaparthotel.com; 89 Triq ix-Xatt; d low/high season €60/93; ❅@☎) This complex of 93 great-value studio apartments, decorated in cool greys and whites, is handy for the bus terminus and the ferry to Valletta. It's not for the claustrophobic – don't expect a lot of living space, but do expect some value for your money: all studios have a private bathroom, kitchenette, phone and flatscreen cable TV (the most expensive studios enjoy a sea view). At ground level is a cafe-bar, and there's a sun terrace on the roof. Breakfast is not included and there's a charge for internet and wifi.

Preluna Hotel & Spa

HOTEL €€

(Map p62; ☎2133 4001; www.preluna-hotel.com; 124 Triq it-Torri; d low/high season from €88/96; ❅@☎☒) Malta's tallest hotel commands views along the coast, attracting plenty of Euro holidaymakers. The attractive lobby and obliging staff create a good first impression; rooms are small but bright and fresh, and facilities are exhaustive (health spa, private beachfront lido, dive school and a choice of bars and restaurants). Superior rooms aren't all that much better than standard rooms but are worth it for the sea view and balcony.

Paceville

TOP CHOICE Hotel Valentina

HOTEL €€

(Map p66; ☎2138 2232; www.hotelvalentina.com; Triq Schreiber; s €50-110, d €55-115; ❅☎) This is a small and appealing choice, tucked away in a relatively quiet Paceville backstreet. Prices at split-personality Valentina are shockingly reasonable. There's a boutique feel about the place, but while older rooms have a bright, rustic feel; newer rooms have clean, contemporary lines and splashes of vivid colour. The bright lobby has a small, buzzing cafe.

Ir-Rokna Hotel

HOTEL €€

(Map p66; ☎2138 4060; www.roknahotel.com; Triq il-Knisja; s from €55, d from €75; ❅☎) Stay within spitting distance of the treats of the glitzy Portomaso marina, but a long way from the Hilton price tag. You're also close to the nightlife, but far enough away from the noise. Ir-Rokna is decent value, and while the rooms are time-worn and bland, the service is friendly and the hotel is home to Malta's oldest pizzeria (mains €7 to €9).

Tropicana Hotel

HOTEL €

(Map p66; ☎2135 9694; www.tropicana.com.mt; Triq Ball; s low/high season from €14/25, d from €22/40; ❅@) Dirt-cheap and in the heart of Paceville, this hotel feels more like a hostel, with small, dark but clean rooms (with facilities including private bathroom, air-con and sometimes-working TV). It's nothing fancy and its party-district location means it's a bit noisy, but for this price, who's complaining?

St Julian's

TOP CHOICE Hotel Juliani

BOUTIQUE HOTEL €€

(Map p66; ☎2138 8000; www.hoteljuliani.com; 12 Triq San Ġorġ; d from €70; ❅@☎☒) This 44-room boutique town house is housed in a restored seafront town house overlooking Spinola Bay, and has chic guestrooms, hued in chocolate brown and pale blue, and equipped with large flatscreen TVs. It's worth paying extra for a more spacious room with a sea view (these come with a jacuzzi), but there's no beating the views from the rooftop pool and terrace. There's an excellent restaurant, Zest (p64), and a cafe.

NORTHWEST MALTA

Buġibba, Qawra & St Paul's Bay

San Antonio Hotel & Spa HOTEL €€€
(Map p80; ☑2158 3434; www.sanantonio-malta.
com; Triq it-Turisti; s/d low season from €80/100,
high season €180/200; ✳@≋) With a Med-
themed, whitewashed exterior and colourful, light-filled lobby, this is one of Buġibba's
best hotels. The high standards carry
through to the restaurants, the pool, the
Moroccan-style spa and the garden areas
as well as the well-kitted-out rooms, simply
furnished with terracotta tiles set against
turquoise and green fabrics.

Dolmen Resort Hotel HOTEL €€
(Map p80; ☑2355 2355; www.dolmen.com.mt;
Triq il-Merluzz; r low/high season from €40/102;
✳@≋) This huge and plush waterfront hotel
has the unique combination of a casino
and its very own prehistoric temple on the
grounds. Rooms are lush-looking yet pleasingly plainly decorated, and some have great
sea views – it's worth paying extra to overlook the ocean. Creature comforts include
four outdoor swimming pools (one solely
for kids), sports facilities, a health spa, an
excellent beach club and a bevy of bars and
restaurants. It draws a mixed international
clientele, from Euro-package families to
older, gambling-focused travellers.

Mediterranea Hotel & Suites HOTEL €€
(Map p80; ☑2157 1118; www.mediterraneahotel
malta.com; Triq Buġibba; tw low/high season
€61/75, 1-bedroom apt low/high season €65/100;
✳@≋) The Mediterranea offers decent
hotel rooms and spacious self-catering studios and apartments (one-/two-bedroom
sleeping up to four/six), with full kitchens. The rustic decor gives it some edge,
with plenty of polished timber and arched
windows. There is a rooftop pool and gym,
and a restaurant, and it's in a good location high above the bay close to St Paul's
Bay village.

Buccaneers Guesthouse GUESTHOUSE €
(Map p80; ☑2157 1671; www.buccaneers.com.
mt; Triq Ġulju; B&B per person €18-20; ✳≋)
This friendly, well-run guesthouse is nicely small scale, with just 30 rooms, and is
surprisingly decent at a bargain price (if
you're on a shoestring budget, the princely
sum of €22 to €24 gets you dinner, bed

and breakfast). Rooms are large, clean and
well equipped – all with phone, air-con and
private shower and washbasin (toilets are
shared). There's a sun terrace on the roof
with a pool that resembles an oversized paddling pool, and a lively bar and restaurant
downstairs.

Sunseeker Holiday Complex APARTMENTS €
(Map p80; ☑2157 5619; www.sunseekerholiday
complex.com; Trejqet il-Kulpara; 1-bedroom apt per
week low/high season €175/280; ≋) Tucked one
block back from the waterfront in a quiet-
ish location, this central complex has indoor
and outdoor pools, a gym, a sauna, a jacuzzi
and a handy minimarket. On offer are one-
to three-bedroom self-catering apartments
for weekly lets (although shorter stays are
welcome); all have ceiling fans (no air-con),
kitchenette and lounge area. Apartments
with families in mind sleep up to seven.
Breakfast, a safety deposit box and a TV are
all available for extra fees.

Golden Bay

Radisson Blu Resort & Spa LUXURY HOTEL €€€
(☑2356 1000; www.goldensands.com.mt; r low/
high season from €90/150; ✳@🛋≋) The
Radisson is something of a glossy carbun-
cle on one of Malta's loveliest beaches, but
is nevertheless inviting. It's a three-tower,
10-storey hotel, chock-full of facilities and
with 329 rooms. The 'Serene' deluxe rooms
are 35 sq m and welcoming, decorated in
soothing, sea colours; fluffy robes, fancy toi-
letries and buffet breakfast are provided. If
you can afford it, fork out for a sea view, but
it'll cost you €30 to €60 more, depending on
the season. The 'Zenith collection' comprises
one-bedroom suites with a separate lounge,
which are a wonderfully roomy 70 sq m. All
are great for families.

Mellieħa

Maritim Antonine Hotel & Spa HOTEL €€
(Map p74; ☑2152 0923; www.maritim.com.mt;
Triq Ġorġ Borg Olivier; B&B per person low/high
season from €31/65; ✳@🛋≋) The glossy
Antonine dominates the main street in the
middle of Mellieħa, and is a great place to
stay, with some sweeping views from its
higher balconies, either over the pool or
down towards the coast. It might not be
characterful, but it's got a more intimate
feel than many of the plush hotels that

directly line the coast. Rooms and suites are decorated in soothing blues or beiges, each with balcony and satellite TV. There are restaurants, a health spa, a rooftop pool and sun terrace, and lovely lush gardens with a large pool.

Splendid Guesthouse GUESTHOUSE €
(Map p74; ☎2152 3602; www.splendidmalta.com; Triq il-Kappillan Magri; per person from €20, apt from €35; ❄@) This pleasant, pink-hued 14-room guesthouse is at the southern end of town in a residential area, a few minutes' walk from the main street. The spick-and-span guest rooms have plain, no-frills furnishings, and all rooms have a private shower and washbasin (some have full en suite). Rates include breakfast in the cheerful breakfast room–bar area, and there's a sunbathing terrace on the rooftop. The friendly owners also have self-catering apartments available, and a large villa sleeping up to 10 people (€1300 to €2000 per week).

Pergola Club Hotel HOTEL €€
(Map p74; ☎2152 3912; www.pergolahotel.com.mt; Triq Adenau; r low/high season €33/100, 2-person studio €45/125, 4-person apt €62/170; ❄@📶≋) Pergola, across the bridge from Mellieħa's main road, offers comfortable if unremarkable hotel rooms and self-catering apartments (entry is at the top of the steps). The views from the sun terraces towards the church are lovely. There is also a health spa, an indoor pool, two outdoor pools and a children's splash pool, as well as a kids' play area, plus bars and restaurants. Studios and apartments are good value, especially for families and especially in low season.

CENTRAL MALTA

Mdina

TOP CHOICE **Xara Palace** LUXURY HOTEL €€€
(Map p88; ☎2145 0560; www.xarapalace.com.mt; Misraħ il-Kunsill; r low/high season from €185/200; ❄📶) This 17th-century palazzo contains 17 beautifully designed, soft-hued duplex suites filled with antiques and original artworks; some have fabulous views. Guests include well-heeled Americans, Europeans, honeymooners and the odd celeb. The rooftop fine-dining restaurant De Mondion (p90), with sweeping views, is considered by many to be Malta's best restaurant.

Point de Vue Guesthouse & Restaurants GUESTHOUSE €
(Map p88; ☎2145 4117; www.pointdevuemalta.com; 5 Is-Saqqajja; B&B per person €32; @) This guesthouse scores goals with a combination of affordable rates and a privileged position, just metres from the walled city. The large, spotless twin and double guest rooms are simply furnished, with tiled floors, whitewashed walls, white bed linen and sparkling bathrooms. There are also great views.

Rabat

Casa Melita HOUSE €€
(Map p88; ☎7958 0800; 39 Triq Melita; per week low/high season €575/890; 📶) This restored town house sleeps six, and is on a lovely little pedestrianised lane. Facilities (including a kitchen and two bathrooms) are basic, and the house can feel damp outside the summer months, but it's reasonably comfortable. The best thing about staying here is the location in the heart of Rabat, with its local feel. Wi-fi is available on request (at an extra charge).

The Three Villages

Corinthia Palace Hotel HOTEL €€€
(☎2144 0301; www.corinthia.com; Vjal de Paule; r low/high season from €130/180; ❄@📶≋) The grand old five-star Corinthia Palace, close to the San Anton Gardens, has an Italian palazzo feel. It is popular with conference organisers and official delegations, and appeals to an older crowd who enjoy the discreet location, lush gardens, health spa and upmarket on-site restaurants. All rooms have a decent-sized balcony – request a pool view. There are often good deals available on room rates; it pays to ask or check the website.

University Residence STUDENT ACCOMMODATION €
(☎2143 0360/6168; www.universityresidence.com; Triq R M Bonnici; 2-bed dm per person from €14; @📶≋) The official student residence for the University of Malta, 200m north of the San Anton Gardens, is 4km away from the centre of town and connected by a free bus service. It's a well-equipped, well-run facility, and a good place to meet local and international students – beware, though, that securing short-term accommodation here can be tough (especially from June to September). The facility sleeps a few hundred students and is in a residential area. There

are self-catering facilities, tennis courts, large grounds, a minimarket, a cafe-bar and a laundrette. There's a three-night minimum on stays and a variety of good accommodation available, including hotel-standard double rooms from €46.

SOUTHEAST MALTA

Marsaxlokk

TOP CHOICE Duncan Guesthouse · GUESTHOUSE €
(☑2165 7212; www.duncanmalta.com; 33 Xatt is-Sajjieda; d from €40; ❄️🐾) Friendly, family-run Duncan's is hands-down the sweetest accommodation deal in southern Malta. It's above Duncan Bar & Restaurant on the waterfront, and the spacious, aqua-hued guest rooms come in family-friendly configurations. They're well kitted out for lengthy stays, each with a sitting area, a TV, a small balcony, a spick-and-span modern bathroom and a kitchenette. Air-con is an optional extra. There's a washing machine for guest use (a rare beast in Malta), and a rooftop sun terrace – the perfect vantage point for sundowner drinks and watching the harbour.

Marsaskala

Summer Nights Guesthouse · GUESTHOUSE €
(☑2163 7956; cutalex@gmail.com; Triq ix-Xatt; d without/with kitchenette €30/35) Basic, good-value rooms are on offer at this central guesthouse in the heart of the town's action (there's a restaurant and a pub downstairs). Rooms have private bathroom, fan, TV and fridge (some have a kitchenette), and all have a balcony with a sea view.

GOZO & COMINO

Victoria (Rabat)

The Gardens · GUESTHOUSE €
(Map p111; ☑2155 3723/7737; www.casal goholidays.com; Triq Kerċem; d €30) This guesthouse has a cascade of bougainvillea down its front, and faces some gardens. It's in a good location west of Victoria's main square, albeit a bit away from the action. The warm, hospitable owners rent out simple, comfort-

able rooms over three floors (connected by a lift). Facilities include guest kitchens and garden terraces. The owners also have self-catering apartments and farmhouses for rent, scattered around Gozo; see the website for more information.

Downtown Hotel · HOTEL €€
(Map p111; ☑2210 8000; www.downtown.com.mt; Triq l-Ewropa; d low/high season €52/70; ❄️@🐾) Victoria's only hotel offers bright, fuss-free, if uninspiring, rooms with respectable three-star amenities (cable TV, hairdryer, minibar). Prices are slightly higher at the weekends, giving an indication of the main clientele – visitors over from Malta. There's a family-friendly feel, with a rooftop pool (with magic views) and soft-play kids' club, where you can drop your children for a fee. In high season there's a free bus service to Gozo beaches.

Mġarr

Grand Hotel · HOTEL €€€
(☑2156 3840; www.grandhotelmalta.com; Triq Sant'Antnin; d low/high season from €60/140; ❄️@🐾) There's only one hotel in Mġarr – the butterscotch-coloured, four-star Grand Hotel, which has a fine position overlooking the harbour; bright, airy rooms; and extensive facilities including a sauna, a gym, a games room, a restaurant and a cocktail bar. Its least expensive rooms have no view; from these it's a small step up to a 'country view' room; sea-view rooms are naturally at the top of the scale and are a worthwhile investment.

Ta'Ċenċ

TOP CHOICE Hotel Ta'Ċenċ · LUXURY HOTEL €€€
(☑2155 6819; www.vjborg.com/tacenc; Triq Ta-Ċenċ; s low/high season €80/130, d €130/200; ❄️@🐾) The ritzy, five-star Hotel Ta'Ċenċ hides in 160 hectares on a remote cliff-top plateau just east of Sannat, and is one of the islands' loveliest hotels. Built out of local stone, the rooms are housed in *trulli*, which are cone-shaped buildings that echo the traditional architecture of Puglia in Southern Italy, and their decor is stylishly simple. The main building has a beckoning array of sofa-filled living spaces, and beyond these are landscaped gardens and two outdoor pools. If those don't appeal, head to the indoor-

outdoor pool at the relaxation-inducing 'wellness spa', or catch the courtesy bus to the hotel's private rocky beach, lapped by azure sea and complete with a bar and restaurant. When you've checked out your surrounds, have a sundowner with a view, or retire to a sought-after table under the carob tree of the hotel's highly regarded restaurant (open for lunch and dinner).

Munxar

Thirtyseven BOUTIQUE HOTEL €€€
(☑2720 0069; www.thirtysevengozo.com; Munxar; r low season €140-200, r high season €160-250; ☎☒) This stylish, rustic place has five rooms set around sunny courtyards in a lovely old farmhouse building in one of Gozo's quietest villages. It's owned and run by a couple who used to work on the Milanese fashion scene – the decor is a kind of boho chic, with artefacts from Morocco, India and Italy dotted around the place. There's an inviting outdoor pool, overlooked by a terrace that's ideal for an evening drink. Patti and Giuseppe offer lots of local information, and meals and cooking courses are available.

Qala

Ferrieha Farmhouse GUESTHOUSE €€
(☑2155 3819; www.ferriehafarmhouse.com; d from €70; ☒) This large house, perched on a hilltop, is built in a traditional style, with lots of space and fantastic views over the sea and over to Comino. There are four spacious guest rooms, all with views, and a great pool and splash pool, plus the Swedish owners have installed a wood-heated sauna in an outhouse.

Xlendi

TOP CHOICE **San Antonio Guesthouse** GUESTHOUSE €€
(☑2156 3555; www.clubgozo.com.mt; Triq it-Torri; s low/high season €33/50, d €50/80; ☎☒) This lovely, leafy guesthouse is a fair climb up the hill on the south side of Xlendi bay, rendering it close enough to Xlendi's habour-front activity when you want it, yet far enough to allow a relaxing holiday. The rates provide marvellous value and get you one of 13 rooms – all large, bright and spotless, decked out in chunky pine furniture. Aircon, TV with some satellite channels, big private bathrooms and balconies/terraces are

GOZITAN FARMHOUSES

One of the best accommodation options for a stay on Gozo, especially if you're looking for a little local colour and rustic charm, is to rent a farmhouse. Often what's termed a farmhouse, however, is a spacious, characterful town house with lots of rustic features. Dozens of these old, square-set buildings have been converted into accommodation, and many retain the beautiful stone arches, wooden beams and flagstone floors of their original construction (some are up to 400 years old). Most rental properties are very well equipped with everything you'll need for an easy holiday, including lush kitchens, a swimming pool, outdoor terrace and barbecue, laundry facilities and cable TV. They can sleep anywhere from two to 16 people, so are perfect for families or groups of friends, and the costs are very reasonable – from around €750 per week for two people in the high season (most high-season rentals are weekly), or from €60 per night for two people in the low season.

The farmhouses are usually inland in pretty, slow-paced villages – Xagħra and Għarb are two of the best places to look out for these kinds of properties. Xagħra is livelier, while Għarb is very tranquil. Almost anyone with a guesthouse or hotel on the island can arrange a farmhouse for visitors; check the following websites for details of properties for rent (note that many agencies also offer cheaper apartments and villas on Gozo, as well as farmhouses):

» www.farmhousegozo.com
» www.gozo.com/gozodirectory/farmhouses.php
» www.gozofarmhouses.com
» www.gozoescape.com
» www.casalgoholidays.com

standard, and there's a garden, a very nice swimming pool (with views) and a kiddies' pool. For optimum views, request a pool-facing room on the 1st floor. The accommodating owners can help arrange transfers, car hire and various extras; they also have self-catering apartments and farmhouses – check the website. It's worth paying around €5 to €8 extra for a sea view.

St Patrick's Hotel
HOTEL €€

(☑2156 2951; www.vjborg.com/stpatricks; Xatt ix-Xlendi; d low/high season from €44/72; ❋@⊠) Bang in the middle of the Xlendi waterfront is the four-star, friendly and helpful St Patrick's, with attractive, well-equipped rooms that are popular with weekending Maltese. The cheaper rooms face a pleasant-enough internal courtyard; the next step up sees larger rooms with a balcony and views over the town car park and valley beyond. It's worth paying more for a room with a balcony and sea view. There's a rooftop terrace with spa and pool, and a ground-level waterside restaurant.

San Andrea Hotel
HOTEL €€

(☑2156 5555; www.hotelsanandrea.com; Xatt ix-Xlendi; d low/high season from €50/70; ❋) This small hotel on the Xlendi waterfront has a great location, with plenty of rooms with balconies looking out to sea (it's worth paying around €8 extra for a sea view). Rooms are unexciting, but made by the views, and are comfortable, if small.

San Lawrenz

TOP CHOICE Kempinski Hotel San Lawrenz
HOTEL €€€

(☑2211 0000; www.kempinski-gozo.com; Triq ir-Rokon; d low/high season from €100/200; ❋@⊠) The Kempinski, close to the attractive village of San Lawrenz and the wondrous coastline around Dwejra, is a swish hideaway set in palm-shaded landscaped grounds. Rooms are warmly decorated in polished wood and making use of smooth, pale, local limestone. You get the feeling nothing is too much trouble for the obliging staff here; the crowd is a mix of honeymooners, families and well-heeled older Europeans. Facilities to help pass the time include a large health spa (with a huge list of de-stress treatments), tennis and squash courts, a gym, indoor and outdoor pools and pool bars. There's also a coffee lounge, trattoria and fine-dining restaurant. The spa and eateries are open to the public.

Marsalforn

TOP CHOICE Maria-Giovanna Hostel
GUESTHOUSE €€

(Map p121; ☑2155 3630; www.gozohostels.com; cnr Triq il-Munġbell & Triq ir-Rabat; s low/high season from €40/60, d €60/90; @) Hostel is misleading. Forget shared dorms and smelly socks: this is a guesthouse, with 15 rooms, each decorated in rustic style, with funky cast-iron or wooden beds, polished wooden furniture and colourful linen and rugs. From the pretty town-house exterior to the fish tank, plants and piano in the communal lounge, this place is all about attention to detail. Guests have use of the establishment's kitchen, dining area, courtyard and TV lounge. Run by helpful twin sisters, who live across the road and can arrange all sorts of extras (for a small fee): laundry, home-cooked local meals, taxi service, a water taxi to Comino – nothing seems too much trouble. The owners can also help with self-catering apartments and farmhouses – check the website for more information. Book well ahead.

Lantern Guesthouse
GUESTHOUSE €

(Map p121; ☑2155 6285; www.gozo.com/lantern; Triq il-Munġbell; B&B per person €25-30; ❋) The Lantern is a cosy guesthouse, with clean, homely rooms, all with en suite, cable TV and fridge (air-con available at extra charge). The friendly owners can also hook you up with reasonably priced apartments around town.

Calypso Hotel
HOTEL €€

(Map p121; ☑2156 2000; www.hotelcalypsogozo. com; Triq il-Port; s low/high season from €45/68, d from €64/100; ❋@🔊⊠) The Calypso is a typical custard-coloured Maltese building on the beach, low-rise and nondescript; however, inside it offers smart, bright rooms hued in warm blues. An international and Maltese crowd makes good use of the handful of on-site restaurants and cafes, plus the lovely pool, bar and sun terrace on the roof. Sea-view rooms cost an additional €10.50 per person.

Xagħra

Cornucopia Hotel
HOTEL €€

(☑2155 6486; www.vjborg.com/cornucopia; Triq Ġnien Imrik; r per person low/high season €37/47; ❋@🔊⊠) Cornucopia and its copious accommodation options are set in and around a converted farmhouse about 1km north of the village square. Four-star accommodation is available in its 48 hotel rooms and suites arranged around a courtyard, pool and pretty garden, or in self-catering villas, bungalows, apartments and farmhouses (two-bedroom bungalow low/high season €135/150); request a valley view for sweeping countryside vistas. It's particularly good for families, with lots of larger room options, and the pool is lovely and big.

Xagħra Lodge GUESTHOUSE €
(Map p122; ☎2156 2362; www.gozo.com/xaghra -lodge/index.html; Triq Dun Ġorġ Preca; d €50-60; ❋❄) This homely guesthouse is fronted by two long balconies. In a quiet neighbourhood, it's run by a friendly English couple and rooms feel as if you could be in a nice British B&B. It's good value, with cable TV and said balconies; a flowering garden with pool and aviary; and an adjacent bar and Chinese restaurant. Located a five-minute walk east of the town square.

Comino

Comino Hotels HOTEL €€€
(☎2152 9821; www.cominohotel.com; half-board s/d low season from €54/70, high season €89/140; ☺Easter-Oct; ❋@❄) An international crowd of sunseekers, scuba divers and those who prefer to holiday without too many distractions make a regular pilgrimage to the well-equipped Comino Hotels, the only place to stay on the island. The four-star hotel has 95 rooms at San Niklaw Bay and 46 bungalows at Santa Marija Bay, but no self-catering options. Bungalows are bigger than the hotel rooms, and have a sitting area. Pack a good book – there are no museums or shops to distract you, and only the hotel's cafe, restaurant and bar to keep you fed and watered. Full board costs an additional €14, a sea view is €7 (both per person per night). The buffet meals are of a good standard.

By day there are hotel-organised activities (at an additional cost) to occupy your time – the most popular is scuba-diving, taking advantage of Comino's excellent dive sites. Instruction and courses for beginners, experienced divers and kids are available through the hotel's dive school.

Other diversions include a private beach (in San Niklaw Bay), swimming pools, tennis courts, bikes, watersports (including rental of windsurfing equipment, sailing and motor boats, and canoes) and boat excursions. Or you can simply recharge your batteries in your bright, bland but perfectly adequate room (featuring air-con, phone, cable TV, fridge and balcony).

Day-trippers can use the hotel's facilities for €39 a day, but this must be booked in advance through the hotel. The price includes buffet lunch, a return boat ticket and use of the pool and private beach. Casual visitors might like to escape the Blue Lagoon and dine at the cafe or buy a drink at the bar.

ACCOMMODATION COMINO

Understand
> # Malta & Gozo

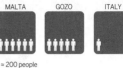

population per sq km

MALTA   GOZO   ITALY

≈ 200 people

Malta & Gozo Today

Malta and Gozo are a microcosm of the Mediterranean, a sponge that has absorbed different dollops of character from its neighbours and conquerors: listen to the local language to hear the Arabic influences; sample its Sicilian-inspired cuisine; and look out for the legacy of 150 years of British rule, and the political influence of the Roman Catholic Church. This eclectic mix is owed to the long roll-call of rulers over the centuries – but Malta is by no means a notional outpost of Italy or a relic of colonial Britain. The character of this diminutive collection of islands is powerful enough to measure up to any larger nation.

The EU, the Euro & the Economy

Malta is the smallest state in the EU, having joined in 2004. The country agonised over joining the Eurozone, fearing it would lead to price increases and runaway inflation. However, Malta's economy has not been as badly battered as other countries in the European storm: EU membership led to a flood of foreign investment, and strict regulations governing the banking sector prevented the kind of financial meltdown seen elsewhere.

That said, the Maltese economy is dependent on foreign trade, manufacturing and tourism, and thus could not escape being hurt by the global economic situation. Public finances have deteriorated since 2011, leading to warnings from the EU, and Malta's credit rating was downgraded in September 2011. The flow of UK tourists – long a mainstay of the Maltese economy – decreased significantly. On the other hand, a weakened euro and the arrival of budget carriers on Malta's deregulated airline scene have helped to keep tourist numbers higher than they might have been.

Nevertheless, locals enjoy a good standard of living, with low inflation and relatively low unemployment. During recent years Malta has

» Population: 410,000

» Area: 316 sq km

» Number of registered vehicles: 310,400

» Number of mobile-phone subscribers: 455,400

» Inflation: 2.7%

» Unemployment: 6.4%

Dos & Don'ts

» Do dress respectfully when visiting a church: keep your shoulders and legs covered.

» Don't go topless on the beach – conservative Maltese would find this offensive.

» Do avoid eating meat on a Friday, traditionally the day Roman Catholics eat fish.

» Don't expect Maltese drivers to stop at roundabouts, indicate or to cease talking on mobile phones while driving.

Top Books

The Great Siege: Malta 1565 (Ernle Bradford) Rip-roaring read that brings alive the epic battle between the Ottoman Turks and the Knights of Malta

belief systems
(% of population)

98 Christian

1.3 Other

0.7 Muslim

if Malta were 100 people

95 would live in cities
5 would live in rural areas

---

witnessed a massive increase in speculative property development – curious, when it's estimated that around a third of its property lies vacant. The government's relaxation of construction laws has in part led to the boom, which was only slowed, not decimated, by the 2008–09 recession.

Immigration

Malta's migrant community is predominantly British, but there are also around 4000 people from the sub-Saharan region. Racial tension has been evident since the relatively recent arrival of irregular migrants from Africa, mainly Somalia. The island's small size and proximity to Africa combine to make unauthorised immigration a controversial issue; in 2011, the Maltese government made an urgent appeal to the EU for help with immigrant numbers. Malta has been criticised by various organisations for its policy of mandatory detention, which Amnesty International and others believe is at odds with international human rights obligations.

Environment

Key environmental concerns in Malta are caused by landuse, increased development and the pressures of the population. The country only grows around 20% of its food and has no domestic energy sources (almost all its electricity is generated using oil-fired power stations), so it is heavily reliant on imports. There is also a severe shortage of fresh water – the only natural supply comes from ground water.

Malta has the highest rate of asthma of all Mediterranean countries, with air (and noise) pollution caused by construction, traffic and discharges from power stations and factories. With such a small land area, disposal of rubbish in landfill sites is increasingly problematic, though recycling is on the rise.

The number of overseas-born residents in Malta has doubled in the past 15 years, but still only amounts to around 4.4% of the population.

Living Standards

Fortress Malta: An Island Under Siege 1940–1943 (James Holland) Evocative account of Malta's fascinating and essential part in WWII.

» Schooling is compulsory in Malta for children between the ages of five and 16, and is provided free in state and church schools (church schools are subsidised by the government).

» A university education is free to Maltese citizens, and students receive an annual stipend.

» In 2011 the Maltese rate of unemployment was, at 6.4%, the fifth lowest in the Eurozone.

History

The diminutive islands of Malta and Gozo have punched a long way above their weight for millennia. Everywhere you look, there are reminders of their remarkable importance as key locations in the Mediterranean, and their consequential tumultuous pasts.

The islands are a particular treasure trove of prehistoric sites. The earliest evidence of human occupation here goes back to 5000 BC, the early neolithic period, reflecting other societies around the Mediterranean. But in the period from 3500 to 2500 BC, the inhabitants of the islands created the most sophisticated architecture known from that period of anywhere in the world.

With Malta's magnificent natural harbours and prime location between Africa and Europe, ever since the Phoenicians mastered the art of sailing in the open sea in around 1000 BC, geography shaped the islands' destiny. Subsequent masters included the Romans, Arabs and Normans.

Perhaps the most influential settlers of all, however, were the Knights of St John, who held sway (most famously beating off the Ottoman Turks in 1565) until the arrival of Napoleon. Later under the British the islands once again became an essential stop on the international trade map. In the aftermath of WWII and the ensuing economic slump, Malta finally achieved independence in 1964.

It's no small feat to cover a country's past in under 300 pages, but *A Concise History of Malta*, by Carmel Cassar, is a readable introduction to Maltese history.

The Mystery of the Temple Builders

About 1000 years before the construction of the Great Pyramid of Cheops in Egypt, the people of Malta were manipulating megaliths that weighed up to 50 tonnes and creating elaborate buildings that appear to be oriented in relation to the winter solstice sunrise. The Maltese megalithic temples built between 3600 and 2500 BC are the oldest surviving free-standing structures in the world. It's thought that their builders were descended from the islands' neolithic inhabitants, rather than being new settlers, yet it appears they started building these structures quite suddenly.

TIMELINE

800–480 BC	480–218 BC	218 BC–AD 395
Malta is colonised by the Phoenicians, a seafaring people based in present-day Lebanon.	Malta is controlled by the Carthaginian Empire, based in present-day Tunisia. The islands may have served as a Carthaginian naval base during the First Punic War against Rome (264–241 BC).	The Romans take over Malta, having destroyed Carthage in the Punic Wars. They build farmhouses and villas, such as the one on display at the Domus Romana museum in Rabat.

It was a seemingly peaceful era, perhaps due to the islands' then geographical isolation, as no evidence of defensive structures remain. The society that built these temples must have been sophisticated, as indicated by the scale and complexity of the buildings and the evidence of delicate sculpture and decoration (mostly now displayed in Valletta's National Museum of Archaeology). The builders were also significantly wealthy enough to pay for the materials and extra labour beyond the needs of everyday life. Although the materials were mainly local, they often were transported from a distance of around 1km. It's thought that the massive slabs of stone were moved by rolling them on ball-shaped rocks – such stones have been discovered at the sites. The buildings have been termed 'temples' but, while there is evidence of ritual activity, it's not known definitively what they were used for.

It's a mystery why the population died out: some theories are drought and famine, an epidemic or an attack from overseas – or perhaps a combination of these afflictions. Whatever the reason, temple building appears to have come to a sudden stop around 2500 BC. The temples fell into disrepair, and the Bronze Age culture that followed was completely different, including its practices (for example, cremation rather than burial) and its artworks, which were heavier and rougher than the fine work of the mysterious temple builders.

Renowned British archaeologist and scholar David H Trump wrote *Malta Prehistory & Temples*, the definitive guide to Malta's prehistory. This comprehensive book includes detailed visual treatment of 30 key sites.

HISTORY A TRADING POST

A Trading Post

Phoenicians & Romans

As sea travel developed, so did Malta's significance. It was impossible for ancient vessels to sail overnight or attempt long, continuous trips, so Malta was the ideal place to stop on a journey between mainland Europe and Africa.

From around 800 to 218 BC, Malta was ruled by the Phoenicians and, for around 250 years of this period, by Phoenicia's principal North African colony, Carthage. There is a direct legacy of this period visible in contemporary Malta: with their watchful eyes painted on the prow, the colourful Maltese fishing boats – the *luzzu* and the *kajjik* – seem little changed from the Phoenician trading vessels that once plied the Mediterranean.

During the Second Punic War (218–201 BC) Rome took control of Malta before finally crushing Carthage in the Third Punic War (149–146 BC). The island was then given the status of a *municipium* (free town), with the power to control its own affairs and to send an ambassador to Rome. However, there is evidence that Malta retained a Punic influence. The 1st-century-BC historian Diodorus Siculus described the island as a Phoenician colony, and the biblical account of St Paul's shipwreck on

41 BC	AD 60	395–870	870–1090
The Romans make Malta a *municipium* (free town). The islands prosper through trade, as an outpost of Roman Sicily.	St Paul is shipwrecked on Malta in what is now St Paul's Bay. He is sheltered by the local people and introduces Christianity to the population.	After the Roman Empire splits in AD 395 Malta is believed to have fallen under Byzantine rule.	North African Arabs occupy Malta, introducing irrigation and the cultivation of cotton and citrus fruits.

Malta in AD 60 describes the islanders as 'barbarous' (that is, they did not speak the 'civilised' languages of Latin or Greek). St Paul's shipwreck was also particularly significant as he brought Christianity to the islands.

Malta seems to have prospered under Roman rule. The main town, called Melita, occupied the hilltop of Mdina but also spread over an area around three times the size of the later medieval citadel. The excavated remains of town houses, villas, farms and baths suggest that the inhabitants enjoyed a comfortable lifestyle and occupied themselves with the production of olives, wheat, honey and grapes.

Arabs

The rapid expansion of Islam in the 7th to 9th centuries saw an Arab empire extend from Spain to India. Arab armies invaded Sicily in 827 and finally conquered it in 878; Malta fell into Arab hands in 870. Both Malta and Sicily remained Muslim possessions until the end of the 11th century. The Arab rulers tolerated the Christian population, and had a strong influence on the Malti language. Apart from the names Malta and Gozo, which are thought to have Latin roots, most Maltese place names date from after the Arab occupation.

Normans

Didier Destremau, former French ambassador to Malta, wrote *Malte Tricolore – The Story of a French Malta 1798-1964*, a lighthearted, satirical history of Malta 'as it might have happened' had Napoleon not got the boot and the country remained under French rule.

For 400 years after the Norman conquest of Malta and Sicily (1090–91), the Mediterranean islands' histories were linked – their rulers were a succession of Normans, Angevins (French), Aragonese and Castilians (Spanish). Malta remained a minor pawn on the edge of the European chessboard, and its relatively small population of downtrodden islanders paid their taxes by trading, slaving and piracy, and were repaid in kind by marauding Turks and Barbary corsairs. This was the scene when the Knights of St John arrived, having been given the islands (much to the islanders' dismay) by the Holy Roman Emperor Charles V; the Knights were to rule the islands until the arrival of the French in the 18th century.

East vs West

Swapped for Falcons

In 1479 the marriage of Catholic monarchs Fernando II of Aragon and Isabella of Castile led to the unification of Spain. Under their grandson, the Holy Roman Emperor Charles V, Malta became part of the vast Spanish Empire. One of the greatest threats to Charles' realm was the expanding Ottoman Empire of Süleyman the Magnificent in the East. Sultan Süleyman had driven the Knights of St John from their island stronghold of Rhodes between 1522 and 1523. When the Knights begged Charles V to find them a new home, he offered them Malta along with

1090–1530	1565	
Normans take over. During their rule, a Maltese aristocracy is established, and the architectural style referred to as Siculo-Norman developed.	The Knights defeat Turkish invaders in the Great Siege of Malta. The Knights' victory on 8 September is still celebrated as a public holiday.	

» *Levée du Siege de Malte*, Charles-Philippe Lariviere

the governorship of Tripoli, hoping that they might help to contain the Turkish naval forces in the eastern Mediterranean. The nominal rent was to be two falcons a year – one for the emperor and one for the viceroy of Sicily. Malta consequently found itself at the heart of a struggle between two different religious philosophies: Islam and Christianity, with both sides convinced of their god-given supremacy. Malta became the location for one of the mightiest clashes between East and West, which was to shape not only the landscape of the island as we see it today, but the nation's future.

The Great Siege of 1565

Grand Master Philippe Villiers de L'Isle Adam (1530–34) of the Knights of St John was not particularly impressed by the gift of the Maltese Islands, which seemed to him barren, waterless and poorly defended.

WHO WERE THE KNIGHTS OF ST JOHN?

The Sovereign and Military Order of the Knights Hospitaller of St John of Jerusalem had its origins in the Christian Crusades of the 11th and 12th centuries.

A hospital for poor pilgrims in Jerusalem was founded by some Italian merchants from Amalfi in 1070. The hospital, operated by monks, won the protection of the papacy in 1113 and was raised to the status of an independent religious order known as the Hospitallers. The Order set up more hospitals along the pilgrimage route from Italy to the Holy Land, and the knights who had been healed of their wounds showed their gratitude by granting funds and property to the growing Order.

When the armies of Islam recaptured the Holy Land in 1291, the Order sought refuge first in the Kingdom of Cyprus. In 1309 they acquired the island of Rhodes, planning to stay close to the Middle East in the hope of reconquering Jerusalem. But here they remained for over 200 years, building fortresses, auberges and a hospital, and evolving from a land-based army into the medieval world's most formidable naval fighting force.

The order consisted of European noblemen who lived the lives of monks and soldiers. Their traditional attire was a hooded monk's habit emblazoned with a white Maltese cross. This eight-pointed cross is said to represent the eight virtues that the Knights strove to uphold: to live in truth; to have faith; to repent of sins; to give proof of humility; to love justice; to be merciful; to be sincere and whole-hearted; and to endure persecution. The Order comprised eight nationalities or langues (literally 'tongues' or languages) – Italy, France, Provence, Auvergne, Castile, Aragon, Germany and England.

The hospitals created by the Order – first in the Holy Land, then in Rhodes and finally in Malta – were often at the forefront of medical development. Ironically, although the Knights had sworn to bring death and destruction to the 'infidel' Muslims, much of the Order's medical knowledge was gleaned from the study of Arabic medicine.

1566	**1600–50**	**1607**	**1798**
Valletta is founded, and is the first planned city in Europe, with a regular grid of streets, underground sewers and massive fortifications.	The Knights extend the fortifications of the Three Cities by constructing the Cottonera Lines, a string of walls and bastions designed by papal engineer Vincenzo Maculano da Firenzuola.	Caravaggio arrives in Malta after fleeing justice in Rome. He is admitted to the Order of St John, and paints his masterpiece, *The Beheading of St John the Baptist*, before fleeing again to Sicily.	Napoleon's fleet calls at Malta and captures the island with hardly a fight. Napoleon departs six days later, leaving Malta under French control.

KNIGHTS

The Order of Malta website (www.orderof malta.org/ english) covers the long, illustrious history of the Knights, as well as information about present-day knightly activities.

Equally unimpressed were the 12,000 or so local inhabitants, who were given no say in the matter; likewise the aristocracy, who remained aloof in their palazzi in Mdina. However, determined to make the best of a bad job and hoping one day to return to Rhodes, in 1530 the Knights settled in the fishing village of Birgu (now Vittoriosa) on the south side of Grand Harbour and set about fortifying their defences.

While in Rhodes, the Knights had been a constant thorn in the side of the Ottoman Turks. In Malta their greatest adversary was the Turkish admiral Dragut Reis, who invaded Gozo in 1551 and carried off almost the entire population of 5000 into slavery. Later, in 1559, the Knights lost half their galleys in a disastrous attack on Dragut's lair on the island of Djerba (Tunisia). With the power of the Knights at a low ebb, Süleyman the Magnificent saw an opportunity to polish off this troublesome crew, while at the same time capturing Malta as a base for the invasion of Europe.

Jean Parisot de la Valette, Grand Master between 1557 and 1568, was a stern disciplinarian and an experienced soldier. He foresaw the threat of a Turkish siege and prepared for it well, renewing Fort St Angelo and building Fort St Michael and Fort St Elmo. The Knights' galley fleet was taken into the creek below Birgu, and a great chain was stretched across the harbour entrance between Fort St Angelo and Fort St Michael to keep out enemy vessels. Food, water and arms were stockpiled, and la Valette sent urgent requests for aid to the emperor, the pope and the viceroy of Sicily. No help came. In May 1565, when an Ottoman fleet carrying more than 30,000 men arrived to lay siege to the island, la Valette was 70 years old and commanded a force of only 700 Knights and around 8000 Maltese irregulars and mercenary troops.

The Turkish force, led jointly by Admiral Piali and Mustafa Pasha, dropped anchor in the bay of Marsaxlokk, and its soldiers set up camp on the plain of Marsa. The entire population of Malta took refuge within the walls of Birgu, Isla and Mdina, taking their livestock with them and poisoning the wells and cisterns they left behind. The Turks began their campaign with an attack on Fort St Elmo, which guarded the entrance to both Grand and Marsamxett Harbours. The fort was small, holding a garrison of only 60 Knights and a few hundred men – Mustafa Pasha was confident that it would fall in less than a week.

However, despite continuous bombardment and repeated mass assaults on its walls, Fort St Elmo held out for over four weeks, and cost the lives of 8000 Turkish soldiers before it was taken. When the fort finally fell, not one of the Christian defenders survived.

Looking across at the looming bulk of Fort St Angelo from the smoke and rubble of St Elmo, Mustafa Pasha is said to have muttered, 'Allah! If

1800	1814	1814–1964	1853–56
The Maltese rebel against the French garrison and ask the British for assistance. Following a naval blockade, the French surrender in September.	Malta becomes a prosperous trading port and entrepôt; after the 1814 Treaty of Paris it is formerly recognised as a Crown Colony of the British Empire.	The British rule Malta, allowing varying levels of Maltese self-government. The island becomes a linchpin in the imperial chain of command.	Malta is the headquarters of the British Mediterranean Fleet, and is used as a base and supply station for the Royal Navy during the Crimean War.

so small a son has cost us so dear, what price shall we have to pay for so large a father?'

Hoping to intimidate the already demoralised defenders of Fort St Angelo, Mustafa Pasha ordered that several of the leading Knights be beheaded and their heads fixed on stakes looking across towards Birgu. The Turks nailed the decapitated bodies to makeshift wooden crucifixes and sent them floating across the harbour. La Valette's response was immediate and equally cruel: all Turkish prisoners were executed and decapitated. The Knights then used their heads as cannonballs and fired them back across the harbour to St Elmo.

Then began the final assault on the strongholds of Birgu and Isla: the Turks launched at least 10 massed assaults, but each time they were beaten back. Turkish morale was drained by the long hot summer, their increasing casualties, and the impending possibility of having to spend the entire winter on Malta (the Mediterranean sailing season traditionally ended with the storms of late September). The ferocity of their attacks decreased. On 7 September, the Knights' long-promised relief force from Sicily finally arrived – 28 ships carrying some 8000 men landed at Mellieħa Bay and took command of the high ground around Naxxar as the Turks scrambled to embark their troops and guns at Marsamxett.

Seeing the unexpectedly small size of the relief force, Mustafa Pasha ordered some of his troops to land again at St Paul's Bay, while the rest marched towards Naxxar from Marsamxett. But the tired and demoralised Turkish soldiers were in no mood to fight these fresh and ferocious Knights and men-at-arms; they turned and ran for the galleys now anchored in St Paul's Bay. Thousands were hacked to pieces in the shallow waters of the bay as they tried to escape. That night the banner of the Order of St John flew once again over the battered ruins of St Elmo.

The part played in the Great Siege by the ordinary people of Malta is often overlooked, but their courage and resilience was a deciding factor in the Turkish defeat. Besides the 5000 or so strong defence force made up of Maltese soldiers, the local women and children contributed by repairing walls, supplying food and ammunition and tending the wounded. The date of the end of the siege, 8 September, is still commemorated in Malta as the Victory Day public holiday.

From Heroism to Hedonism

The Knights of St John, previously neglected, were now hailed as the saviours of Europe. Money and honours were heaped on them by grateful monarchs, and the construction of the new city of Valletta – named after the hero of the siege – and its enormous fortifications began.

The Great Siege: Malta 1565, by Ernle Bradford, is a page-turning account of the epic 1565 battle between the Ottoman Turks and the Knights of St John.

1887	1914–18	1919	1921
For the first time in its history, Malta acquires representative government through a legislative council, composed of a majority of Maltese elected members. This is later revoked in 1903.	Malta serves as a military hospital during WWI. Known as the 'Nurse of the Mediterranean', it provides 25,000 beds for casualties from the disastrous Gallipoli campaign.	There is a growing desire for Maltese self-government. Tension comes to a head on 7 June when riots break out.	The British respond to Maltese unrest by granting a new constitution that provides for a limited form of self-government. Joseph Howard becomes the first prime minister of Malta.

Although sporadic raids continued, Malta was never again seriously threatened by the Turks.

The period following the Great Siege was one of building – not only massive new fortifications and watchtowers, but also churches, palaces and auberges. The military engineer Francesco Laparelli was sent to Malta by the pope to design the new defences of Valletta, and Italian artists arrived to decorate its churches, chapels and palazzi. An influx of new Knights, eager to join the now prestigious Order, swelled the coffers of the treasury. The pious Grand Master Jean de la Cassière (1572–81) oversaw the construction of the Order's new hospital, the Sacra Infermeria, and the magnificent St John's Co-Cathedral.

However, in later years, with the Turkish threat removed, the Knights occupied themselves less with militarism and monasticism, and more with piracy, commerce, drinking and duelling.

Following their 1798 expulsion from Malta by Napoleon and the loss of their French estates, the Knights sought refuge first in Russia and later in Italy. After several years of uncertainty, they finally made their headquarters in the Palazzo di Malta (the former Embassy of the Hospitallers) in Rome. The Order continues to this day; since 2008 the Grand Master has been Englishman Fra' Matthew Festing.

A Military Linchpin

Napoleon in Malta

The Malta Story (1953), starring Alec Guinness and Jack Hawkins, involves men in spiffy uniforms fighting dangerous battles, performing heroic acts and winning hearts (of course). Surprisingly, it's the only movie made about the dramatic WWII events in Malta.

In the aftermath of the French Revolution, Grand Master Emmanuel de Rohan (1775–97) provided money for Louis XVI's doomed attempt to escape from Paris. By the late 18th century around three-quarters of the Order's income came from the Knights of the French langue; when the revolutionary authorities confiscated all of the Order's properties and estates in France, the Order was left in dire financial straits.

In 1798 Napoleon Bonaparte arrived in Malta aboard his flagship *L'Orient* at the head of the French Navy, on his way to Egypt to counter the British influence in the Mediterranean. He demanded that he be allowed to water his ships, but the Knights refused. The French landed and captured the island with hardly a fight – many of the Knights were in league with the French, and the Maltese were in no mood for a battle. On 11 June 1798 the Order surrendered to Napoleon.

Napoleon stayed in Malta for only six days (in the Palazzo de Parisio in Valletta), but when he left, *L'Orient* was weighed down with silver, gold, paintings and tapestries looted from the Order's churches, auberges and infirmary. (Most of this treasure went to the bottom of the sea a few months later when the Royal Navy under Admiral Nelson destroyed the French fleet at the Battle of the Nile.) The French also abolished

1934	1930s–'50s	1940	1940–43
Malti becomes the co-official language of Malta, alongside English, and the use of Italian is officially dropped. The first ever grammar of the Malti language is published.	Economic depression and political turmoil result in large numbers of Maltese immigrating to America, Australia, Canada and the UK.	Mussolini's Italy enters WWII on 10 June. On 11 June Italian bombers strike at Malta's Grand Harbour. Three ageing biplanes take to the air to defend the islands.	Malta assumes huge strategic importance as a WWII naval and air-force base, and the country experiences heavy bombing and great hardship.

the Maltese aristocracy, defaced coats of arms, desecrated churches and closed down monasteries.

Napoleon left behind a garrison of 4000 men, but they were taken unawares by a spontaneous uprising of the Maltese and had to retreat within the walls of Valletta. A Maltese deputation sought help from the sympathetic British, who enforced a naval blockade. The French garrison finally capitulated in September 1800 – and the British government, having taken Malta, was somewhat unsure what to do with it.

Read *Malta: Phoenician, Punic & Roman,* by Anthony Bonanno, to learn about the island's early history.

British Rule

The Treaty of Amiens (March 1802) provided for the return of Malta to the Order of St John, but the Maltese, not wanting it back, petitioned the British to stay. Their pleas fell on deaf ears; arrangements had been made for the return of the Order when war between Britain and France broke out again in May 1803. Faced with the blockade of European ports against British trade, the British government soon changed its mind regarding the potential usefulness of Malta.

While the latter stages of the Napoleonic Wars wore on, Malta rapidly became a prosperous entrepôt, and with the Treaty of Paris in 1814 it was formally recognised as a Crown Colony of the British Empire.

The end of the Napoleonic Wars brought an economic slump to Malta as trade fell off and little was done in the way of investment in the island. But its fortunes revived during the Crimean War (1853–56), when it was developed by the Royal Navy as a major naval base and supply station. With the opening of the Suez Canal in 1869 Malta became one of the chief coaling ports on the imperial steamship route between Britain and India.

The early 19th century also saw the beginnings of Maltese political development. In 1835 a Council of Government made up of prominent local citizens was appointed to advise the governor and a free press was established.

In the second half of the 19th century vast sums were spent on improving Malta's defences and dockyard facilities as the island became a linchpin in the imperial chain of command. The Victoria Lines and several large dry docks were built during this period. Commercial facilities were also improved to cater for the busy trade route to India and the Far East. In 1883 a railway was built between Valletta and Mdina (it closed in 1931).

The day after Mussolini's Italy entered WWII, one of that country's first acts of war was to bomb Malta.

During WWI Malta served as a military hospital, providing 25,000 beds for casualties from the disastrous Gallipoli campaign in Turkey. But prices and taxes rose during the war and the economy slumped. During protest riots in 1919, four Maltese citizens were shot dead by panicking British soldiers and several more were injured.

HISTORY A MILITARY LINCHPIN

1942

King George VI awards the George Cross, Britain's highest award for civilian bravery, to the entire population of Malta.

1943

In July Malta serves as the operational headquarters and air support base for the Allied invasion of Sicily. Captured Italian warships are anchored in Marsaxlokk Bay.

1947

A measure of self-government is restored with a general election in 1947, but a post-war economic slump creates more political tension.

KEYSTONE/STRINGER/GETTY IMAGES ©

» British warships, 1944

The British government replied to the unrest by giving the Maltese a greater say in the running of Malta. The 1921 constitution created a diarchic system of government, with a Maltese assembly presiding over local affairs and a British imperial government controlling foreign policy and defence.

WWII

The outbreak of WWII found Britain undecided as to the strategic importance of Malta. The islands' need for defence did not seem crucial at a time when Britain was itself poorly armed. The Italian threat was remote until the Fall of France in June 1940. Thus Malta was unprepared and undefended when on 11 June, the day after Mussolini entered the war, Italian bombers attacked Grand Harbour.

The only aircraft available on the islands at this time were three Gloster Gladiator biplanes – quickly nicknamed Faith, Hope and Charity – whose pilots fought with such tenacity that Italian pilots estimated the strength of the Maltese squadron to be in the region of 25 aircraft. The Gladiators battled on alone for three weeks before squadrons of modern Hurricane fighters arrived to bolster the islands' air defences. The remains of the sole surviving aircraft, Faith, can be seen at Valletta's National War Museum.

Malta effectively became a fortified aircraft carrier, a base for bombing attacks on enemy shipping and harbours in Sicily and North Africa. It also harboured submarines that preyed on Italian and German supply ships. Malta's importance was clear to Hitler, too, and crack squadrons of Stuka divebombers were stationed in Sicily with the objective of pounding the island into submission.

Malta's greatest ordeal came in 1942, when the country came close to starvation and surrender. In April alone some 6700 tonnes of bombs were dropped on Grand Harbour and the surrounding area. On 15 April, King George VI awarded the George Cross – Britain's highest award for civilian bravery – to the entire population of Malta.

Just as Malta's importance to the Allies lay in disrupting enemy supply lines, so its major weakness was the difficulty of getting supplies to the island. At the height of the siege in the summer of 1942 the governor made an inventory of remaining food and fuel, and informed London that Malta could only withstand until August without further supplies. A huge relief convoy known as Operation Pedestal, consisting of 14 supply ships escorted by three aircraft carriers, two battleships, seven cruisers and 24 destroyers, was dispatched to run the gauntlet of enemy bombers and submarines. It suffered massive attacks, and only five supply ships made it into Grand Harbour – the crippled oil tanker *Ohio*,

Malta suffered 154 days and nights of nonstop bombing in 1942. By comparison, at the height of London's Blitz there were 57 days of continuous bombing.

1964	1974	1984	1989
On 21 September, Malta gains its independence from Britain, but Queen Elizabeth II remains the head of state.	Under pivotal and pugnacious Prime Minister Dom Mintoff, Malta becomes a republic, with a president appointed by parliament replacing the British queen as head of state.	Dom Mintoff resigns as prime minister, but continues to play an important backbench role until 1998.	Neutral Malta hosts a summit between Mikhail Gorbachev and George Bush Sr, marking the end of the Cold War.

with its precious cargo of fuel, limped in on 15 August, lashed between two warships.

Malta was thus able to continue its vital task of disrupting enemy supply lines. The aircraft and submarines based in Malta succeeded in destroying or damaging German convoys to North Africa to the extent that Rommel's Afrika Korps was low on fuel and ammunition during the crucial Battle of El Alamein in October 1942, a situation that contributed to a famous Allied victory and the beginning of the end of the German presence in North Africa.

In July 1943 Malta served as the operational headquarters and air support base for Operation Husky, the Allied invasion of Sicily, and the Italian Navy finally surrendered to the Allies on 8 September, after which Malta's role in the war rapidly diminished.

Independence to the Present Day

WWII left the islands with 35,000 homes destroyed and the population on the brink of starvation. In 1947 the war-torn islands was given a measure of self-government and a £30-million war-damage fund to help with rebuilding and restoration. But the economic slump that followed Britain's reductions in defence spending and the loss of jobs in the naval dockyard led to calls either for closer integration with Britain, or for Malta to go it alone. On 21 September 1964, with Prime Minister Dr George Borg Olivier at the helm, Malta gained its independence. It remained within the British Commonwealth, with Queen Elizabeth II as the head of state represented in Malta by a governor-general.

Borg Olivier's successor as prime minister in 1971 was the Labour Party's Dominic (Dom) Mintoff, a fiery and controversial politician who had previously served as prime minister from 1955 to 1958. During Mintoff's second period as prime minister (1971–84) Malta became a republic (in 1974). In 1979 links with Britain were reduced further when Mintoff expelled the British armed services, declared Malta's neutrality and signed agreements with Libya, the Soviet Union and North Korea.

Malta was the scene for a historic meeting between USSR and US leaders Mikhail Gorbachev and George Bush Sr in 1989, which signaled the end of the Cold War.

In 2004 Malta joined the EU, and in 2008 became part of the Eurozone, which brought much inward investment and helped diversify the local economy. More recently the islands have been buffeted by the European financial crisis and have experienced ongoing controversy over increased immigration from Africa.

In 2012, when Mintoff died, thousands of Maltese united in mourning and assessed the legacy of their most prominent contemporary politician.

When Malta gained independence in 1964 it was the first time since prehistory that the country had been ruled by the native Maltese and not by an outside power.

2003–04	**2005**	**2008**	**2012**
In a 2003 referendum with a voter turnout of 92%, just over half the electorate votes to join the EU. On 1 May 2004 Malta joins the EU, along with nine other states.	Tensions rise as around 1800 African irregular immigrants arrive on Maltese shores. By 2009, 5000 have settled in in Malta, and 7000 have been repatriated.	On 1 January Malta kisses goodbye to the Maltese lira, its currency since 1972, and adopts the euro. Maltese euro coins proudly display the Maltese cross.	Former Prime Minister Dom Mintoff dies, aged 96.

The Maltese Table

Like the Malti language, Maltese cuisine is an exotic mix of flavours. Different types of food were introduced by the many cultures that dominated Malta over its long history, with the Italian, French, British and Arabic cuisines have a particularly strong impact. Traditional local food is rustic; meals are generally based on seasonal produce, rabbit and the fisherman's catch. It's not an internationally renowned cuisine: Maltese dishes are usually at their finest at home, while locals often go out to eat a mix of international flavours – Italian, French and Asian restaurants abound. However, there are also many traditional Maltese restaurants across the islands, and many creative eateries offer a twist on local specialities.

Italian cooking has perhaps the strongest influence. Most restaurants serve pasta and pizza, albeit with a Maltese flavour – for example, there are lots of pasta dishes with rabbit sauce, or pizzas featuring Maltese sausage. Portions in Malta tend to be large, unless you're eating at a high-end restaurant.

You'll also find plenty of traditional English standards (grilled chops, roast with three veg) in touristy areas. Restaurants aimed chiefly at tourists sometimes churn out bog-standard fare that's reminiscent of old-school pub grub – to avoid a disappointing meal, follow this guide or ask for local recommendations.

Perfect Picnics

Ftira is traditional Maltese bread baked in a flat disc. It makes for delicious sandwiches when stuffed with a substantial, punchy mixture of tomatoes, olives, capers and anchovies. Another traditional, any-time-of-day snack is *ħobż biż-żejt*, which are slices of bread rubbed with ripe tomatoes and olive oil until they are pink and delicious, then topped with a mix of tuna, onion, capers,olives, garlic, black pepper and salt.

Malta's national gap-filler is the *pastizza*. This is a small parcel of flaky pastry, Arabic in origin, which is filled with either ricotta cheese or mushy peas, usually served warm. A couple of *pastizzi* make for a tasty and substantial breakfast or afternoon filler. You'll probably pay around €0.30 for one, so they're great for budget travellers. They're available in most bars or from special takeaway *pastizzerijas* (usually hole-in-the-wall places in villages – follow your nose).

For bread-and-cheese picnics, search local bakeries for the famously delicious traditional bread *ħobż*. It is made in a similar manner to sourdough bread, using a scrap of yesterday's dough to leaven today's loaves. To accompany it, pick up some *ġbejniet*, a small, hard, white cheese traditionally made from unpasteurised sheep's or goat's milk. It is dried in

Food-lovers, don't eat out without the *Definitive(ly) Good Guide to Restaurants in Malta & Gozo*. It's updated annually and includes objective reviews of 150 of Malta's best restaurants. It's available from most major bookshops (€8); information is also online at www.restaurantsmalta.com.

Smoking is banned in all enclosed public places in Malta, including restaurants and bars.

baskets and often steeped in olive oil flavoured with salt and crushed black peppercorns. It's said the best comes from Żebbuġ (Gozo).

Big Broth

Maltese traditional cuisine includes a large range of soups that make the most of local ingredients. Several recipes cook meat in the broth, so the soup serves as a starter, followed by the meat as a main course. This practice became popular as, in times past,many homes in the past didn't have traditional ovens.

Aljotta, a delicious fish broth made with tomato, rice and lots of garlic, is the soup you'll most commonly see on menus. You also may encounter *kusksu,* a soup made from broad beans (at their best in May for this recipe) and small pasta shapes. To make this a complete meal, it's served with a soft, fresh *ġbejniet,* ricotta and an egg floating in the middle. *Minestra* is a thick soup of tomatoes, beans, pasta and vegetables, similar to some variations of Italian minestrone.

Soppa tal-armla means 'widow's soup' (probably named because of its inexpensive ingredients). It's traditionally made only with components that are either green or white: a tasty mix of cauliflower, spinach, endive and peas, with protein provided by a poached egg, a *ġbejniet* and a lump of ricotta.

Matty Cremona has written several books on Maltese cuisine, including *Cooking with Maltese Olive Oil: Maltese and Mediterranean Dishes* and *A Year in the Country: Life and Food in Rural Malta.* Both are available locally.

The Main Attraction

Carb Heaven

Two dishes that were born out of Italian cuisine, but then made particularly Maltese, are *ravjul/ravjuletti* (pasta pouches filled with ricotta, parmesan and parsley, basically a Maltese variety of ravioli) and *timpana,* a rich pie filled with macaroni, cheese, egg, minced beef, tomato, garlic and onion. *Timpana,* perhaps most carb-laden of all Maltese cuisine, is a Sicilian dish similar to the Greek *pastitsio,* and is usually cooked for special occasions.

From Rabbit to Roast Beef

Maltese main courses tend to be on the hearty side. Meat pies and roast beef, lamb and pork feature heavily; *braġioli,* another favourite, is prepared by wrapping thin slices of beef around a stuffing of breadcrumbs, chopped

MALTA & GOZO'S BEST RESTAURANTS

Glorious gastronomic experiences on Malta and Gozo range from fine dining to simple-yet-brilliant. Here is a selection of the best.

» Ambrosia (Valletta) Warmly welcoming, with top use of fresh, local produce.

» Trattoria da Pippo (Valletta) An old-boys'-club feel and simple yet fine Italian cooking.

» De Mondion (Mdina) Fine dining under a starlit sky on a Mdina bastion.

» Assaggi (St Julian's) Classy Italian place, famous for its aged beef.

» Ir-Rizzu (Marsaxlokk) Fabulously fresh seafood, straight off the local fishing boats.

» Patrick's (Victoria) Stylish Gozitan option that woos locals and visitors with great choices.

» Kitchen (Sliema) An award-winning chef presides over the modern menu.

» Restaurant Ta'Frenċ (outside Marsalforn) Gorgeous country restaurant – gloriously top rate, yet welcoming to all.

» Zest (St Julian's) Funky decor and an inspiring menu of treats from East and West.

» Rew Rew (Mgarr) Great seafood on the beach.

MALTA'S FAVOURITES

Helen Caruana Galizia, co-author of the culinary classic *Food & Cookery of Malta*, highlights some local specialities.

What foodstuffs would you particularly recommend? What people love here is the abundance of seasonal fruit and vegetables. They look forward to the new *qara baghli* (zucchini), broad beans, aubergines and peppers.

The melons and watermelons, white-skinned peaches and *bambinella* (miniature pears) are all exquisite. Figs are unsurpassed. The season starts in June (to coincide with the feast of St John the Baptist!) and continues into August. They come in different colours, from pale green to dark purple.

Maltese blood oranges are famously luscious and fragrant. The variety is believed to be produced by grafting the orange bud on to pomegranate stock, but there is also a natural variety of Citrus sinensis which gives the pigment its dark red colour.

Pastizzi (filled pastries) and *lampuki* (dolphin fish) are both greatly cherished. The *pastizzi* pastry is really special and it takes years to learn to make it well.

Where should visitors look out for specialities? Qormi – formerly known as Casal Fornaro, from the Italian for 'farmhouse bakery' – is famous for its bread, and locals hold an annual bread festival. Maltese bread is internationally renowned – look for traditional bakers who do not use chemical additives.

As Gozo is the smaller island, there can be strong feelings and comparisons made between the two societies, with the people of Gozo sometimes regarded as more innovative and inspired than their Maltese neighbours. Gozitan cooks tend to adhere more to traditional recipes; they specialise in pie-making and have their own unique versions of Maltese dishes.

bacon, hard-boiled egg and parsley, then braising these 'beef olives' in a red wine sauce. Quail and duck are also common.

Another dish traditionally prepared for a special occasion, but also a staple on many Maltese menus, is *fenek* (rabbit). The rabbit, introduced by the Normans, became a symbol of feudal repression as the Knights, to save enough game for the hunt, banned the peasantry from eating it. Adding insult to injury, rabbits persistently attacked the farmers' crops. The Maltese have certainly got their own back: it's the island's favourite national dish, whether fried in olive oil, roasted, stewed, served with spaghetti or baked in a pie. *Fenek bit-tewm u l-inbid* is rabbit cooked in garlic and wine, *fenek moqli* is fried rabbit and *stuffat tal-fenek* is stewed rabbit.

Food & Cookery of Malta by Anne and Helen Caruana Galizia is the definitive guide to Maltese cuisine, packed with recipes and information on local ingredients.

Riches of the Sea

Unsurprisingly given that the island is skirted by sea, Maltese cooking often uses fresh seafood. The most favoured fish is the *lampuka* (dolphin fish), in season from August to November. *Torta tal-lampuki* – also known as *lampuki* pie – is the local fish speciality. It's typically baked with tomatoes, onions, black olives, spinach, sultanas and walnuts – although there are lots of other recipes, too. *Ćerna* (grouper) is another versatile and popular fish that you'll find on lots of menus. Cod is not found in the Mediterranean, so Maltese recipes sometimes make use of *bakkaljaw* (salt cod). Octopus and cuttlefish are also excellent menu additions.

Sweets

Kannoli are a Sicilian import. These tubes of crispy, fried pastry are best eaten when they've been freshly filled with ricotta (to avoid the tubes going soggy); sometimes they're also sweetened with chocolate chips or candied fruit. *Mqaret* are almond-shaped pastries stuffed with chopped, spiced dates and deep fried – they're particularly good accompanied by vanilla ice cream.

Deliciously chewy Maltese nougat, flavoured with almonds or hazelnuts and traditionally sold on festa (feast) days, is known as *qubbajt*. *Gagħħ tal-għasel,* honey or treacle rings made from a light pastry, are served in small pieces as an after-dinner accompaniment to coffee.

Drinks

Non-Alcoholic Drinks

Good Italian coffee is widely available in cafes and bars. In the main tourist areas you'll also be able to find a cup of old-school British tea, heavy on the milk and sugar.

Cold soft drinks are available everywhere. Kinnie (its advertising signs are all over the place in Malta) is the brand name of a local soft drink flavoured with bitter oranges and aromatic herbs. It also slips down nicely when mixed with rum or vodka.

Alcoholic Drinks

Maltese bars serve up every kind of drink you could ask for, from pints of British beer to shots of Galliano liqueur. The good, locally made beers, Cisk Lager and Hopleaf Ale, are cheaper than imported brews.

The main players on the local wine scene are Camilleri Wines, Emmanuel Delicata, Marsovin and Meridiana. These companies make wine from local grapes and also produce more expensive 'special reserve' wines – merlot, cabernet sauvignon, chardonnay and sauvignon blanc – using imported grapes from Italy. The result can be surprisingly good and the quality is improving all the time.

Maltese liqueurs pack a punch and make good souvenirs. Look out for Zeppi's potent liqueurs concocted from local honey, aniseed or prickly pear. Gozo-produced *limunċell* (a variant on the Italian lemon liqueur *limoncello*) is delicious; there are orange and mandarin variants, too.

Mona's just the kind of in-the-know local we'd want pointing us in the right gastronomical direction. Check out her spot-on restaurant reviews at www.planetmona.com before making dinner plans.

Celebrations

A *fenkata* is a big, communal meal of rabbit, usually eaten in the countryside. It supposedly originated as a gesture of rebellion against the occupying Knights, who hunted rabbits and denied them to the local population. The most important *fenkata* is associated with the L-Imnarja harvest festival at the end of June, when hundreds of people gather at

A TASTE FOR THE GRAPE

When Malta joined the EU in 2004, it said goodbye to government levies charged on sales of imported wine. Wine became cheaper, sales grew by an estimated 25%, and wine bars started popping up all over the country. Some of these are simply cafes that have added 'wine bar' to their name and a few bottles to their menus, while other places have embraced the culture surrounding wine-drinking and have gone the whole hog, with lengthy lists of imported and locally produced drops, available by the glass or bottle. Some restaurants have made a feature of an attached bar, or even, as in the case of Trabuxu in Valletta, vice versa. And it seems no wine bar is complete without a menu of platters – local nibble-worthy produce such as sausage, olives, cheese and sun-dried tomatoes feature prominently.

You'll no doubt find a favourite of your own, but recommended options include Trabuxu in Valletta, Il-Forn in Vittoriosa, Grapes Wine Bar in Gozo's Victoria, and Capuvino in Buġibba. These all make a good alternative to English- or Irish-style pubs or brash Paceville nightclubs, and attract a mix of ages.

Buskett Gardens to eat rabbit, drink wine, sing folk songs and dance all night. *Fenkata* is also eaten on special occasions, with family and friends taking over a country restaurant for an afternoon of celebration. *Timpana* is another great festive dish.

Other celebratory foods include *prinjolata* (a cake made of pastry, candied fruit, cream, pine nuts, chocolate and meringue), a gloriously gaudy pre-Lent sweet that makes pancakes look like diet food; *kwarezimal* (almond cakes without fat or eggs), traditional for Lent; and *qubbatjt Gagħħ tal-għasel* and *imbuljuta* (sweet chestnut soup) at Christmas.

> The Catholic tradition of not eating meat on Friday still holds strong; most travellers tend to eat fish on Fridays rather than risk disapproving looks.

Where To Eat & Drink

Many travellers to Malta opt for packages that include breakfast and dinner at their hotel. If you'd prefer to sample local specialities, enjoy Malta's many fine restaurants, feast on views, and chow down on rabbit with the locals, you'll find that a bed and breakfast will allow you more flexibility.

Restaurants

Restaurants usually open for lunch between noon and 3pm, and for dinner between 7pm and 11pm. It's common for fine-dining restaurants to open only in the evening; conversely, some of Valletta's best eateries open only for lunch. Many restaurants open only six days a week, but days of closure vary (Sunday and Monday are popular – it may be worth calling ahead to find out if a place is open).

Cafes

Cafes are usually open all day. Some cafes, such as Café Jubilee in Victoria and Café Juliani in St Julian's, morph from daytime cafe to night-time cafe-bar, staying open until midnight or later, serving cocktails, wine and snacks.

Quick Eats

Look out for small hole-in-the-wall *pastizzerijas* selling authentic *pastizzi* and other pastries – Triq San Pawl in Valletta has some excellent central outlets. You can also buy decent snacks from the many kiosks outside Valletta's main gate.

> RICOTTA
>
> Ricotta cheese is used in many Maltese recipes, both sweet and savoury. The name, of Italian origin, means 'twice cooked'.

Vegetarians & Vegans

Until relatively recently meat was a rare luxury on many Maltese tables, and there are plenty of traditional, vegetarian Maltese dishes, using ingredients such as artichokes, broad beans, cauliflower and cabbage, depending on the season.

Visitors will find that vegetarians are reasonably well catered for, vegans less so. Some restaurants offer meat-free dishes as main courses, and most have vegetarian pizza and pasta options (these usually include egg and/or dairy ingredients). Alternatively, vegetarians and vegans can make a beeline for the local Chinese or Indian restaurant for a greater selection of dishes. At off-the-beaten-track village restaurants that specialise in rabbit, vegetarians may draw a blank: the menu will most likely also feature lamb, beef and quite possibly horse.

The Maltese Way of Life

The Maltese have many passions: Roman Catholicism, band clubs, sport, cars, fireworks, swimming, sailing, eating and drinking, children (who are adored and treasured), and family gatherings – many families meet for a long lunch every Sunday.

This is a deeply traditional society in many respects, and there are strong class divisions, which are perhaps a hangover from British rule. The elite tend to speak English and attend English schools. Some locals say Maltese people suffer from a collective inferiority complex, in part a product of the diminutive size of the islands, in part born out of the many years of occupation and colonialism the islands have endured.

When Malta gained its independence in 1964 it was the first time since prehistory that the islands had been ruled by the native Maltese and not by an outside power. Since early in the 1st millennium BC Malta had been occupied successively by the Phoenicians, Carthaginians, Romans, Byzantines, Arabs, Normans, Sicilians, the Knights of St John, French and the British. All of these temporary powers have influenced Maltese culture to varying degrees, yet during all this time the population has managed to preserve a distinctive identity and a strong sense of continuity with the past.

Malta is among the most densely populated countries in the world, with 1304 people per sq km (the comparable figure for the Netherlands, the second most populous country in the EU, is 402).

Psyche

The Maltese are friendly, laid-back and welcoming, though people are a little more reserved than you might expect in a Mediterranean country (in comparison to the Italians and Greeks, for example). People remain conservative in their outlook; the Catholic Church still exerts a strong influence, and church buildings and parish activities remain at the core of village life. If you're here during an important religious festival such as Holy Week you'll experience first hand how people of all ages take part, from young children in costume to the frailest elderly locals lined up in wheelchairs to watch the procession pass.

It is estimated that there are as many Maltese living abroad as there are in Malta.

Family values are held in high regard, as is the love of socialising that is common to southern European countries – Sunday in particular is the day to gather with family and friends, and enjoy good food and company.

Locals talk about the slightly claustrophobic feeling of living in a tiny country with the population of a mid-size regional town: on one hand, there's a great sense of community, on the other, a lack of privacy, and a tendency for gossip (everyone seems to know everyone else's business). People speak of 'six degrees of separation', but in Malta, given the small population, it's invariably two degrees – if I don't know you, I'm bound to know someone who does...

The Maltese are justifiably proud of their small country's historical importance and the local grit and determination (well demonstrated

A LINGUISTIC MELTING POT

The native language of Malta is called Malti (also called Maltese). Some linguists attribute its origins to the Phoenician occupation of Malta in the 1st millennium BC, but most link it to North African Arabic dialects. The language has an Arabic grammar and construction but is formed from a morass of influences, laced with Sicilian, Italian, Spanish, French and English loanwords. Until the 1930s, Italian was the official language of the country, used in the Church and for all administrative matters, even though only the aristocracy could speak it. Malti only became an official language in 1934.

English is taught to schoolchildren from an early age, and almost everyone in Malta speaks it well. Many also speak Italian, helped by the fact that Malta receives Italian TV. French and German are also spoken, though less widely.

during WWII). Understandably, they have relished their independence since 1964 and the vast majority of the population takes great interest in political matters. The people love discussing politics – a small population and the accessibility of politicians probably plays a large part. And the locals put their money where their mouth is, too: voter turnout is among the highest in the world (over 90%) but, interestingly, margins are usually very close – the country seems fairly evenly split on major issues. Perhaps local political passions are partly fuelled by the Maltese love of taking sides. As well as fierce support for political parties, there is fierce competition between the local band clubs, the local football teams, as well as which is the best local festa.

An estimated crowd of 100,000 people (one quarter of the population) attended the Mass celebrated by Pope John Paul II on his visit to Malta in 2001.

The Church

In some ways Roman Catholicism has an even stronger hold here than in Italy. One indicator of the powerful influence of the Church is the fact that divorce only became legal here in 2011 (it's been legal in Italy since 1974). Under the Maltese constitution, Roman Catholic Christianity is the official state religion and must be taught in state schools, but the constitution guarantees freedom of worship.

The Roman Catholic Church still plays a major role in everyday life, but there is evidence that its influence is waning. Although around 95% of Maltese are Catholic, the most recent Sunday Mass attendance census (2005) showed that just over half the population regularly attend Mass on Sunday – a drop of around 11% in 10 years. The bitter debate over the divorce referendum exposed dissatisfaction with the Church and saw an unusual and unprecedented rebellion against its influence. However, also telling is that the battle was won only by a slim margin: 53% voted in favour of the reform, 46% against.

Divorce was only made legal in Malta in 2011.

Church ceremonies are sombre affairs, full of tradition and reverence, which may explain why many of the younger generation prefer not to attend every week. Still, christenings, first communions, weddings and funerals continue to be celebrated in church (weddings in the parish where the bride was born), and the most important event in the calendar is the annual parish festa, which is held on different dates depending on the village.

Women in Malta

Women are traditionally expected to stay at home to look after their children or elderly parents. Childcare costs are high – there simply isn't an entrenched culture of paying for this kind of service in such a traditional, family-oriented society. Malta's female participation rate in the labour market remains relatively low when compared to that of other

EU member states, standing at 39.9% in 2010, though it's been increasing at a slow but steady rate in recent years.

According to a 2008 study, the main reasons given for women not working was personal or family reasons. Among the more conservative members of Maltese society (and society in general), women who go out to work are not only seen as failing their families but are also largely held responsible for the dysfunction in modern society.

Interestingly, the birth rate is fairly low at around 1.5 children per woman of child-bearing age, a little higher than its famously non-procreative neighbour Italy, but not much. This also points to the fact that statistics don't paint the full picture. Locals talk of low official wages spurring the creation of a parallel economy of cash work on the side. Second jobs are common (teachers giving private lessons, policemen working as house painters on their days off), and many qualified women work from home, in positions such as hairdressing and dressmaking, which is another contributor to the low official percentage of women in employment.

Malta at Play

Music

The Maltese are great music lovers and the *għana* (*ah*-na; folk song) is Maltese folk music at its most individual and traditional. A tribute to Malta's geographic location, *għana* verses are a mixture of the Sicilian ballad and the rhythmic wail of an Arabic tune, and were traditionally viewed as the music of the farmers, labourers and working classes. In the truest form, lyrics are created fresh each time and tell stories of village life and events in local history. The verses are always sung by men with guitar accompaniment.

Intrigued by *għana*? Read all about it – and listen to samples – at www. allmalta.com.

BIRD HUNTING

One of Malta's favourite traditional sports is hunting and trapping birds – there are almost 12,000 registered hunters in the country, plus around 4600 licensed trappers. Most birds are shot or trapped while migrating between Africa and Europe; Malta is one of the major flyways for migrating birds and over 384 species have been recorded here. Despite its international importance with regard to the Africa–Europe migration route, the Maltese continue to hunt and shoot to an alarming degree.

The spring hunting season is open between 12 and 30 April. Two species of bird – turtle dove and quail – may be legally hunted; shooting at any other bird is illegal. It does occur though; for example, in May 2011 eight white storks were shot while flying over the islands.

In 2005, following Malta's accession to the EU, BirdLife Malta, a large organisation of bird-lovers, sought a ban on spring hunting and trapping. Malta is the only EU member state that still allows hunting during the spring season, invoking a derogation (an exemption of sorts) granted by the EU's Birds Directive, which prohibits bird hunting and trapping in spring. The battle between the pro-hunting lobby, represented by the Federation for Hunting and Conservation (FKNK) and those against, has raged ever since. The Maltese government is loathe to alienate the hunters – 12,000 people count for a lot of votes in a small country – and in 2010 the prime minister stated that the government would 'be prepared to go back to the European Court of Justice over the issue of spring hunting to defend Malta's rights'.

In addition, illegal hunting continues to be a major concern. In September 2009 a bird 'cemetery' was discovered containing over 200 bodies of protected species, including night heron, honey buzzards and falcons. Since 2007 BirdLife Malta has kept a centralised database on illegal hunting and trapping incidents witnessed by ornithologists, members of the public and the organisation's staff and volunteers.

The St James' Cavalier Centre for Creativity in Valletta organises *għana* nights, as do other venues across Malta, especially in the centre and south. You might see performances at various heritage events, or even chance upon an impromptu *għana* performance in a rural bar. Għanafest takes place in mid-June in Floriana, with three days of live concerts.

Etnika is one traditional folk group who has revived ethnic Maltese musical forms and instruments. Its music, using traditional bagpipes, horns and drums, was once part of Malta's daily life, and was used in a variety of social contexts, including weddings and funerals. Etnika re-interprets this musical heritage for a contemporary audience and some-times fuse it with *għana,* jazz and flamenco for a unique sound. You should be able to pick up a CD of the music of Etnika at music stores throughout Malta.

Traditional band music is one of the most popular traditions on the is-lands, with bands playing a vital role in the village festa and other open-air events. Every town and village has at least one band club, sometimes two, and they are often engaged in strong rivalry.

Malta also has a popular contemporary music scene, with live music in many pubs and clubs.

The Cultural Events section of the Malta Council for Culture & the Arts (www. maltaculture. com) is a great starting point for information about forthcoming cultural events, including literary recitals, tradi-tional folk music performances and lunchtime concerts.

Craft

Malta is noted for its fine crafts, especially its handmade lace, handwoven fabrics and silver filigree.

Lacemaking probably arrived with the Knights in the 16th century. It was traditionally the role of village women, particularly on Gozo. Al-though the craft has developed into a healthy industry, it is still possible to find women sitting on their doorsteps making lace tablecloths.

The art of producing silver filigree was probably introduced to the islands in the 17th century via Sicily, which was then strongly influenced by Spain. Malta's silversmiths still produce beautiful filigree by tradition-al methods, yet in large quantities to meet tourist demand.

Other handicrafts include weaving, knitting and glass-blowing; the latter is an especially healthy small industry that produces glassware ex-ported throughout the world. Head to Ta'Qali Crafts Village near Rabat or its smaller Gozitan equivalent, Ta'Dbieġi, for the opportunity to see locals practising their craft and to buy souvenirs.

The highs! The lows! The bright outfits and big hair! Read all about Malta's performance at Eurovision over the years at www.eurovision malta.com.

Sport

Football (Soccer)

The Maltese are staunch, passionate football fans and follow the for-tunes of local sides and international teams (especially British and Ital-ian) with equal fervour – countless bars televise matches. The local and Maltese Premier League season runs from October till May; League and international matches are held at the 20,000-seat National Stadium (☑2143 6137; www.mfa.com.mt), which is situated between Mosta and Rabat; results are reported in the local newspapers. The Malta Football Association (www.mfa.com.mt) and Malta Football (www.maltafootball. com) are good resources.

Water Polo

As the heat of summer increases, football gives way to water polo. Between July and September, the fans who were once shouting on the terraces now yell from the poolside. Games are fierce and physical – it's worth trying to take in a match during your stay. The important clashes are held at the National Swimming Pool Complex on Triq Maria Teresa Spinelli in Gżira. Further information is available from the Aquatic Sports Association (www.asaofmalta.org).

Racing

Another of Malta's most popular spectator sports is horse racing. Race meetings are held at the Marsa Racecourse (part of the Marsa Sports Club outside Valletta) every Sunday, and sometimes on Friday and Saturday, from October to May. Races are mostly harness racing – and the betting is frantic. In season, some tour operators offer a day trip to the races. For more information see www.maltaracingclub.com.

In car-loving Malta, motor racing is also hugely popular; the Valletta Grand Prix takes place annually.

5000 Years of Architecture

Malta and Gozo's architecture is partly shaped by their geology: the islands are predominantly made up of layers of limestone. This type of stone, with its natural faults, allows rocks to be levered out with simple tools and divided into building blocks. Prehistoric builders exploited the weaknesses in the rock to carve out their mammoth slabs. The stone, while soft when first quarried, becomes harder when it dries out, making it ideal for carving and moulding.

Landscape and historical context are also of huge importance. Grand defensive structures are abundant across the islands, signalling how much they were fought over throughout a tumultuous history. There are the great forts and walled cities constructed by the Knights of St John; the Victoria Lines, built by the British, running across the Maltese hills; and numerous watchtowers, which stalk the coastline like sentinels.

Prehistoric Innovation

The islands are home to a series of extraordinary megalithic monuments constructed between the 4th and the 3rd millennia BC. A model made by the temple builders has been discovered, which shows the corbelled roof of a temple made of stone, indicating the extraordinary sophistication of the ancient builders.

The Hal Saflieni Hypogeum, a multi-levelled underground burial complex hewn out of globigerina limestone, dates from 5000 years ago. The builders carved out the stone in such a way as to imitate structures above ground, with rock-cut decoration, smoothed walls and curved ceilings. The well-preserved forms of this underground complex have also cast light on the less enduring monuments above ground, such as the Tarxien Temples and Ħaġar Qim on Malta and Ġgantija on Gozo. Where the roofs of the above-ground temples have collapsed, their paralleled subterranean architecture provides an invaluable reference point.

At Ġgantija temple, the interior, finer work was created from globigerina limestone, dragged from over a kilometre away.

Early Prosperity

Malta's urban architecture developed during prosperous times. The Carthaginians built Malta's first towns, although little architecture remains from this period. Some significant Roman relics have been preserved, including the grand villa complex at Rabat in central Malta, a typically Roman structure centred on a peristyle courtyard. Although its cultural impact was extremely significant, the later Islamic period left little architectural trace.

For over 2000 years Mdina was the island's major town. Originally a Phoenician settlement, it was enlarged and built upon by the Romans, and developed further by the Byzantines, Arabs, Normans and Aragonese.

Mdina reached its current form in the 15th and 16th centuries, though the 1720s saw major redevelopment as the fortifications were bolstered.

Military Might

When the Knights of St John arrived in Malta in the 16th century they set about building defences, particularly around Birgu (Vittoriosa); they also rebuilt the fortifications around Mdina. They based themselves at Birgu, and here constructed splendid hostels, or auberges, where the members of the Order lived.

After the Knights fought off the Ottoman threat in the Great Siege of 1565, grateful European allies poured money into Malta. With this largesse the Knights built Valletta, surrounding it with huge bastions. Because the island is so rocky, the fortifications were often carved into the rock, rather than built upon it, which helped increase their strength. The well-connected Knights had access to all the leading courts of Europe, so were able to call on all the great military engineers of the era to create cutting-edge defences, which remain vastly impressive today. These constructions are not merely intimidating, but also beautiful, with delicate, decorative elements that exalt their builders – intricacies that helped reinforce the power of the Order.

However, the extent of the building was vastly expensive, and by the late 1600s the Order was bankrupted by its cost. Built but untested by conflict, these fortifications were the nuclear weaponry of their day, acting as a deterrent to potential invaders.

Baroque Splendours

Together, the Knights of St John and the Church created a distinctive variation of baroque, the ornate style that dominated Europe from the 16th to the 18th centuries. This frenzy of decoration was a visual form of propaganda, exalting God, Christianity and the nobility of the builders.

The greatest Maltese architect of the 16th century was Gerolamo Cassar (1520–86). He was born in the fishing village of Birgu 10 years before the Knights of St John arrived from Rhodes, and worked as an assistant to Francesco Laparelli, the military engineer who designed the fortifications of Valletta. Cassar studied architecture in Rome and was responsible for the design of many of Malta's finest buildings, including the Grand Master's Palace, the facade of St John's Co-Cathedral and many of the Knights' auberges.

Prolific architect Tommaso Dingli (1591–1666) created many of Malta's parish churches. His masterpiece is the Church of St Mary in Attard, which he designed when he was only 22 years of age. Lorenzo Gafa (1630–1704) designed many of the finest examples of Maltese baroque, among them the cathedrals of Mdina and Gozo.

Valletta's Manoel Theatre is an architectural treasure, with a magnificent auditorium. Founded by the Portuguese Grand Master Antonio Manoel de Vilhena in 1731, it was used regularly by the Knights for their productions, and is one of the oldest working theatres in Europe.

Great Mansions

Malta is not only rich in ecclesiastical and military architecture, but has some splendid noble houses, several of which are open to the public. These include Casa Rocca Piccola in Valletta and Palazzo Falson in Mdina, which provide a glimpse into the gilded world of the Maltese aristocracy. The grandest of them all is the largely 19th-century Palazzo Parisio in Naxxar, once a summer house belonging to Maltese Sicilian gentry, and later transformed by a wealthy Maltese marquis, who added extravagant murals and a mirror-lined ballroom to create a mini-Versailles.

Best Prehistoric Sites

» Hal Saflieni Hypogeum, Malta

» Tarxien Temples, Malta

» Ħaġar Qim & Mnajdra, Malta

» Ġgantija, Gozo

Best Baroque Architecture

» St John's Co-Cathedral, Valletta

» Church of St Paul's Shipwreck, Valletta

» St Paul's Cathedral, Mdina

» Gozo Cathedral, Victoria

5000 YEARS OF ARCHITECTURE MILITARY MIGHT

MALTA'S CHURCHES

The Maltese claim to be one of the oldest Christian peoples in the world, having been converted by St Paul after his shipwreck on Malta in AD 60, and ecclesiastical architecture certainly dominates the landscape.

There are 64 Catholic parishes and 313 Catholic churches on Malta, and 15 Catholic parishes and 46 Catholic churches on Gozo. The main period of church-building on Malta took place after the arrival of the Knights of St John, in the 16th, 17th and 18th centuries; the oldest surviving church is the tiny medieval Chapel of the Annunciation at Ħal Millieri near Żurrieq, which dates from the mid-15th century.

In the 16th century the Knights imported the Renaissance style from Italy. This was supplanted by the more elaborate forms of Maltese baroque, which evolved throughout the 17th century and culminated in the design of St Paul's Cathedral in Mdina. The 19th and 20th centuries saw the addition of several large churches in the neogothic style, including St Paul's Anglican Cathedral (1839–41) in Valletta and the Church of Our Lady of Lourdes (1924–75) in Mġarr, Gozo. Two huge rotundas were also built by public subscription: the seemingly oversized Church of St Mary (1833–60) at Mosta and the Church of St John the Baptist (1951–71) at Xewkija, Gozo.

Contemporary Style

Malta has been blighted in the modern period by overdevelopment, which has rampaged in some places seemingly unfettered. While the contemporary scene is not all bad news, every new major development has been dogged by controversy.

The country's best-known contemporary architect is Richard England (www.richardengland.com), whose work has included transforming Valletta's St James Cavalier, originally designed by military engineer Francesco Laparelli, into its contemporary guise as the Centre for Creativity, a project that divided the Maltese on its inauguration.

Another divisive development is Tigné Point in St Julian's, comprising a shopping mall, restaurants and accommodation. The apartment blocks have been derided as resembling stacks of boxes, and criticised both for their juxtaposition against the elegant buildings of Sliema, and the view they present from Valletta. However, the apartments command the highest property prices on the island – perhaps because their views are outwards, across Valletta. A linked project on Manoel Island has stalled, indicating the force of disapproval.

Also controversial are Italian architect Renzo Piano's new developments in Valletta, which combine the redesigned city entrance, a new parliament building, and a state-of-the-art open-air theatre atop the ruins of the city's opera house. Piano's new entrance to the city consists of a breach in the walls, replacing the 1960s development that previously framed the entrance. Like the islands' prehistoric builders, Piano has been inspired by the local stone; his parliament-building design supports huge blocks on a steel structure.

5000 Years of Architecture in Malta, by Leonard Mahoney, provides comprehensive coverage of Malta's archaeological history, from neolithic temples to the auberges of the Knights and beyond.

Survival Guide

Directory A–Z

Activities

Sports Facilities

The **Marsa Sports Club** (☎2123 3851; www.marsasports club.com) is used by various national sport associations. The complex, about 4km southwest of Valletta, includes a horse-racing course and the National Athletics Stadium. Facilities include five turf pitches, a rugby pitch, a baseball pitch, two netball courts, two basketball courts and one full-size football ground. It also includes an 18-hole golf course (the only one in Malta), 19 tennis courts, five squash courts, a swimming pool, a cricket ground and a gymnasium. Visitors may use these facilities; a day membership costs €7, a week membership €35.

Golf

The **Royal Malta Golf Club** (☎2123 9302; www.royalmalta golfclub.com; 9/18 holes €47/65) is a private members' club established in 1888, located at the Marsa Sports Club at Marsa. Visitors are welcome to play the 18-hole, par-68 course, but reservations are essential (it's best to avoid Thursday

and Saturday morning, as these days are reserved for members' competitions). Club facilities include a pro shop, a bar, a restaurant and a driving range.

Running

Several major running events are held each year in Malta, including triathlons and half-marathons, culminating in the Malta Marathon and half-marathon, held in late February/early March (you really wouldn't want to be running too far in the heat of summer!). Application forms are available from www.maltamarathon.com; the entrance fee for Maltese/UK/other nationalities is €25/30/35.

Business Hours

Standard opening hours for businesses and services in Malta are given below. Our reviews only list opening hours where they differ significantly from these guidelines.

Banks

» 8.30am to 12.30pm Monday to Friday (some banks will stay open until 2pm, or even slightly longer, on Friday) and 8.30am to around noon on Saturday.
» From 8am mid-June to September.

Museums

» Museums and historic site, administered by Heritage Malta: 9am to 5pm daily (last entry at 4.30pm).
» Closed 24, 25 and 31 December, 1 January and Good Friday.
» Hours vary at privately run museums.

Pharmacies

» 9am to 1pm and 4pm to 7pm Monday to Saturday.
» Duty pharmacists that open late and on Sunday or public holidays are listed in local newspapers.

Restaurants

» Lunch: noon to 3pm; dinner: 7pm to 11pm.
» Many fine-dining restaurants open for dinner only.
» Some of Valletta's best eateries open for lunch only.
» Many restaurants open only six days a week, but days of closure vary (often Sunday or Monday), so call ahead to find out if a place is open.
» Some restaurants close for three or four weeks in August.

Shops

» 9am to 1pm, and 4pm to 7pm Monday to Saturday.
» In tourist areas in summer shops are often open all day.
» Most shops are closed on Sunday and public holidays.

Customs Regulations

No restrictions if you're travelling from another EU country, though you're likely to be questioned if amounts seem excessive. If you're entering Malta from outside the EU, the duty-free allowance per person is 1L of spirits, 4L of wine, and 200 cigarettes or

Climate

Valletta

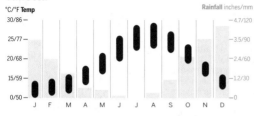

°C/°F **Temp**   Rainfall inches/mm

100 cigarillos or 50 cigars or 250g of tobacco. Duty will be charged on any gifts over €430 that are intended for local residents.

Discount Cards

Passes

Heritage Malta (www. heritagemalta.org) Individual/family Multisite pass is €30/65 – covers admission to most Heritage Malta sites. Buy at any of the individual sites covered.

Malta Pass (www.maltapass.com.mt) One/two/three-day €25/40/50 – allows admission to over 40 attractions, plus a harbour cruise and open-bus tour. Buy online.

Senior Cards

» In Malta people over 60 are entitled to discounted admission to all government-owned museums.

Student & Youth Cards

» A valid ISIC card (www.isic.org) or European Youth Card (www.eyca.org) will get you discounts.

» The **National Student Travel Service** (NSTS; ☑2558 8257; www.nsts.org; 220 Triq San Pawl, Valletta; ☉8.30am-4.30pm Mon-Fri) can provide information about where you can get student reductions.

» Admission to state-run museums is discounted for card-carrying students.

Electricity

240V/50Hz

Embassies & Consulates

Full lists of Maltese embassies abroad and foreign embassies in Malta can be found at www.foreign.gov.mt.

Countries with representation in Malta include the following:

Australia (☑2133 8201; www.malta.embassy.gov.au; Villa Fiorentina, Rampa Ta'Xbiex, Ta'Xbiex)

France (☑2248 0600; www.ambafrance-mt.org; 130 Triq Melita, Valletta)

Germany (☑2133 6531; www.valletta.diplo.de; Entrance B, 1st fl, Il-Piazzetta, Triq it-Torri, Sliema)

Ireland (☑2133 4744; www.embassyofireland.org.mt; Whitehall Mansions, Ix-Xatt Ta'Xbiex, Ta'Xbiex)

Italy (☑2123 3157-9; www.amblavalletta.esteri.it; 5 Triq Vilhena, Floriana)

Netherlands (☑2131 3980; http://netherlands.visahq.com/embassy/Malta/; Whitehall Mansions, Ix-Xatt Ta'Xbiex, Ta'Xbiex)

UK (☑2323 0000; http://ukinmalta.fco.gov.uk/en/; Whitehall Mansions, Ix-Xatt Ta'Xbiex, Ta'Xbiex)

USA (☑2561 4000; http://valletta.usembassy.gov; Ta'Qali, Attard)

Gay & Lesbian Travellers

Homosexual sex was legalised in Malta in 1973, and the age of consent for males and females is 16. Attitudes towards homosexuality in Malta are much the same as elsewhere in southern Europe. Younger people and women are usually more tolerant than older people and straight men. Remember that it's a very Catholic country and public affection (straight or gay) is generally frowned upon.

Still, while Malta is not a very 'out' destination, it is gay-friendly. Although there are only a handful of gay venues, a few clubs have the occasional gay night. The best way to find out more about the local scene is to visit www.gaymalta.com.

Malta Gay Rights Movement (www.maltagayrights.org) staged its first Gay Pride march in Valletta in July 2004, and has staged one annually ever since. Although the march and surrounding festivities are tiny in comparison to the large gatherings elsewhere in Europe, they're a chance for Malta's LGBT community to gather, celebrate diversity and push for an end to discrimination.

Health

Availability of Health Care in Malta

High-standard health care is readily available in Malta, and for minor illnesses pharmacists can give valuable advice and sell over-the-counter medication. They can also advise when more specialised help is required and point you in the right direction.

There are pharmacies in most towns; these are generally open from 9am to 1pm and 4pm to 7pm Monday to Saturday. On Sundays and public holidays they open by roster in the morning – the local Sunday newspapers print details of the roster, or it can be found online at www.ehealth.gov.mt.

Malta's public general hospital is **Mater Dei Hospital** (☑2545 0000, emergency 112; www.ehealth.gov.mt; Tal-Qroqq), 2km southwest of Sliema and accessible by bus 75 from Valletta. Gozo's smaller **General Hospital** (Craig Hospital; ☑2156 1600; Triq l-Arċisqof Pietru Pace) may also be of use. GP service is also available at a network of health centres (at Floriana, Gżira, Qormi, Paola, Cospicua, Mosta, Rabat and on Gozo).

English is spoken at all pharmacies, hospitals and health centres.

The standard of dental care is usually good; however, it is sensible to have a dental check-up before a long trip.

Medical Insurance

Citizens of the EU, plus Iceland, Liechtenstein, Norway and Switzerland, receive free or reduced-cost state-provided health care with the European Health Insurance Card (EHIC) for medical treatment that becomes necessary while in Malta. The EHIC will not provide cover for non-emergencies or emergency repatriation home. Each family member will need a separate card. The EHIC replaced the E111 in

2006, and is free; full details are online at www.ehic.org.uk.

Malta has reciprocal health agreements with Australia and the UK. Australians are eligible for subsidised health care for up to six months from their date of arrival in Malta; UK residents for up to 30 days. Details of these arrangements and various health services can be found on the website of the Maltese **Ministry of Health** (www.ehealth.gov.mt).

If you need health insurance, strongly consider a policy covering the worst possible scenario, such as an accident requiring an emergency flight home. Find out in advance if your insurance company will make payments directly to providers or reimburse you later for overseas health expenditures.

Insurance

A travel insurance policy to cover theft, loss and medical problems is always a good idea. Worldwide travel insurance is available at www.lonelyplanet.com/bookings/index.do. You can buy, extend and claim online anytime – even if you're already on the road.

Some insurance policies specifically exclude 'dangerous activities', which can include scuba-diving (a popular holiday activity in Malta). If 'risky' activities are on your agenda, as they may well be, you'll need the most comprehensive policy.

You may prefer to have an insurance policy that pays doctors or hospitals directly rather than you having to pay on the spot and claim later. If you have to claim later, make sure you keep all documentation. Some policies ask you to call back (reverse charges) to a centre in your home country, where an immediate assessment of your problem is made. Check that the policy covers ambulances or an emergency flight home.

Internet Access

Malta has notable wi-fi coverage – most towns and even some of the sleepiest villages have a wi-fi hotspot in their main square. Many establishments, including hotels, cafes, bars and restaurants, also offer wifi hotspots. There are also numerous internet cafes, and most hotels have at least one computer available for guest use; typical charges for internet access are around €2 to €4 an hour.

If you're travelling with your laptop, check that it is compatible with the 240V current in Malta; if not, you will need a converter.

Language Courses

The Maltese Islands are renowned as an enjoyable place to study English, and young people flock to the more than 40 language schools across the islands. Schools are mainly clustered in Valletta, St Julian's and Paceville. For a comprehensive list, see the website of the **Malta Tourism Authority** (www.visitmalta.com).

Legal Matters

All towns and most villages have their own police station; the smaller ones are manned by a single officer and often marked by a traditional British-style blue lamp.

If you are arrested or detained by the police you have the right to be informed, in a language that you understand, of the reasons for your arrest or detention, and if the police do not release you they must bring you before a court within 48 hours. You also have the right to inform your consulate and to speak to a lawyer.

For an emergency requiring help from the police (*pulizija* in Malti), call 112.

Useful contacts:

Gozo's Main Police Station (☑2156 2040; Triq ir-Repubblika)

Malta Police Headquarters (☑2122 4001; Pjazza San Kalcidonju)

Money

Malta abandoned the Maltese lira (Lm) and adopted the euro (€) on 1 January 2008. To prevent retailers from rounding up prices, the rate of exchange was fixed at Lm1 to €2.33, which is why you'll sometimes see euro prices in fractions or multiples of 2.33.

The reverse sides of Maltese coins feature a uniquely Maltese design (a Maltese cross, for example), but are legal tender in all countries in the Eurozone. (See p12 for information on costs and exchange rates.)

ATMs

There are ATMs at Malta International Airport, Valletta Waterfront and in all the main towns in Malta, where you can withdraw euros using a credit or debit card and PIN.

ATM transactions may incur a 'handling charge' of around 1.5% of the amount withdrawn – check with your bank before departing (and bear in mind that if you're withdrawing from a credit-card account, you'll be paying interest on the cash advance until you pay off your credit-card bill).

Cash

Cash can be changed at hotels, banks, exchange bureaus and some tourist shops. There are also 24-hour exchange machines at banks in the main tourist towns, including Valletta, Sliema and Buġibba, where you can feed in foreign banknotes and get euros back.

You'll need to carry cash as many smaller restaurants and hotels don't accept cards.

PRACTICALITIES

Newspapers

» *The Times* (www.timesofmalta.com) Good mix of local, European and world news; English-language daily.

» *The Independent* (www.independent.com.mt) Coverage of domestic social issues; English-language daily.

» *Malta Today* (www.maltatoday.com.mt/en/home) Covers local and international news. Issued twice weekly (Wednesday and Sunday); Sunday edition includes forthcoming week's listings of TV, cinema and events.

Radio & TV

» More than 20 local radio stations broadcast, mostly in Malti but occasionally in English.

» TVM is the state-run TV channel.

» Most of the main Italian TV stations, such as RAI-1, RAI-2, and RAI-3 are received in Malta.

» Satellite and cable TV are widely available in hotels and bars.

Weights & Measures

» Metric system, like elsewhere in Europe. The British legacy persists in the use of pint glasses in some pubs.

Credit Cards

Visa, MasterCard and Amex credit- and charge-cards are widely accepted in larger hotels, restaurants and shops, though smaller places only deal in cash. Travel and car-hire agencies accept cards.

Taxes & Refunds

VAT (value-added tax) was reintroduced to Malta in 1999, with two rates of tax: accommodation is charged at 5% (and is usually included in the rates quoted) and the rate for other items is 18%. Food, medicine, education, maritime services and air, sea and public transport are exempt from VAT.

Visitors to Malta can reclaim VAT on their purchases provided they are residents outside the EU and will be taking the goods outside the EU when they depart from Malta. Repayment of VAT applies only on single items valued at not less than €55 and bought from a single registered outlet as shown on the receipt, and where the total value of all items is not under €315. If you wish to get a VAT refund, you should fill out an application form, available at the customs exit points at the airport or sea port. The next steps on how to obtain your refund are described on the form and at the customs offices.

Tipping & Bargaining

» Tipping etiquette is like mainland Europe (ie tipping is not expected, but appreciated). In restaurants where no service charge is included in the bill, leave 10% for good service. Baggage porters should get about €0.50 per piece of luggage, car-park attendants around €0.50. Taxi drivers don't expect a tip, but it's nice to round up a fare in order to leave a small tip (up to 10%) if warranted.

» You may bargain for handicrafts at stalls or markets, but shops have fixed prices.

» You can often angle for lower prices from hotels and car-hire agencies in the low season between October and mid-June – stays/rentals of a week or more will often get a 10% discount.

Travellers Cheques

The main brands of travellers cheques can be easily exchanged at hotels, banks and bureaux de change, but are not accepted in shops and restaurants. Euros, pounds sterling and US dollars are the favoured denominations.

Photography

Memory cards, mini-DVDs and camera equipment are easily obtained at photographic shops in all the main towns in Malta. Print film is available only from a few specialist stores.

For tips on taking the perfect holiday snaps, look out for Lonely Planet's *Travel Photography* book.

Post

Malta Post (www.maltapost. com) operates a reliable postal service. Post office branches are found in most towns and villages (in some towns the local newsagent/ souvenir shop acts as a branch agent).

Local postage costs €0.20 up to 50g; a 20g letter or postcard sent airmail to the UK or Europe costs €0.37,

to the USA €0.51 and to Australia €0.63. You can get stamps from post offices, as well as some hotels and souvenir shops.

Safe Travel

Hunting

If you go walking in the countryside, be aware of the common pastime with shooting and trapping birds – the little stone shacks that pepper the cliff tops are shooters' hides. You will hear the popping of shotguns before you see the shooters. There are usually two short hunting seasons, in spring and autumn, but official dates are routinely ignored by hunters, and the law is poorly enforced.

If you do encounter hunters, the best thing is to greet them and keep walking – certainly don't confront them if you disapprove of their activities (hunters won't take kindly to this, and things could get ugly). By all means express your opinions elsewhere – letters of support to BirdLife Malta, (☎2134 7646; www.birdlifemalta.org) or of disapproval to the local newspapers or government departments can't hurt.

Road Conditions & Driving

Much of the road network in Malta is badly in need of repair, which means that driving is often an uncomfortably bumpy experience. Rules of the road are rarely observed, which adds to the stress of driving in unfamiliar territory, especially during rush-hour conditions around Sliema and St Julian's.

Take special care on roundabouts and always wait to see what other drivers are doing, even if it's your right of way (never assume they will stop for you!). A satnav will also enormously reduce the stress of driving, particularly as signposting can be erratic off the main routes.

Theft

Malta has a low rate of violent crime, and crimes against visitors are a rarity. Incidents involving pickpockets and purse-snatchers are uncommon, but in past years there have been increasing reports of thieves breaking into cars parked in quiet areas such as Marfa and Delimara Point. Lock your car and don't leave anything of value in it.

Although Valletta is far safer than most European capitals, it's sensible to exercise a degree of caution, especially in the quieter side streets late at night.

Smoking

Banned in any enclosed private or public premises open to the public, except in designated smoking rooms. People can smoke freely outside.

Telephone

Mobile Phones

There are 125.4% mobile phones per 100 people in Malta, so not only are mobiles widespread, many locals have more than one number. Mobile-phone numbers begin with either 79 or 99. Malta uses the GSM900 mobile phone network, which is compatible with the rest of Europe, Australia and New Zealand, but not with the USA and Canada's GSM1900. If you have a GSM phone, check with your service provider about using it in Malta and beware of calls being routed internationally (expensive for a 'local' call).

You may consider bringing your mobile phone from your home country and buying a Maltese SIM card, which gives you a Maltese mobile number. (Your mobile may be locked-in to the local network in your home country, so ask your home network for advice before going abroad.)

Prepaid vouchers for topping up credit are available at many stores and kiosks throughout Malta.

Phone Codes

The international direct dialling code is 00, followed by the relevant country code and then the number. To call Malta from abroad, dial the international access code, 356 (the country code for Malta) and then the number.

There are no area codes in Malta; all Maltese phone numbers are eight-digit numbers.

Public Phones & Phonecards

Public telephones are widely available, and most are card-operated (there are also coin-operated phones, but these are not as common). You can buy phonecards at many kiosks, post offices and souvenir shops. Easyline cards can be used from any line (including payphones, mobiles and even from hotels) and can be used in a range of overseas destinations. They are available in denominations of €5, €10 and €20.

Local calls from public phones using an Easyline card cost €0.08 per 2.5 minutes from 8am to 6pm and €0.16 per 30 minutes from 6pm to 8am to landlines, and €0.09 per 15 seconds to mobiles.

International calls are discounted between 6pm and midnight Monday to Friday, and all day Saturday and Sunday (offpeak rate); the discount increases between midnight and 8am (night rate) daily.

Time

Malta is in the same time zone as most of Western Europe (one hour ahead of the UK). The country is two hours ahead of GMT/UTC from the last Sunday in March to the last Sunday in October (the daylight saving period) and one hour ahead for the rest of the year.

Toilets

Malta is well equipped with public toilets, often at the entrance to a public garden or near the village square. They are usually clean and in good order. If there is an attendant, it is good manners to leave a tip of a few cents in a dish by the door.

Tourist Information

Local Tourist Offices

The head office of the Malta Tourism Authority (2291 5000; www.visitmalta.com; Triq il-Merkanti, Auberge d'Italie), in Valletta, is for postal and telephone enquiries only. Your best source of information is its comprehensive website, with directories, interactive maps and loads of holiday and practical information.

There are tourist information offices in Valletta, at Malta International Airport and in Victoria on Gozo.

Tourist Offices Abroad

The Malta Tourism Authority has overseas representation that can help with enquiries from potential holidaymakers. Contact the following.

Germany (069-285890; www.visitmalta.com/de; Fremdenverkehrsamt Malta, Schillerstrasse 30-40, D-60313 Frankfurt-am-Main)

UK (020-8877 6990; office.uk@visitmalta.com; Malta Tourist Office, Unit C, Park House, 14 Northfields, London SW18 1DD)

Travellers with Disabilities

It's Maltese government policy to improve access for people with disabilities, but many of Malta's historic places – notably the steep, stepped streets of Valletta – remain difficult, if not impossible, to negotiate for those with restricted mobility. Several sights are accessible, however, including the Malta Experience and the National Museum of Archaeology in Valletta. A good number of the more expensive hotels have wheelchair access and some have rooms specially designed for guests with disabilities. Sliema, with its long promenade, is a good place to be based. The new Malta and Gozo bus service, run by Arriva, operates a sleek fleet of wheelchair-accessible buses.

The Malta Tourism Authority can provide information on hotels and sights that are equipped for wheelchair users.

The National Commission for Persons with Disabilities (Centru Hidma Socjali; 2278 8555; www.knpd.org; Triq Braille, Santa Venera) can provide information on facilities and access in Malta for travellers with a disability.

Visas

Everyone is required to have a valid passport (or ID card for EU citizens) to enter Malta. EU citizens are entitled to travel freely around the member states of the EU, and settle anywhere within its territory.

Citizens of Australia, Canada, Israel, Japan, New Zealand and the USA can stay for up to three months without a visa; other nationalities can check their visa requirements at www.foreign.gov.mt (click on the Services/Travelling to Malta link).

Malta is part of the Schengen Zone. Citizens from some non-EU countries are required to hold a visa when travelling to the Schengen Area. Generally, a short-stay visa issued by one of the Schengen States entitles its holder to travel throughout the 25 Schengen States for up to three months within a six-month period. Visas for visits exceeding that period are at the discretion of the Malta authorities.

If you wish to stay for more than three months you should apply for an extension at the **immigration office** (☑2122 4001; sb.police@gov. mt; Pjazza Vicenzo Buġeja) at the police headquarters in Floriana at least four weeks before your three months are up. You will need four recent passport photographs and proof that you have enough money to support yourself and not be a burden on the state. Extensions can be difficult to obtain. Applications for temporary residence should also be made at police headquarters. More information is available at www.mfa.gov.mt.

Visit Lonely Planet's website for up-to-date visa information at www.lonely planet.com/malta/practical -information/visas.

Transport

GETTING THERE & AWAY

Flights, tours and rail tickets can be booked online at lonely planet.com/bookings.'

Entering the Country

Citizens of EU member states can travel to Malta with their national identity cards. Travellers from countries that don't issue ID cards, such as the UK, must carry a valid passport. All non-EU nationals must have a full valid passport.

Air

Malta is well connected to Europe and North Africa, but there are no direct flights into Malta from places further afield. If you're flying from elsewhere, it's best to travel to a major European hub, such as London, Amsterdam or Brussels, then join a direct connecting flight to Malta.

Airports & Airlines

All flights arrive and depart from Malta International Airport (MLA; ☑2124 9600; www.maltairport.com) at Luqa, 8km south of Valletta. The airport has good facilities, including ATMs and currency exchange, internet access, a tourist office (open daily), left luggage and regular, inexpensive bus connections to Malta's major towns, as well as to the Gozo ferry. The Maltese national airline is Air Malta (KM; ☑2166 2211; www.

airmalta.com), a small airline with a good safety record. The following airlines fly to and from Malta:

Alitalia (AZ; www.alitalia.com)
Brussels Airlines (SN; www.brusselsairlines.com)
easyJet (EZY; www.easyjet.com)
Egyptair (MS; www.egyptair.com.eg)
Emirates (EK; www.emirates.com)
JAT Yugoslav Airlines (JU; www.jat.com)
KLM Royal Dutch Airlines (KL; www.klm.com)
Lufthansa (LH; www.lufthansa.com)
Ryanair (FR; www.ryanair.com)

Tickets

High season in Malta is mid-June to September and ticket prices are at their highest during this period. A month or two either side is the shoulder season (April, May, October), while low season is November to March.

Middle East

Emirates has around five flights a week between Dubai and Malta via Larnaca, with connections to/from destinations in other parts of the Middle East as well as Australia, India and Asia. Air Malta flies twice a week between Malta and Istanbul.

Recommended agencies in the region:
Al-Rais Travels (☑04-393 3333; www.alrais.com) In Dubai.
Israel Student Travel Association (ISSTA; ☑03-7777 777; www.issta.co.il) In Jerusalem.

CLIMATE CHANGE & TRAVEL

Every form of transport that relies on carbon-based fuel generates CO_2, the main cause of human-induced climate change. Modern travel is dependent on aeroplanes, which might use less fuel per kilometre per person than most cars but travel much greater distances. The altitude at which aircraft emit gases (including CO_2) and particles also contributes to their climate change impact. Many websites offer 'carbon calculators' that allow people to estimate the carbon emissions generated by their journey and, for those who wish to do so, to offset the impact of the greenhouse gases emitted with contributions to portfolios of climate-friendly initiatives throughout the world. Lonely Planet offsets the carbon footprint of all staff and author travel.

Orion-Tour (📞212-232 6300; www.oriontour.com) In Istanbul.

North Africa

There are frequent flights between Malta and various North African cities, including Cairo and Tripoli. One recommended travel agency in the area is **Egypt Panorama Tours** (📞02-2359 0200; http://eptours.com/) in Cairo.

UK & Ireland

Flights depart from various London airports, as well as Dublin, Manchester and Leeds. Bargains are frequently available, even in high season.

Land

Bus

You can travel by bus from most parts of Europe to a port in Italy and catch a ferry from there to Malta. **Eurolines** (www.eurolines.com) is a consortium of coach companies that operates across Europe, with offices in all major European cities.

As the saying goes, all roads lead to Rome; from there you will have to continue to Malta by bus or train to one of the ferry ports in northern and southern Italy.

Car & Motorcycle

With your own vehicle, you can drive to northern Italy and take a car ferry from Genoa, or drive to southern Italy and take a car ferry from Salerno or from Pozzallo or Catania (Sicily) to Malta. From northern Europe the fastest road route is via the Simplon Pass to Milan, from which the Autostrada del Sole stretches all the way to Reggio di Calabria. From London the distance is around 2200km.

Car drivers and motorbike riders will need the vehicle's registration papers, a Green Card, a nationality plate and their domestic licence. Contact your local automobile association for details about necessary documentation.

Sea

Ferry

Malta has regular sea links with Sicily (Pozzallo and Catania), central Italy (Civitavecchia) and northern Italy (Genoa). Ferries dock at the Sea Passenger Terminal beside the Valletta Waterfront in Floriana, underneath the southeast bastions of Valletta.

Virtu Ferries (📞2206 9022; www.virtuferries.com)

offers the shortest, fastest Malta–Sicily crossing with its catamaran service (carrying cars and passengers) to/ from Pozzallo and Catania. The company also operates day excursions to Sicily.

The Pozzallo–Malta crossing takes 1½ hours and operates year-round, with daily sailings from June to August, dropping to four or five days a week from November to April, weather permitting. The Catania–Malta crossing takes three hours and operates from March to October (five days a week in August, down to one day a week in March). The return passenger fare in high/low season on both routes is €145/100 (day return €120/68).

Children under four travel free of charge; children aged four to 14 pay around 50% of the adult fares.

Grandi Navi Veloci (www. gnv.it) has a daily Palermo–Malta service, and a car ferry service between Genoa, Palermo and Valletta (34½ hours, with a four-hour stopover in Palermo). The local agent is **Gollcher & Sons** (📞2569 4550; www.gollcher.com; 19 Triq San Zakkarija, Valletta).

Public transport links with the ferry terminal in Floriana

BIG YELLOW BUSES

Malta's old buses were a tourist attraction in themselves, and it's a sad thing, in terms of local colour and photo opportunities, that they're no longer rattling around the islands. The average age of the old buses was 35 years. They were run as independent businesses by their drivers, lovingly customised with handmade parts and decorations, and used to hurtle around Malta's potholed roads with unsettling speed. They were known as 'xarabank', a derivation of 'charabanc' (a carriage or an old-fashioned term for a motor coach).

The buses probably also contributed to Malta being the most car-dense country in Europe. Quaintness is not necessarily an endearing quality when you have to use the buses day to day, and the new Arriva Malta bus system is a great boon for local transport. You will spot the occasional old bus on the road: the classic Bedfords, Thames, Leylands and AECs dating from the 1950s, '60s and '70s, brightly painted in a livery of yellow, white and orange, have not completely disappeared. Numerous well preserved vintage buses have been retained as tourist attractions, and are now used for sightseeing trips around the islands. Try **Citysightseeing Malta** (📞2346 7777; www.citysightseeing.com.mt; adult/ child €15/9; ⊙half-hourly 9am-3pm Mon-Sat, 9am-1pm Sun), which offers a tour from Sliema around the Three Cities. A vintage bus also runs from Valletta Waterfront up to Floriana.

The Malta Buses by Michael Cassar and Joseph Bonnici is an illustrated history of the islands' celebrated public transport.

should have improved by the time you read this, when the new panoramic lift up to Valletta is complete. However, with luggage, many will prefer to catch a taxi to your destination. Set fees are established – head to the information booth at Valletta Waterfront (to Valletta it's €10, to Sliema/St Julian's €18).

Yacht

Malta's excellent harbour and its strategic location at the hub of the Mediterranean has led to its development as a major yachting centre.

There are berths for 720 yachts (up to 22m length overall) in the Msida and Ta'Xbiex marinas near Valletta; and Mġarr Marina on Gozo has space for over 200 boats. There are also marinas at the **Portomaso complex** (www.portomasomarina.com) in St Julian's, and the **Grand Harbour Marina** (www.cn marinas.com/en/marinas/grand -harbour-marina) in Vittoriosa.

For more information on these marinas and details of the logistics and formalities of sailing to Malta, contact **Transport Malta** (☑2122 2203; www.transport.gov.mt).

Malta's popularity with the yachting fraternity means that it is possible to make your way there as unpaid crew. Yachts tend to leave Gibraltar, southern Spain and the Balearics in April and May to head towards the popular cruising grounds of the Greek Islands and the Turkish coast. It's possible to just turn up at a marina and ask if there are any yachts looking for crew, but there are also agencies that bring together yacht owners and prospective crew (for a fee). One such agency is UK-based **Crewseekers** (☑01489 578 319; www.crewseekers.net), which charges £70/95 for a six-/12-month membership.

Tours

There are dozens of tour operators in the UK, Europe and North America that offer package holidays and organised tours to Malta. Package holidays, which include flights and accommodation, can offer some real bargains, particularly in winter.

There are also many tour operators catering to a wide range of special-interest groups, including walking, diving, history, archaeology, architecture and religion, and others offering holidays designed for senior travellers. The comprehensive website of the **Malta Tourism Authority** (www.visitmalta.com) allows you to search for tour operators based on country and speciality. Click on 'Plan Your Trip', then 'Tour Operators'.

GETTING AROUND

Air

Harbour Air (☑2122 8302; www.harbourairmalta.com) operates a floatplane service between Valletta (leaving from the Floatplane Terminal alongside Valletta Waterfront) and Mġarr Harbour on Gozo. There are two flights daily (weather and sea conditions permitting), with a flight time of 10 minutes. At the time of research, all flights were grounded while it replaced their fleet, but when it's functioning again fares will cost approximately €150 return.

Bicycle

Cycling on Maltese roads can be nerve-racking – the roads are often narrow and potholed, there's lots of traffic, and drivers show little consideration for cyclists. However, things are considerably better on Gozo – the roads can still be rough, but there's far less traffic.

You can rent bikes for around €5 per day from **Magri Cycles & Spares** (☑2141 4399; www.magricycles.com; 135 Triq il-Kungress Ewkaristiku, Mosta, Malta) and **Victoria**

Garage (☑2155 6414; www.victoriagaragegozo.com; Triq Putirjal, Victoria, Gozo).

Bus

In 2011, **Arriva Malta** (☑2122 2000; www.arriva.com.mt) took over Malta and Gozo bus services and revolutionised bus travel on the islands. The shaking, charming, brightly painted vintage buses that were so characteristic of Malta have gone, and have been replaced with the boring-looking, but ineffably more efficient, sleek, comfortable and quiet Arriva vehicles, which have access for travellers.

Many bus routes on Malta originate from the Arriva bus terminus in Valletta and radiate to all parts of the island, but there are also many routes that bypass the capital, making cross-country journeys much more convenient than in the past. Services are faster and more regular. On Gozo, where once buses were of little use to visiting tourists, they're now an efficient way of getting from place to place.

Tickets

You can buy tickets either as you board the bus; from ticket machines, which are found near numerous bus stops; at ticketing booths at Valletta terminus, Sliema bus terminus and the airport; at Lotto, Maltapost or Agenda bookshop outlets, and from various other outlets; as well as online. If you're caught travelling without a ticket, there's a penalty charge of €10.

Those who hold an official Malta Identity Card, a Registration Certificate/Residence Card (for EU citizens and their family members) or a Long-Term Residence Permit receive discounts on tickets. Malta bus tickets are not valid on Gozo, and vice versa.

Fares:
» €2.20 single (valid 2 hours)
» €2.60 day

» €2.50 night single
» €12 seven-day ticket

Routes & Timetables

Full bus timetables and route maps are online, and the best routes for getting from A to B are detailed in this book. There are six different express services running between the airport and various parts of the island, including St Julian's, Sliema and Ċirkewwa. The X7 runs to/from Valletta and the airport, and takes just over 20 minutes.

Most buses run from around 5.30am to 11pm, and frequency varies depending on the popularity of the route. In towns and villages the bus terminus is usually found on or near the parish church square.

Car & Motorcycle

The Maltese love their cars. At weekends (Sunday in particular) they take to the road en masse, visiting friends and family or heading for the beach or a favourite picnic site. This means that there is often serious congestion on the roads around Valletta, Sliema and St Julian's. Friday and Saturday night in Paceville is one big traffic jam. However, renting a car gives you more flexibility, particularly to discover out-of-the-way beach coves.

Distance isn't a problem – the longest distance on Malta is 27km and the widest point is around 15km. On Gozo the longest distance is about 14km, the widest is only 7km.

Automobile Associations

If you're renting a car, you'll be provided with a telephone number to contact in the event of mechanical difficulties or breakdown. If you're bringing your own vehicle, it's a good idea to take out European breakdown cover (offered in the UK by both the RAC and the AA). For roadside assistance in Malta, contact **RMF** (☑2124 2222; www.rmfmalta.

com) or **MTC** (☑2143 3333; www.mtctowingmalta.com).

Bringing Your Own Vehicle

Tourists are permitted to use their vehicles for a maximum of six months in any given year without the need to apply for a permit. A motor vehicle entering a foreign country must display a sticker identifying its country of registration.

Driving Licences

All EU member states' driving licences are fully recognised throughout Europe. For those with a non-EU licence, an International Driving Permit (IDP) is a useful adjunct, especially if your home licence has no photo or is in a language other than English. Your local automobile association can issue an IDP, valid for one year, for a small fee. You must carry your home licence together with the IDP.

Fuel

The price of fuel is set by the government and at the time of research was €1.51/1.39 a litre for unleaded/diesel petrol. Petrol is dispensed by attendants and garages are generally open from 7am to 7pm (6pm in winter) Monday to Saturday; most are closed on Sunday and public holidays – though a few are open from 8am to noon on a roster system. Larger stations have a self-service, cash-operated pump (€5, €10 and €20 notes accepted) for filling up outside opening hours.

Hire

Car rental rates in Malta are among the lowest in Europe, and hiring a car allows you to see a lot more of the islands if your time is limited. If you hire a car on Malta you can take it over to Gozo on the ferry without a problem. Rental rates on Gozo are lower (but with an extra charge for taking the car to Malta), but if you're visiting both islands the inconvenience of hiring a car in both places would outweigh any benefits.

Most of the car-hire companies have representatives at the airport, but rates vary so it's worth shopping around. Make sure you know what is included in the quoted rate – many of the local agencies quote very low rates that do not include full insurance against theft and collision damage.

Obviously rates will vary with season, length of rental period and the size and make of car (plus extras such as air-con). Daily rates for the smallest vehicles start from around €25 a day (for rental of seven days or longer) in the high season.

The age limit for rental drivers is generally 21 to 70, and drivers between 21 and 25 may be asked to pay a supplement of up to €10 a day. You will need a valid driving licence that you have held for at least two years. Rental rates often include free delivery and collection, especially in the Valletta-Sliema-St Julian's area.

There are dozens of local car-hire agencies, and many accommodation providers also offer car-rental arrangements – it pays to ask when you're making a booking. Most will drop off and collect cars (usually for a small fee). As well as all the major international companies, such as Avis, Budget and Hertz, there are the following local companies:

Billy's (☑2152 3676; www.billyscarhire.com; 113 Triq Ġorġ Borg Olivier, Mellieħa, Malta)

Mayjo Car Rentals (☑2155 6678; www.mayjo.com.mt; Triq Fortunato Mizzi, Victoria, Gozo)

Wembleys (☑2137 4242/4141; www.wembleys.net; 50 Triq San Ġorġ, St Julian's, Malta)

Windsor Car Rentals (☑2134 6921; www.windsorgarageservices.com; 10 Triq San Franġisk, Sliema, Malta)

Insurance

Car-hire companies offer collision damage waiver (CDW) and/or theft damage protection insurance with rental vehicles at extra cost (usually charged per day). Be sure to read the fine print and understand what you're covered for, and what excess charges you'll be up for in the case of an accident.

Normally cars registered in other European countries can circulate freely in Malta; check with your local insurance company before you leave to make sure you are covered.

Parking

Parking can be tricky in the Sliema-St Julian's and Buġibba-Qawra areas. While there are car parks available, it's far more difficult to find parking in high season. In Valletta only residents are allowed to park within the city walls, but you can use the large MCP underground car park near the bus terminus, close to the Hotel Phoenicia, which is only a short walk from Valletta's main gate and sights. Parking in the MCP costs €2.50 for up to two hours and €5 for over four hours. Parking elsewhere costs €1 to €2 per hour.

Local traffic police are swift and merciless in the imposition of on-the-spot fines. Most main towns, tourist sights and beaches have a car park, with an attendant dressed in a blue shirt and cap and usually wearing an official badge. These attendants will expect a tip of around €0.50 upon your departure.

Road Rules & Conditions

Unlike most of Europe, the Maltese drive on the left. Speed limits are 80km/h on highways and 50km/h in urban areas, but are rarely observed. Wearing a seat belt is compulsory for the driver and front-seat passenger. Any accidents must be reported to the nearest police station (and to the rental company if the car is hired); don't move your vehicle until the police arrive, otherwise your insurance may be nullified.

Road signs and regulations are pretty much the same as the rest of Europe, with one

KARROZZIN

The *karrozzin* – a traditional horse-drawn carriage with seats for four passengers – has been in use in Malta since 1856. Many of the carriages are treasured family possessions passed down through generations, and are cared for with obsessive pride.

You can catch a *karrozzin* in Valletta at City Gate, Marsamxetto Ferry, Fort St Elmo and at Valletta Waterfront, and at Mdina's Main Gate. There is an unfortunate tendency in some drivers to overcharge unwitting tourists. Haggle with the driver and be sure to agree on a fare before getting in. The usual fare is €35 for 35 minutes.

important difference – in Malta no-one seems to pay the least attention to any of the rules. Be prepared for drivers overtaking on the inside, ignoring traffic lights, refusing to give way at junctions and hanging on your rear bumper if they think you're going too slowly. All rental cars have registration numbers ending in K, so tourists can be spotted easily. Vehicles coming from your right are supposed to have right of way at roundabouts, but don't count on vehicles on your left observing this rule.

You should also be aware that many of the roads are in pitiful condition, with cracks and potholes, and there are very few road markings. In winter, minor roads are occasionally blocked by wash-outs or collapsed retaining walls after heavy rain. Signposting is variable – some minor sights are easy to find, while major towns remain elusive. It's worth getting hold of a detailed road map.

The maximum allowable blood-alcohol concentration in drivers in Malta is 0.08%.

Ferry

The **Marsamxetto Ferry Service** (☎2346 3862; single/return €1.50/3) operates regularly between Valletta and Sliema; you can also take **Malta Water Taxis** (☎7999 0001; www.maltawatertaxis.com.mt) on the same route. For the most scenic way to travel be-

tween Valletta and the Three Cities, try **A&S Water Taxis** (☎2180 6921; www.maltese watertaxis.com; ⊙9am-5pm, or until dark in summer).

To/From Gozo & Comino

Gozo Channel (☎2158 0435; www.gozochannel.com) operates the car ferry that shuttles between Malta's Ċirkewwa and Gozo's Mġarr every 45 minutes from 6am to around 6pm (and roughly every 1½ hours throughout the night). You pay on your return leg, when leaving Mġarr (Gozo), so there's no need to buy a ticket in Ċirkewwa on the way out. Return fares per foot passenger/child aged three to 12/car and passengers cost €4.65/1.15/15.70.

There's also a car ferry from Sa Palma near Valletta to/from Gozo (90 minutes; usually thrice weekly, on Monday, Tuesday & Thursday), which takes some foot passengers.

For information on ferries, boat trips and water taxis to/from Comino from Gozo and Malta, see p127.

Taxi

Official Maltese taxis are white (usually Mercedes, with a taxi sign on top). To combat regular complaints of overcharging, taxi drivers must by law use the meter to determine the fare (except from the airport and sea port, where there are set fares).

Details of the fixed fares from the airport are available at the taxi desk in the arrivals hall, where you can pay in advance and hand a ticket to the driver.

There are taxi ranks at City Gate and outside the Grand Master's Palace in Valletta, and at bus stations and major hotels in main tourist resorts. Within Valletta, a private company provides an electric-powered taxi service for a flat fare of €3 to €5 per person.

As an alternative to the official Maltese white taxis (Taxi Licensed White Amalgamated, TLWA; ☑2182 3017; www.maltataxi.net), unsigned black taxis are owned by private companies and usually offer cheaper set fares (similar to the UK's minicabs). To order a taxi, it's best to ask at your hotel reception for the name and number of their preferred service, or try one of the following 24-hour companies:

Belmont Garage (☑2155 6962; Nadur, Gozo)

Freephone Taxis (☑2138 9575, 8007 3770; www.free phonetaxis.net; St Julian's, Malta)

Wembley's (☑2137 4242/ 4141; www.wembleys.net; St Julian's, Malta) Wembley's provides a reliable 24-hour radio taxi service. Rates are generally cheaper than official taxi rates.

Tours

There are loads of companies offering tours around the islands, by boat/bus/4WD or a combination of the three. Prices vary (as does what's included), so shop around. If you're pushed for time these trips can be a good way to see the highlights, but itineraries can often be rushed, with little free time.

Tours include half-day tours to the Blue Grotto or Valletta's Sunday market; full-day trips to the Three Cities, Mosta and Mdina; or evening trips to take in festa celebrations. Day trips to Gozo and Comino are

TAXI FARES FROM THE AIRPORT

DESTINATION	FARE
Buġibba/St Paul's Bay	€25
Ċirkewwa	€32
Golden Bay area	€25
Mdina/Rabat	€18
Mellieħa	€30
Sliema/St Julian's area	€20
Three Cities area	€18
Valletta/Floriana	€15

also common. Tours can be arranged through most hotels and travel agents.

Captain Morgan Cruises (☑2346 3333; www.captain morgan.com.mt) is the biggest tour operator in the Maltese Islands, offering a wide range of boat excursions. There's a water-taxi tour of the Grand Harbour, leaving on Wednesday or Saturday, which allows time to visit Valletta, Vittoriosa and Fort Rinella, and costs €30/25 per adult/child. There is also an all-day cruise around Malta and Comino (six times a week from May to October, three times a week in March, April and November), which will set you back €45 per adult (under 12s go free!); a buffet lunch is included. Other options include day trips to the Blue Lagoon on Comino (adult/under 12s €40/free). These trips depart from the ferry area in Sliema; some trips include transfers to/from your accommodation in the area. There are also 'underwater safari' cruises (adult/child €15/11) out of Sliema and Buġibba, on boats with underwater viewing areas.

Captain Morgan also offers popular year-round, chauffeur-driven jeep safaris to remote parts of Malta (adult/child €55/45) and Gozo (adult/child €62/52). Lunch is included, as is the Malta–Gozo return ferry ticket for Gozo tours. Book ahead as places are limited.

Hera Cruises (☑2133 0583; www.heracruises.com) also offers cruises around Malta, including all-day cruises and trips to Comino and the Blue Lagoon in a Turkish *gulet* (old-style sailing boat). It also has yacht charters (a catamaran costs €800 per day, with crew) and 4WD jeep tours.

Citysightseeing Malta (☑2346 7777; www.citysightsee ing.com.mt; adult/child €15/9; ☺half-hourly 9am-3pm Mon-Sat, 9am-1pm Sun) offers hop-on, hop-off, open-top bus tours around both islands. There are two different routes on Malta: north (blue) and south (red). It also offers 'Malta by Night' (starting at 7pm, and lasting for four hours, with a 60-minute stop in Mdina) and Gozo tours; all cost the same.

Excursions to Sicily

Virtu Ferries (☑2206 9022; www.virtuferries.com) runs 90-minute passenger catamaran services to Pozzallo and Catania that enable travellers to make a day trip to the Italian island of Sicily. You take the boat at 6.45am and return on the 9.30pm boat; the itinerary takes in Mt Etna and the town of Taormina (adult/child aged four to 14 €107/75).

Prices include taxes but exclude the cost of lunch; transfers in Malta cost €10. You can book a trip online or through most hotels and travel agents in Malta.

Language

Malti – the native language of Malta – is a member of the Semitic language group, which also includes Arabic, Hebrew and Amharic. It's thought by some to be a direct descendant of the language spoken by the Phoenicians, but most linguists consider it to be related to the Arabic dialects of western North Africa. Malti is the only Semitic language that is written in a Latin script.

Both Malti and English are official languages in Malta, and almost everyone is bilingual. Travellers will have no trouble at all getting by in English at all times. This chapter provides a basic introduction to Malti.

Pronunciation

Most letters of the Maltese alphabet are pronounced as they are in English, with the following exceptions:

ċ	as the 'ch' in 'child'
ġ	soft, as the 'j' in 'job'
għ	inaudible; lengthens the preceding or following vowel
h	inaudible, as in 'hour'
ħ	as the 'h' in 'hand'
ij	as the 'ai' in 'aisle'
j	as the 'y' in 'yellow'
q	a glottal stop, which is similar to the pause in the middle of 'uh-oh'
x	as the 'sh' in 'shop'
z	as the 'ts' in 'bits'
ż	soft, as in 'zero'

Basics

Hello.	Merħba.
Good morning/day.	Bonġu.
Good evening.	Bonswa.
Goodbye.	Saħħa.
Yes.	Iva.
No.	Le.
Please.	Jekk jogħġbok.
Thank you.	Grazzi.
Excuse me.	Skużani.
How are you?	Kif inti?
I'm fine, thank you.	Tajjed, grazzi.
Do you speak English?	Titkellem bl-ingliż?
What's your name?	X'ismek?
My name is ...	Jisimni ...
I love you.	Inħobbok.

Accommodation

Do you have any rooms available?	Għad fadlilkom xi kmamar vojta?
Can you show me a room?	Tista' turini kamra?
How much is it?	Kemm hi?
I'd like a room ...	Nixtieq kamra ...
with en suite	bil-kamra tal-banju
with one bed	b'sodda waħda
with two beds	b'żewġ sodod

Emergencies

Help!	Ajjut!
Police!	Pulizija!
Call a doctor!	Qibgħad ghat-tabib!
I'm lost.	Ninsab mitluf.
ambulance	ambulans
hospital	sptar

Shopping & Services

At what time does it open/close?	Fix'ħin jiftaħ/jagħlaq?
How much?	Kemm?
bank	bank
... embassy	ambaxxata ...
hotel	hotel/il-lukanda
market	suq
pharmacy	ispiżerija
post office	posta
public telephone	telefon pubbliku
shop	ħanut

Time, Dates & Numbers

What's the time?	X'ħin hu?
morning	fil-għodu
afternoon	wara nofs in-nhar
yesterday	il-bieraħ
today	illum
tomorrow	għada
Monday	it-tnejn
Tuesday	it-tlieta
Wednesday	l-erbgħa
Thursday	il-ħamis
Friday	il-gimgħa
Saturday	is-sibt
Sunday	il-ħadd
January	Jannar
February	Frar
March	Marzu
April	April
May	Mejju
June	Ġunju
July	Lulju
August	Awissu
September	Settembru
October	Ottubru
November	Novembru
December	Diċembru

0	xejn
1	wieħed
2	tnejn
3	tlieta
4	erbgħa
5	ħamsa
6	sitta
7	sebgħa
8	tmienja
9	disgħa
10	għaxra
11	ħdax
12	tnax
13	tlettax
14	erbatax
15	ħmistax
16	sittax
17	sbatax
18	tmintax
19	dsatax
20	għoxrin
30	tletin
40	erbgħin
50	ħamsin
60	sittin
70	sebgħin
80	tmienin
90	disgħin
100	mija
1000	elf

Signs

Dħul	Entrance
Ħrug	Exit
Magħluq	Closed
Miftuħ	Open
Nisa	Women
Rġiel	Men
Sqaq	Lane/Alley
Twaletta	Toilet
Vjalq	Avenue

Transport & Directions

I'd like a ticket.	Nixtieq biljett.
When does the boat leave/arrive?	Meta jitlaq/jasal il-vapur?
When does the bus leave/arrive?	Meta titlaq/jasal il-karozza?
I'd like to hire a car/bicycle.	Nixtieq nikri karozza/rota.

Where is a/the ...?	Fejn hu ...?
Go straight ahead.	Mur dritt.
Turn left.	Dur fuq ix-xellug.
Turn right.	Dur fuq il-lemin.
far	il-boghod
near	il-viċin
left luggage	hallejt il-bagalji

GLOSSARY

(m) indicates masculine gender, (f) feminine gender and (pl) plural

AFM – Armed Forces of Malta

auberge – the residence of an individual langue of the Knights of St John

bajja – bay

bastion – a defensive work with two faces and two flanks, projecting from the line of the rampart

belt – city

bieb – gate

cavalier – a defensive work inside the main fortification, rising above the level of the main rampart to give covering fire

ċimiterju – cemetery

curtain – a stretch of rampart linking two bastions, with a parapet along the top

daħla – creek

dawret – bypass

demi-bastion – a half-bastion with only one face and one flank

dgħajsa – a traditional oar-powered boat

festa – feast day

fortizza – fort

foss – ditch

Grand Master – the title typically given to the head of an order of knights, including the Knights of Malta

għajn – spring (of water)

għar – cave

ġnien – garden

kajjik – fishing boat

kappillan – parish priest

karrozzin – traditional horse-drawn carriage

kastell – castle

katidral – cathedral

kbira – big, main

knisja – church

kwartier – quarter, neighbourhood

langue – a division of the Knights of St John, based on nationality

luzzu – fishing boat

marsa – harbour

medina – fortified town, citadel

mina – arch, gate

misraħ – square

mitħna – windmill

mużew – museum

palazzo – Italian term for palace or mansion

parroċċa – parish

passeggiata – evening stroll (Italian term)

pjazza – square

plajja – beach, seashore

pont – bridge

pulizija – police

rabat – town outside the walls of a citadel

ramla – bay, beach

ras – point, headland

razzett – farm, farmhouse

sqaq – alley, lane

suq – market

sur – bastion

taraġ – stairs, steps

telgħa – hill

torri – tower, castle

triq – street, road

trulli – cone-shaped buildings that echo the traditional architecture of Puglia in Southern Italy

vedette – a lookout point, watchtower

vjal – avenue

wied – valley

xatt – wharf, marina

behind the scenes

SEND US YOUR FEEDBACK

We love to hear from travellers – your comments keep us on our toes and help make our books better. Our well-travelled team reads every word on what you loved or loathed about this book. Although we cannot reply individually to postal submissions, we always guarantee that your feedback goes straight to the appropriate authors, in time for the next edition. Each person who sends us information is thanked in the next edition – the most useful submissions are rewarded with a selection of digital PDF chapters.

Visit **lonelyplanet.com/contact** to submit your updates and suggestions or to ask for help. Our award-winning website also features inspirational travel stories, news and discussions.

Note: We may edit, reproduce and incorporate your comments in Lonely Planet products such as guidebooks, websites and digital products, so let us know if you don't want your comments reproduced or your name acknowledged. For a copy of our privacy policy visit lonelyplanet.com/privacy.

OUR READERS

Many thanks to the travellers who used the last edition and wrote to us with helpful hints, useful advice and interesting anecdotes:

Chris Abela, Georgina Arrambide, Goran Axelsson, Ashley Beck, Jennifer Boger, Mark Cameron, Anja de With, Bec Deacon, Ken Donaldson, Mary Frances Doran, Rowin Dreef, Robby Geyer, Nancy Griffith, Melody Jeannin, Alison King, Andrew Lane, Tony McIntyre, Martin Mercieca, George Nelis, Anthony Paul Norton, Fred Pach, Jasmina Popin, Stephen Potts, Mike Quinn, Paolo Razzanelli, Cinzia Redaelli, Phil Staff, Luciana Trentanove, David Wright, Dirck van Dongen, Ignacio Villanueva, Marvic Zarb

AUTHOR THANKS

Abigail Blasi

Many thanks to Julia Tomkins, Helen Caruana Galizia, Philip Manduca, Denise Briffa and Stephen Caruana for all their generous and invaluable help with research, and to Remco Slik and Patti Piazzi for their local tips. Grateful thanks also to Malta Tourism Authority CEO Josef Formosa Gauci for filling me in on Malta's upcoming developments. And an enormous thank you to my family, Luca, Gabriel, Jack and Valentina, for coming along for the ride.

ACKNOWLEDGMENTS

Climate map data adapted from Peel MC, Finlayson BL & McMahon TA (2007) 'Updated World Map of the Köppen-Geiger Climate Classification', *Hydrology and Earth System Sciences*, 11, 163344.

Cover photograph: *Luzzu* (traditional fishing boats) and churches, Marsaxlokk, Malta; Degree/4Corners.

This Book

This 5th edition of Lonely Planet's *Malta & Gozo* guidebook was researched and written by Abigail Blasi. The previous two editions were written by Neil Wilson. This guidebook was commissioned in Lonely Planet's London office, and produced by the following:

Commissioning Editor Joe Bindloss

Coordinating Editors Mardi O'Connor, Jeanette Wall

Coordinating Cartographer Laura Matthewman

Coordinating Layout Designer Katherine Marsh

Managing Editors Barbara Delissen, Brigitte Ellemor

Senior Editor Catherine Naghten

Managing Cartographers Anita Banh, Amanda Sierp

Managing Layout Designer Jane Hart

Assisting Editors Fionnuala Twomey, Tracy Whitmey

Assisting Cartographers Alex Leung, Jacqueline Nguyen, Samantha Tyson

Cover Research Naomi Parker

Internal Image Research Kylie McLaughlin

Language Content Branislava Vladisavljevic

Thanks to Shahara Ahmed, Dan Austin, Carolyn Boicos, Ryan Evans, Larissa Frost, Jouve India, Asha Ioculari, Annelies Mertens, Trent Paton, Lieu Thi Pham, Anthony Phelan, Raphael Richards, Averil Robertson, Fiona Siseman, Andrew Stapleton, Diana von Holdt, Gerard Walker

index

how to use this book

These symbols will help you find the listings you want:

👁 Sights	☞ Tours	🍷 Drinking
🏃 Beaches	🎉 Festivals & Events	★ Entertainment
🏃 Activities	🛏 Sleeping	🔒 Shopping
🎓 Courses	🍴 Eating	ℹ Information/Transport

These symbols give you the vital information for each listing:

☎ Telephone Numbers	📶 Wi-Fi Access	🚌 Bus
⊙ Opening Hours	🏊 Swimming Pool	🚢 Ferry
Ⓟ Parking	🥗 Vegetarian Selection	Ⓜ Metro
⊝ Nonsmoking	📖 English-Language Menu	Ⓢ Subway
❄ Air-Conditioning	👪 Family-Friendly	🚋 Tram
@ Internet Access	🐾 Pet-Friendly	🚆 Train

Reviews are organised by author preference.

Look out for these icons:

TOP CHOICE — Our author's recommendation

FREE — No payment required

🍃 — A green or sustainable option

Our authors have nominated these places as demonstrating a strong commitment to sustainability – for example by supporting local communities and producers, operating in an environmentally friendly way, or supporting conservation projects.

Map Legend

Sights
- 🏖 Beach
- Buddhist
- Castle
- Christian
- Hindu
- Islamic
- Jewish
- Monument
- Museum/Gallery
- Ruin
- Winery/Vineyard
- Zoo
- Other Sight

Activities, Courses & Tours
- Diving/Snorkelling
- Canoeing/Kayaking
- Skiing
- Surfing
- Swimming/Pool
- Walking
- Windsurfing
- Other Activity/Course/Tour

Sleeping
- Sleeping
- Camping

Eating
- Eating

Drinking
- Drinking
- Cafe

Entertainment
- Entertainment

Shopping
- Shopping

Information
- Post Office
- Tourist Information

Transport
- Airport
- Border Crossing
- Bus
- Cable Car/Funicular
- Cycling
- Ferry
- Monorail
- Parking
- S-Bahn
- Taxi
- Train/Railway
- Tram
- U-Bahn
- Underground Train Station
- Other Transport

Routes
- Tollway
- Freeway
- Primary
- Secondary
- Tertiary
- Lane
- Unsealed Road
- Plaza/Mall
- Steps
- Tunnel
- Pedestrian Overpass
- Walking Tour
- Walking Tour Detour
- Path

Boundaries
- International
- State/Province
- Disputed
- Regional/Suburb
- Marine Park
- Cliff
- Wall

Population
- Capital (National)
- Capital (State/Province)
- City/Large Town
- Town/Village

Geographic
- Hut/Shelter
- Lighthouse
- Lookout
- Mountain/Volcano
- Oasis
- Park
- Pass
- Picnic Area
- Waterfall

Hydrography
- River/Creek
- Intermittent River
- Swamp/Mangrove
- Reef
- Canal
- Water
- Dry/Salt/Intermittent Lake
- Glacier

Areas
- Beach/Desert
- Cemetery (Christian)
- Cemetery (Other)
- Park/Forest
- Sportsground
- Sight (Building)
- Top Sight (Building)

OUR STORY

A beat-up old car, a few dollars in the pocket and a sense of adventure. In 1972 that's all Tony and Maureen Wheeler needed for the trip of a lifetime – across Europe and Asia overland to Australia. It took several months, and at the end – broke but inspired – they sat at their kitchen table writing and stapling together their first travel guide, *Across Asia on the Cheap*. Within a week they'd sold 1500 copies. Lonely Planet was born.

Today, Lonely Planet has offices in Melbourne, London and Oakland, with more than 600 staff and writers. We share Tony's belief that 'a great guidebook should do three things: inform, educate and amuse'.

OUR WRITER

Abigail Blasi

Originally from London, Abigail has also lived in Hong Kong and Rome, and has been travel writing since 2002. She mainly divides her time between London, Rome and Puglia and, as often as she can, takes her young family on the road with her to assist with research. As well as writing for many newspapers, magazines and websites, Abigail has worked on Lonely Planet guidebooks to numerous Mediterranean destinations, including Italy, Portugal, Tunisia and now Malta. Having been bewitched by this cluster of islands, dotted by historic wonders and surrounded by intensely sparkling sea, she can't wait to go back.

Published by Lonely Planet Publications Pty Ltd
ABN 36 005 607 983
5th edition – February 2013
ISBN 978 1 74179 916 3
© Lonely Planet 2013   Photographs © as indicated 2013
10 9 8 7 6 5 4 3 2 1
Printed in China